## Praise for *The Chotchk*

*"Barry Dennis brilliantly mines our everyday habits
to make a major contribution to humanity. A must-read for
anyone interested in raising the quality of our environment and
the quality of our consciousness. His humor and humility are
indispensable in this timely work that deserves wide attention."*

— **Dr. Harold Bloomfield,** the best-selling author of
*Making Peace with Your Past*

*"What a superb entertainer/author/teacher! Bristling with
spiritual insights, laced with humor and personal authenticity,
here is proof that 'musicians do it better' when they turn their
talents to writing books that sing out with truth like this."*

— **John Maxwell Taylor,** the author of *The Power of I Am*
and *Eros Ascending: The Life-Transforming Power of Sacred Sexuality,*
and . . . a musician

*"Life is all about relationships. **The Chotchky Challenge** shows us
how our relationship to our material things affects the relationships
to our friends, families, and coworkers. Barry Dennis offers a
fresh, original book that will make you laugh out loud and
reflect on your own life and relationships."*

— **John Gray, Ph.D.,** the best-selling author of
*Men Are from Mars, Women Are from Venus*

*"With inspiring honesty, Barry Dennis has woven together a rich
tapestry of engaging stories and exercises to help us reveal the masterpiece of our own lives. As a sculptor carves away stone to reveal its
inner beauty, so **The Chotchky Challenge** guides us to remove that
which distracts from our soul's highest purpose. Packed with endearing
humor and penetrating observations, this book joyfully elevates us to
awaken to the harmony of who and what we really are."*

— **James Papp,** the author of *Inquire Within:
A Companion Guide to Living in Spirit*

THE
# CHOTCHKY
## CHALLENGE

THE

# CHOTCHKY
## CHALLENGE

Clear the Clutter from Your Home,
Heart, and Mind . . . and Discover
the True Treasure of Your Soul

# BARRY DENNIS

INSIGHTS

**HAY HOUSE, INC.**
Carlsbad, California • New York City
London • Sydney • Johannesburg
Vancouver • Hong Kong • New Delhi

*Published and distributed in the United States by:* Hay House, Inc.: www
.hayhouse.com® • *Published and distributed in Australia by:* Hay House Australia Pty. Ltd.: www.hayhouse.com.au • *Published and distributed in the United
Kingdom by:* Hay House UK, Ltd.: www.hayhouse.co.uk • *Published and distributed in the Republic of South Africa by:* Hay House SA (Pty), Ltd.: www.hayhouse
.co.za • *Distributed in Canada by:* Raincoast: www.raincoast.com • *Published in
India by:* Hay House Publishers India: www.hayhouse.co.in

*Cover design:* thebookdesigners • *Interior design:* Tricia Breidenthal
*Interior illustrations:* Elizabeth Mason

Library of Congress Control Number: 2012930216

Tradepaper ISBN: 978-1-4019-3578-8
Digital ISBN: 978-1-4019-3579-5

15  14  13  12    4  3  2  1
1st edition, April 2012

Printed in the United States of America

To my children's, children's,
children's, children's, children's,
children's children. May they inherit
a world that we have yet to even imagine.

# CONTENTS

## LEVEL IV: SOUL

# PREFACE

"Well Barry, I'm sorry, but . . . you're retarded."

These are the words I heard from the "office lady" the day I was late for school in fourth grade. She's the one who stapled papers and answered the phone behind the big counter with the swinging door in the main office. I guess I wasn't too surprised, given that I went to some of the "special" classes for "slow" kids. Those road signs that say "slow children ahead" were there, I thought, to make sure other people knew I was around. After all, every time I saw one, I *was* there.

Needless to say, I never thought I would be a writer. Heck, I got F's in the three R's. For quite some time I even thought that section in the alphabet beginning with *L* and ending with *P* was one letter called "elaminopee." Really, I did. (In my defense, that *is* how it sounds when you sing the alphabet song.) There's actually a very logical reason why I found the alphabet so confounding. We will get to that. For now, know that the day I was late in fourth grade did not sit well with me. I had never been late before. I was filled with anxiety as my mom drove me to school because I had messed around and missed the bus. I wanted to be good. Being late wasn't good. I guess maybe the anxiety, combined with my insecurities around learning, obstructed my ability to hear. You see, what the office lady actually said was, "Well, Barry, I'm sorry, but . . . you're *tardy.*"

It was several years before I realized her true words. In the meantime, I accepted my lot in life. Instead of moping about, I became something of a class clown. I was rather quick on my feet, which often resulted in hysterical outbursts of laughter in the classroom.

Over the years, I got involved in music and acting and in college I studied film, music, and speech. I also played in a rock band and did stand-up comedy.

Underneath it all, I was searching for the meaning of life. I wanted to understand the universe and my place in it. I wanted to know "God." I began to read voraciously. I'd pick up anything on the subject of spiritual growth, scientific breakthroughs, psychology, and the like while I wrote a never-ending stream of songs. I traveled the country speaking to kids of all ages, using comedy and music to inspire them to make positive life choices. I eventually started my own church called Celebration, as well as Coexist Celebration, a multicultural, interfaith movement whose mission is to create peace of mind and peace of planet.

After many years of writing the talks I'd give every week, I wondered, *Does this mean I could write a book?* It turns out that there is a correlation. Once I started the process, it was often suggested that I hire a ghostwriter, which, I've been told, is what many successful speakers do, but that didn't sit well with me. If I was going to write a book, I needed to do it myself—otherwise, the humor, the nuances, and the heart and soul wouldn't find their way onto the pages.

In the end, I had to write this book. I didn't have a choice. You see, I finally found the meaning of life, my place in it, and God. As difficult as it was, I couldn't stop. My life, your life, is the greatest gift, the greatest miracle in all the universe. It is my hope that somewhere in these pages, you will find and know that miracle.

Oh, and one last thing. I do read self-improvement/spiritually oriented books like a man lost in a desert might drink fresh water. I thirst for truth. The books are interesting, stimulating, and useful for cogitation. That's a good thing. Very few, however, take the next step and ask the reader to change or take action. To break out of old patterns and beliefs by actually doing something.

Rest assured, this book is *your* catalyst for change—a thought-provoking conversation starter that will empower and motivate you. And if you're "in," it can change your life forever. Are you in? The way I see it, you and I are in the same class, here at the University of the Third Planet from the Sun. It's high time we got crackin'. Don't you think? I mean, take a look around. If you ask me, as a whole, we are all a little tardy.

# THE
# PARABLE
## OF THE
## SANNYASI

The sannyasi (wise man) had reached the outskirts of the village and settled down under a tree for the night when a villager came running up to him and said, "The stone! The stone! Give me the precious stone!"

"What stone?" asked the sannyasi.

"Last night, the Lord Shiva appeared to me in a dream and told me that if I went to the outskirts of the village at dusk, I should find a sannyasi who would give me a precious stone, a treasure beyond compare, that would make me rich forever."

The sannyasi rummaged in his bag and pulled out a stone.

"He probably meant this one," he said as he handed the stone over to the villager. "I found it on the forest path some days ago. You may certainly have it."

The man gazed at the stone in wonder. It was a diamond; probably the largest diamond in the whole world, for it was as large as a person's head. He took the diamond and walked away.

That night the man tossed about in bed, unable to sleep. The next day at the crack of dawn, he returned to the outskirts of the village and woke the sannyasi.

"Please," the man said, "give me the wealth that makes it possible for you to give this diamond away so easily."

# BACKWARD

*"For where your treasure is, there your heart will be also."*

— A GUY WHO WALKED ON WATER
(IN A ROBE AND SANDALS)

Yes, I know it is common practice to begin a book with the "Foreword." However, it has become clear that many of our common practices are, well, backward. It's what the villager came to realize as he tossed and turned through the night. For me, unfortunately, it took a lot longer than one night. Here is the story of the eight things I wrestled with that began my search for true treasure. As you read, try to see if you can identify those eight things. Think of them as the sannyasi's diamonds, and a bit later we will examine each one. I'll even drop in a number like this "(1)," as a hint as they draw near.

## *Reaching Critical Mass*

What I first remember on that gray winter's morning was stepping into the shower and being disoriented by all of the *shampoos*. (1) A smorgasbord of shampoos. Which one to use? Two were

1

shampoo/conditioners in one, and there were a few other plastic bottles of plain old conditioners. I thought, *Why use any of the conditioners when I could just use one of the all-in-one combos?*

Then I had a deep thought: *Maybe it doesn't work as well as shampoo-rinse-condition-rinse. Hmm.* I continued to look for the right shampoo. Then I got distracted by the soap dilemma. There were several bars of soap, plus a few dispensers of gel soaps. Then a little voice in my head said, *Maybe you can just use the gel for everything. Even for your hair!* The thought seemed radical . . . as if even thinking it was breaking the rules. After expending no small amount of mental energy, I went for it, like a prisoner running for the fence when the spotlights are turned the other way. "Gel for everything!"

Then it was time to shave. I accidentally knocked one of two kinds of shaving cream off the thin shower shelf. Those cans have smashed my toes in similar situations. My heart racing, I jumped out of the way, banging my funny bone on the glass door. My arm was now vibrating and tingling like I had just received electroshock therapy as a punishment for using body wash on my hair.

After I combed my hair I had to decide which lotion to use. There were several on the counter, but none of them seemed to be specifically for the face. I wanted something for my face. For some reason, I felt sure that using the other lotions might harm my face.

I opened several drawers and waded through canisters, crumpled toothpaste tubes, five or six other hair gels, and seven or eight different hair sprays; then I cut my thumb on a stray razor. Ouch.

Each time I got a trim at the local barber, there seemed to be a better hair gel I had to buy—"New and Improved" in some way. These gels have their own special place two drawers down and seemed to be multiplying. I use gel about once a month, and each time I do I am confused anew.

I went to a cupboard looking for a bandage for my thumb. There were two bottles of DayQuil, two bottles of NyQuil, and a slew of outdated prescriptions. There was Pepto-Bismol in chewable tabs, liquid form, and in both pink and blue. But I just wanted a Band-Aid.

I found the Band-Aids, but they were huge. You could patch together a whale with these things. I just needed a small one. Really small. Like the size the Munchkins from Munchkin Land would use for a paper cut. After some fumbling around, I picked out a reasonably sized bandage and put it on the cut. It covered my entire thumb.

Next I went to the closet and froze. There it sat on a shelf in between shelves that I actually use for clothes. This shelf is full of doodads, trinkets I had collected over time for reasons I could not explain. On that shelf sat the *Shelf Elf.* (2) It was a gift. The elf is creepy. I would like to throw it off the edge of the Grand Canyon or maybe hire someone else to do it. Can you hire a hit man for a Shelf Elf? I feel guilty for not liking it—hence, the frozen state.

*What would possess anyone to purchase such a thing? And give it?*

Once I was finally able to disengage from the Shelf Elf . . . I froze again.

*Oh my hell . . . my closet!* (3) What do I wear?

Most of what was crammed into my closet hadn't seen the light of day in two or three dog years. Who put the idea in my head that I needed enough clothing for an average-size village in Kenya? The entire gay community was coming out of the closet with more frequency than my clothes. My clothing could have learned a thing or two from the gay community: my clothes, too, have nothing to be ashamed of.

*I, however, did.*

From among the warehouse of shirts I had stored in drawers and shelves I grabbed whatever was on top. It was an old Devo T-shirt from a concert I went to *before computers.*

Geez, I still had shoes, socks, and pants to go; and I was exhausted *before* pants. Not a good sign. But the most arduous moment came after I put my pants on.

*It was a footwear nightmare!* When did I become the Imelda Marcos of my own domain? *I don't wear 98 percent of these things!* Many, I'm sure, don't fit me. But how would I know?

Next, I made my way to the breakfast table and yelled to my sons, CJ and Z (Alexander), for about the fifth time, to get ready

for school. I opened the *cereal cupboard.* (4) There were four different kinds of Cheerios, three kinds of Honey Bunches of Oats, *and*
Grape-Nuts. There were Puffins (the cereal of course, not the bird),
an assortment of granola, one giant bag of generic Fruit Loops,
and a few other kinds with nuts and freeze-dried berries. After
much consideration, I chose the Grape-Nuts. As soon as I started
chewing, it sounded like Armageddon in my head. Massive explosions with each chomp. I mixed in a bunch of one of the cereals with freeze-dried strawberries to try and squelch the sound.
Then I made a cup of peach-flavored tea that I warmed up in the
microwave.

I picked up the *newspaper.* (5) As usual, a bunch of coupon-
type flyer things fell out of the paper. I waded through the pages
like I did my closet, trying to find something relevant. As I read,
I thought, *What in the world is going on?* Some of it seemed like it
might matter, but it was hard to weed out, like trying to get to
the roots of a dandelion in between the cracks of the sidewalk. It
wasn't worth it. So I just read the sports section.

I yelled to my sons again, "Z, CJ! Hurry up! We're going to be
late."

I went to check my *e-mail* (6) while the boys ate their cereal
with freeze-dried strawberries. As soon as my AOL account came
up and said, "You've got mail," I was bombarded with the latest-
breaking celebrity "news."

The truth is that I don't really care. Really. I don't. So why, in
the name of all that is good and holy, do I know? Why do I know
what starlet just broke up with which leading man? Seriously!
*What about the things that do matter?*

I had to click off several pop-ups and windows to burrow
down to my 69 unread e-mails. As I began opening them, I found
that very few had any relevance. Why are these people sending
me all this useless stuff? I don't need to be copied on every single
electronic discussion, and I have no interest in shrinking this or
enlarging that.

Then the *phone* rang. (7) The caller ID said in a robotic voice,
"Out of area." Then my cell phone vibrated on the counter. I

picked up the house phone. "Can you hold for a minute?" Then I picked up my cell phone and said, "Just a second, I need to get the house phone."

For the life of me, I can't remember who was on the house phone. I had to take a message, though. Looking for a pen, I opened a drawer in which there were several . . . *phones!* This drawer was devoted to doodads that had nowhere else to go, and it was crammed solid. If I had to put one more thing in that drawer, it would reach critical mass rendering it unclosable. The cell phone call was about my 8:30 appointment with an *old friend* (8), who said it was really important and was just checking to make sure I would be there even though I had just confirmed our meeting by responding to his e-mail. Ugh.

The boys finished their freeze-dried-strawberry cereal. Z, who was 15 at the time, rode his bike to school. CJ, who was 7, was playing video games. We have at least three different video game–type systems, which require myriad cartridges and discs. They seem to have a life of their own. And their drawers had long since reached critical mass.

I told CJ to turn it off and finish getting ready for school.

He began making progress, slowly, distracted by this and that. It seemed there was always *something* in the way of this progress.

At the time I had no name for it, this hindrance to progress. Have you ever felt it? And it wasn't just his progress. It was progress in general. Moving forward with life. Getting on with "it." *What is this "something"?*

Seven-thirty rolled around quickly, and CJ and I got in the car to go to his bus stop. We live in the country, and the bus stop is half a mile away. On the way to the car, he said, "Oh shoot, Dad, I forgot my backpack. It's in my room. I'll go get it. Just wait in the car." So I waited . . . and waited. I honked my horn. After about eight minutes, at which time we were really close to missing the bus, I began to get impatient.

Every "thing" was piling up. It had started with all those darn shampoos, seven-eighths empty, wasting away in their plastic bottles. The problem is that if we missed the bus, I would have to drive my son to school. This would probably make me late for my appointment, which I had now confirmed both by e-mail and phone.

Frustrated, I ran up to CJ's room and opened the door. The first thing I remember was feeling completely overwhelmed. His bedroom resembled one of those islands where they test nuclear bombs. Not unlike any other kid's bedroom, from time to time, in suburban America. There were toys on the floor, some broken. Clothes scattered and jammed in drawers that were half open due to being beyond critical mass. On his desk the chaos extended itself—several calculators; innumerable erasers, pens, and pencils; and old homework assignments he had brought home to show us. An iPod and *three* sets of headphones slowly came into focus in this veritable sea of entropy as I began to raised my voice: "CJ, where are you? What's going on? We have to go right now!"

When he answered me, his voice sounded shaky. Almost teary. "I'm . . . I'm in the closet, Dad."

"What are you doing in the closet?" I yelled. "We have to leave. *Come on!*"

"I can't find my backpack, Daddy. I've looked everywhere. And I want to change my pants, but I can't find the pants I want to wear."

I opened the door to his closet and there he was, on the floor sitting with his head on his knees, arms wrapped around his legs surrounded by stuff: a jump rope, Frisbees, shin guards . . . and crammed in the corner, protruding out into the limited space, was a small puppet theater. It was teetering as if it were about to fall on CJ's head. There was even a marionette wrapped up in and dangling by its strings, contorted and broken. Somehow, the perfect image.

CJ was overwhelmed, crying silent tears of exasperation. I couldn't see that at the time. In that moment, I was blind, turning green.

*"CJ, what are you doing on the floor of your closet? GET UP! WE DON'T HAVE TIME TO CHANGE YOUR PANTS. WE HAVE TO FIND YOUR BACKPACK! COME ON! RIGHT NOW!"*

For the first time, I *really* yelled at one of my children. I'd made a solemn commitment when I became a father that I would never parent in anger. That I would not yell or hit. That my children would not live in fear of me. But there it was: *real* anger, *coldness.* CJ tried to hold back the tears as I frantically scrambled through the nuclear fallout in his room, throwing shoes, underwear, toys, and balls, digging like a crazed archeologist in search of a backpack. My son just sat on the floor and cried.

We missed the bus. So I drove him to school . . . in silence. We didn't say a word the whole way. That had never happened before.

The rest of the morning I felt sick to my stomach. I went to my meeting, but I wasn't *present.* Besides, the guy wanted to borrow money that I didn't have. Yuck.

When I got back to my office at home, I couldn't work. My Incredible Hulk breakdown just kept haunting me. It was one of those moments in time I would have given *anything* to take back.

At 11:30 I hopped in my car and drove with a little more weight on the gas pedal than usual. I headed to my son's school to surprise him and take him to lunch. Usually when I show up unannounced, he waves and smiles, but as soon as he saw me walk into the cafeteria that day, he began to cry. Then he ran to me, clear across the cafeteria, and jumped into my arms. We squeezed the stuffing out of each other, and then he looked me straight in the eyes and said, "Daddy, I'm sorry. It's so good to see you!"

"CJ, it's so good to see you, too. I am so sorry."

We hadn't really *seen* each other all morning. There was something in the way.

That day, I became more aware. The drawers of my mind had reached critical mass. What had caused it? I searched my mind. Had my cup of peach tea been exposed to a radiation leak in the microwave, turning my skin green, my pants purple and shredded at the knees? What transformed me into the Hulk? Just what do those eight things have in common? It was that "something," that thing I couldn't put my finger on. It was . . .

*Chotchky!*

## Let's Begin

Soon, we will analyze my morning of reckoning and the eight "diamonds." Before we do, however, it's important for you to know that you are in for quite a journey. The stories throughout are true. A few of the names have been changed to protect the eccentric. A couple of stories I have condensed and combined for clarity and brevity. The truth is that reality *is* stranger than fiction. So strange, in fact, that it takes what might be the most bizarre word in any language to capture this reality. While researching, I found that the word *chotchky* is spelled at least seven different ways. I have chosen this lesser-known spelling simply because it is easier for those who have never laid eyes upon it to sound it out. The most common spelling is *tchotchke*. Crazy, I know.

The "Chotchky Challenge" is not as much the title of this book as it is *the overarching issue of our time*. This book then is a how-to manual, a guide for the 21st-century human being, helping us acquire the necessary skills to accept and victoriously take The Challenge. Together we will explore the ways in which our Chotchky is not only a cause of great personal stress, but it is also the underlying cause of the environmental, personal health, and general financial challenges we face as one humanity. Through the work of changing our relationship with this one thing, we can heal it all.

As you read, you will awaken a latent superpower, that of Chotchky Vision. Soon only that which is truly important in your life will stand out, like words that have been *highlighted* on a page. All the rest will fall away, bringing a kind of freedom that most people never knew was possible. Chotchky Vision brings an extremely heightened level of awareness, and with this awareness comes the purpose of the book: to attain nothing short of . . .

*Liberotchky: the complete and total freedom from all things Chotchky.*

(Note: "Liberotchky" has no intended connection to the former flamboyant pianist, although he did wear a lot of "Blingotchky." Hmm, coincidence? I think not.)

As you have just experienced, I have created a whole new vocabulary to help in the development of this Vision. By simply taking the "otchky" section of this most unusual of words and slapping it on the back of any noun, you have a new, powerfully descriptive word revealing the deeper truth of the thing you are perceiving. For example, a lot of *information* quickly turns into *"informotchky": the never-ending stream of useless info designed to hijack your attention, causing your thoughts to dwell upon trivial, frivolous matters.*

We all know informotchky exists. We just never had a word for it before. These words are empowering.

For those who may already have some familiarity with the concept of "Chotchky" you, like me, have probably felt the subtle nuance. Something inferred that lives behind the literal meaning. I discovered that this nuance is an ancient wisdom locked inside the word for hundreds if not thousands of years waiting to be released, unraveled, and fully comprehended. The story of how the deeper meaning was revealed is a few page turns ahead.

So, you're in Chotchky Training now. You will need a writing implement—in fact, I encourage you to write all over this book like when you were a kindergartener and the world was your canvas. (If you're reading an e-book, don't write on the screen . . . it won't make sense once you turn the page.) And don't worry, no adult is going to get mad. It's your book! It's *your* life. Have fun.

There are also "Mini Challenges," such as quizzes, throughout the book. They're fun and will strengthen your ability to take on the ever-present Big Challenge: resisting the temptation to waste your time, money, and energy on Chotchky. These Mini Challenges will give you the motivation and skills needed to transform your life in any way you desire.

To assist in comprehension, I have divided this "manual" into five parts. The first section, "The Philosophy," delves deeply into the overall concepts that make up the Chotchky Challenge. It is a philosophy all its own. As your understanding deepens, it will bring greater meaning to the four levels. Moving from the densest form of Chotchky to the most ethereal, they are:

*Level I: Things* (stuff, junk, and other physical manifestations). This is our starting point because it's the easiest to identify. *Thingotchky* is the doorway that will help us understand and see Chotchky in its other less obvious and often more debilitating forms. Any combination of atoms, the building blocks of all things physical, can be thingotchky.

*Level II: Body.* The second level of Chotchky is *Bodyotchky.* It's clear to see how things can be Chotchky, creating dysfunction and confusion in a home. Well, the body is "home" to the most important thing in the Youniverse. Therefore, it is vulnerable to its own kind of Chotchky. *Foodotchky* is one prevalent form of bodyotchky; for example, think Twinkies or cigarettes.

*Level III: Mind.* Our mind is the home of our thoughts, our consciousness. What we put in it and what is placed there creates our experiences. *Mindotchky* is probably more prevalent than Thingotchky, yet it goes relatively unnoticed. Spooky.

*Level IV: Soul.* And finally, there is *Soulotchky.* Everything ends up affecting the soul, or spirit, of our being. Our life is like a funnel. The first three levels pour through that funnel into our soul, which causes great confusion as we go about searching for meaning and purpose in our lives. *Emotionalotchky* is a direct assault on the soul.

During our journey we will "take a moment" from time to time in order to integrate what you have learned with a short affirmation. There are also "Deep Thoughts," which spin a concept inside out, expanding your awareness and leaving you with much to ponder. On occasion, you will be asked the question "Truth or

Fiction?" This is always followed by a tidbit of information that generally seems quite absurd . . . or is it? You get to guess.

Finally, a website link is at the end of every chapter so that you and I can hang out virtually and explore the subject matter even deeper. Sometimes the link will include clips of me telling the very story you just read in front of a live audience. As you will see, we have a lot of fun! The links provide updated information to further assist and inspire you toward creating a more joyful, peaceful, and meaningful life. I will update the videos as my life—and your life—evolves, reflecting the profound wisdom that naturally comes with time. Don't skip ahead to the links though. Read the chapter, take the Mini Challenges, and then check out the link. Oh, and, as I mentioned, be sure to write your own notes in and outside the margins. That's where we're headed: *outside the margins!*

### But First, a Fair Warning . . .

Soon you will be given an opportunity to turn or not turn the page, much like a very powerful scene in the movie *The Matrix*. Morpheus, the wise master, offered Neo, the main character and hero, a choice between two pills. If Neo chose the blue pill, he would quietly go back to the way things were, as if nothing had happened. Back to sleep. Choosing the red one, on the other hand, would mean that he'd find out "how deep the rabbit hole goes." Faced with this choice, Neo paused. It wasn't an easy decision. He knew something was wrong; he did not, however, know that he was plugged into a machine being fed a false reality! Morpheus couldn't explain what would happen if Neo chose the red pill. He simply said, "I offer you the truth, nothing more."

This book *is* a Red Pill. *I offer you the truth, nothing more.*

Read on, and the way you see the world will change forever.

So what's it going to be? Put the book down now and walk quietly back to the masses . . . or turn the page?

Okay, Neo. Excellent choice.

As the pill takes effect, you will begin to see the truth. It's a slow process. For example, soon you will start to see "Small Plastic Gophers" en masse. I know it sounds strange, but they are everywhere. They are taking away your time, your money, and your energy in a most insidious and subtle way. I would go so far as to say these gophers are most likely standing right smack dab in the middle of the path that leads to the life you have always known was possible, yet has always eluded you—shimmering just out of reach. They are sucking your very life force, just like the computers and demonic machines that were plugged into Neo. It's worse, though, because they're *gophers*. But soon you will be able to identify them, and it will make all the difference in the world.

### *The Masterpiece*

I'm guessing that Michelangelo could see the gophers. It seems he had developed phenomenal Chotchky Vision. He once said, "The idea is there, locked inside, and all you have to do is remove the excess stone." Michelangelo crafted the statue *David*, probably the single greatest marble masterpiece ever created. I have seen it. To me, it is close to inconceivable how such a thing could be done, especially when one realizes that if he made one mistake, one chisel tap removing *too much*, the work would have been ruined. Yet he was able to trust and allow himself to see the finished work in his mind, inside the marble, with such perfection that he meticulously removed the excess that hid the masterpiece from the rest of the world. Thank God for Michelangelo.

*You are the Michelangelo of your life.*

Inside your life *is* a masterpiece. And I would assert that it is more miraculous than anything Michelangelo ever put his hand to. It's there. Just like *David* was inside a big chunk of marble, our lives are big chunks of marble. It's time we allow ourselves to see our lives as Michelangelo saw *David*. It's a process of chipping away, one piece at a time, that which is covering up the masterpiece until the masterpiece is revealed. It's a willingness to let go of the insane thinking that we need *all* the marble.

There is no greater metaphor for our lives. The masterpiece is waiting to be revealed. And there is no better way to understand the Chotchky Challenge. The general consciousness of a backward world is trying to constantly and forever *pile on more marble,* smothering our *David.* Right now, by consciously choosing to take the Chotchky Challenge, we become the Michelangelo of our own experience. Now we will be able to see the masterpiece and detect the excess marble so we can begin chipping it away. It's through committing to our own masterpiece that we create the greatest possible work of all: a true "master peace."

The chisel has just been placed in your hands. What will your Master Peace look like? Can you think of one thing that would represent its completion? What do you want to create? Anything goes. A more loving relationship? A healthier body? Peace of mind? The money to start the work your soul longs for? The ability to play the piano? It could be as simple as "the time to spend creating a beautiful garden," or as dramatic as "a new job, a new spouse, and a new attitude." Please write down one thing that represents your Master Peace. Have fun.

_____

_____

_____

_____

_____

Writing down your wishes creates clarity and therefore is a huge step toward creation. Taking the next step, moving from thought to form, is at times quite difficult because we've got it backward. We're always told to move in the direction of our masterpiece without first removing the excess. This is impossible. Remove the excess, and the rest becomes second nature.

Please note: The picture of your masterpiece may alter dramatically by the end of our journey together. If so, that in itself could be the miracle in waiting. Understand that there is nothing specifically you need to do to make it happen. Just fully dive into this material. It will then naturally occur like one season changing to the next. Leaves just fall. New life just comes. Ah, your Master Peace, like *David,* is locked inside, but you're about to remove the excess stone.

Here's link #1: I have created a secret page on my website that only those reading this book know exists. Go to **www.barrya dennis.com** and choose the tab that says "Books/Stories." Then click on the image of this book. Abracadabra, there it is. The secret site. Our first adventure is inside the Chotchky Gnome. Click on it now. Then hurry back to begin our journey. You're about to meet a living cousin of Moses. Yeah, the guy with the tablets. It appears there was a commandment missing.

# THE PHILOSOPHY

# CHAPTER 1

# SMALL PLASTIC GOPHERS

When slavery existed in America, it was against the law to teach slaves to read or write. Ignorance is enslaving. That's how powerful words are. In the Bible, the Word is given credit for the beginning of all creation: "In the beginning was the Word." Words give us an ability to have power over what they represent. So if we don't have a word for something, we are ignorant. We have no power over it. We don't recognize it—like a stranger's face in a crowd, it is invisible to us. The word *Chotchky* gives us power over something that we didn't even know was enslaving us. For clarification, I give you the Small Plastic Gopher.

*There's a reason they call them gift shops. There's nothing in them one would actually want to keep.*

The subtle, profound, and deeper meaning of the word was revealed to me after I bared my soul to my good friend Dr. Harold Bloomfield. Harold is a direct descendent of Moses. I figure if you're going to bare your soul to someone, it may as well be a distant cousin of the author of the Ten Commandments. I told Harold about that morning with my son and how I felt that it was all connected to something—some "thing" I couldn't put my finger on. As I tried to put words to my emotions, he interrupted me with an urgent yet almost defeated look on his face. He glanced at me and then looked at the floor, unable to hold eye contact as if there was something he knew but wasn't sure if he was allowed to speak it. For quite some time, he stared at his feet where his toes sat still at the end of his Birkenstocks. Then he lifted his hand, motioning me to be silent.

I responded by saying nothing.

In a whispered tone, he said, "Barry, you're talking about . . . *Chotchky.*"

I was taken aback. I knew he was right even though I didn't know what he was talking about. My soul screamed, *Aha! That's it!* I knew this was big. Bigger than the two of us put together (which would be over 12 feet tall and tip the scales at nearly 400 pounds—something had to be done!).

It turns out that his familiarity with the word is rooted in the fact that it is of Yiddish origin, a Jewish term. Since Harold is related to Moses, he would know such things. At this point, I figured it must have something to do with "Thou shall not . . ." something or other. Today I can clearly see that all of the Ten Commandments were Moses's effort to squelch Chotchky desires. After Harold gave me a bit of a history lesson, I desperately asked, "Well, what is it? What is Chotchky exactly?"

Again with the sheepish look, he shook his head. "Barry, no one really knows . . . and yet *we all know.*"

What Harold was saying is that there's something about Chotchky we're in denial of. It is the elephant in the room, *and he's wearing a skirt.*

It has been said that ignorance is bliss, and in some ways that may be true. But when we apply that wisdom to Chotchky, all we get is a whole lot of wasted time, money, and energy. When those three things have been wasted, we have wasted nothing less than life itself.

In an effort to get a true definition, Harold suggested I call one of his good Jewish friends, Rev. Dr. Jeanine Behrens in New York City.

"Hello, Jeanine. It's Barry, from Oregon. I have a question for you and, given your Jewish heritage, I thought you might have an answer. What is *Chotchky?*"

She hesitated for quite some time on the phone. I can only imagine that she, too, would have been unable to hold eye contact, staring at her feet, toes motionless at the end of her heels. I can't prove this. I just think so.

Then she responded, "Oh, well, you know . . . it's just *stuff* . . . stuff that gets out of control. I don't know. Let me call my mother and father."

So while I was on the line, she called her parents on her cell phone. "I've got this guy on the phone from Oregon who wants to know what Chotchky is." Her father paused, probably looked at his feet in slippers, and then replied, "Oh, well, you know . . . it's just stuff. Trinkets. It's odds and ends—collectibles with no real value. Other stuff, too. It's hard to say. It goes on and on."

You see, no one could fully put a finger on it, which is why we must *get a grip on it!*

After our phone conversation, Harold seemed to be having fun with the sheltered Irish boy (that would be me) who stood baffled before him as he disclosed the following, as if it was common sense: "It can be a woman, too."

"Chotchky?"

"Yeah."

*"What?!"*

"I know," he replied, shrugging. We stood there speechless. Befuddled. After a mutually acceptable length of silence, his Birkenstocks began walking as he nearly sang, "Let's go find some Chotchky!"

I was excited and yet filled with trepidation as we hopped in the car on this mystifying mission. No sooner than Dorothy could have clicked her ruby red slippers, we stood before the mother lode: "Junk Bros. Antique Mall." There was only one other person walking the cluttered aisles. She had on a Big, Floppy, Flowered Sun Hat, the kind ladies wear at the Kentucky Derby. It bounced up and down just over the top of the display racks like a bobber in a lake when a fish is nibbling. The floppiness of the hat drooped just below her eyes and cast a formidable shadow over her nose, mouth, and chin, leaving her mysteriously faceless. For a fleeting moment I wondered how, or even if, she could see. The three of us moved through the aisles in a way that, from Google Earth, would have looked like a giant game of Ms. Pac-Man.

Suddenly Harold stopped. His eyes lit up as he pointed in a northeasterly direction and said, "Now, *that* is Chotchky." And there it sat: a Small Plastic Gopher on a dusty glass shelf.

I, in no way, wish to offend any Small Plastic Gopher collectors . . . but really. Why? Who in their right mind . . . ? We picked it up and looked at it. Who would ever manufacture such a thing? Who would spend money on it? Who would put this in their house? Who would buy it as a gift? And when you bought it, would you use paper or plastic? If it *were* a gift, how would you present it to someone?

*Husband:* "Honey, close your eyes. You won't believe what I got you . . . okay, open your eyes!"

*Wife:* "What is it?"

*Husband:* "What do you mean, 'What is it'? It's a Small Plastic Gopher. Come on."

*Wife (long pause, followed by a confused and fed-up look):* "That's it. I want a divorce!"

Harold and I laughed our heads off. It can't be! Then, for a moment, we became Small Plastic Gopher collectors.

"Harold," I remarked in a highbrow tone, "*This* is a nice Small Plastic Gopher. I mean, I've seen some plastic gophers in my day, but this one. Look at the lack of detail. It's almost van Gogh–like. Why aren't there more Small Plastic Gophers on Earth?"

As we placed it back on the shelf and began walking away, we felt a great sense of satisfaction, knowing we had found possibly the most useless, worthless thing ever made. And for me, it was an epiphany. I finally understood. The only word that could describe it was . . . *Chotchky.*

*Then the unthinkable happened.*

The woman in the Big, Floppy, Flowered Sun Hat approached the Small Plastic Gopher. Slowly, at first. Cautiously, like one might approach an extraterrestrial after it proclaimed, "We come in peace." Looking at it. "Mole-ing" it over. I'm sure she'd heard us talk about its incredible "lack of detail" and other endearing qualities. Then she picked it up, walked over to the checkout stand and, well, put actual money on the counter for the gopher. She bought it. She selected paper for the bagging. (Apparently the hat *did* impair her vision.)

Now that piece of plastic is in her house taking up valuable space. Or maybe it was a gift she gave to a friend, telling her she overheard "collectors" or "experts" saying it was a masterpiece.

Who knows? Whatever the case, I couldn't believe my five senses.

Later that night after the dust settled, I had an epiphany on top of the epiphany. Exponential epiphanies. It was one of those moments in which, had I been in a movie, intriguing, "mystical" music would play underneath as the director slowly zoomed in on my face, kind of like in *A Field of Dreams,* when Kevin Costner's character began hearing strange words whispered, telling him to go build it.

It was just like that. Except I didn't hear voices . . . and there wasn't a sound track under me . . . and I'm not a farmer. Okay, so it wasn't like that at all.

But I did "get it." Suddenly, it all began to make sense. I began to *see.* Anything and everything has the potential to be or transition into a Small Plastic Gopher. Something that has no use whatsoever. No intrinsic or even artistic value. Something that simply takes up space. And yet *because it exists, because it is, we justify a place for it in our lives.* Because, well, it is "As Seen on TV," or we've heard "experts" or "celebrities" extol its virtues. Therefore, we must need it. There's this subtle yet clear line, and once it's crossed there's no going back.

And here's the startling fashion statement: Each and every one of us, at different times and places, is the woman in the Big, Floppy, Flowered Sun Hat! I finally identified the faceless woman who bought the Small Plastic Gopher. *She is us.*

## The 8 Items from the Worst Day of My Life

Remember those eight "diamonds"? Let's take a closer look at them, and see how, if we give each section a letter, it will actually spell *Chotchky.*

#1. "It" may have been bottles of shampoo and other stuff, but that day there were something like 12 plastic squeeze bottles full of goop with varying degrees of hold. A dozen! They're not roses. I must have been wearing the Big, Floppy, Flowered Sun Hat when I picked up those things, as most of them are Small Plastic Gophers. That's the first item from the worst day of my life and gives us our first letter: **C**

#2. "It" may have been a gift at one time; however, the guilt I felt that morning about not liking the Shelf Elf was causing a subtle debilitation that had been creeping up on me for years. That day it was as if it jumped off the shelf, wrapped its little arms around my neck, and refused to let go, while whispering negative affirmations in my ear: *You should feel guilty for not liking me. I was a gift!* **H**

#3. "It" may have been a T-shirt from my first concert. But I haven't worn the shirt for 27 years. It's just taking up space in my drawer, making it harder and harder to find the few T-shirts I actually like *and* wear. A problem has come along and now I must "whip it." **O**

#4. "It" may look like food, at least kind of. But about 20 minutes after eating the Grape-Nut/sugarcoated, freeze-dried-strawberry combo, I began to feel a little dizzy. Like I was on one of those rides at the fair that spins so fast they pull the floor out from under you. It's actually a box of Small Plastic Gophers that we put milk on and eat. **T**

#5. "It" might be called "news," but under the sensational headlines and buried in ads and coupons often lurks some pretty smooth talkin' ground squirrels whispering in our ears and obscuring our vision. **C**

#6. "It" may be called the Internet, but with all the spam, pop-ups, and gossip, it transmutes into Small Plastic Gophers in my mind! (Not to mention the magazines at checkout stands. Those images linger! I know I didn't go to the grocery store that morning, but they were still with me. They are always with us, stuck to the surface of our minds like gum on the bottom of a third grader's desk.) **H**

#7. "It" may have been a phone at one time, but now I have enough to open my own AT&T outlet store. And with all the other random technological devices in cupboards and drawers in my house, I could stock the local Radio Shack. **K**

#8. "It" may have been a friend at one time. We have a history, but I've grown. I've changed! And when we're together, I revert back to old habits. I do and say things that aren't me anymore. Besides, all he wants from me now is money that I don't have. When we're together, I'm wasting my time, energy, and money. Yes, my "friend" has now become a Small Plastic Gopher. **Y**

What does that spell? *Chotchky.*

Yes, everything has the potential to be or become Chotchky: *anything that crowds, intrudes, clutters, or in any way distracts from our soul's highest purpose.* An incredible amount of what we actually buy, accept, and allow into our lives is Chotchky already. Somehow we were wearing the Big, Floppy, Flowered Sun Hat when we saw it. CJ's bedroom was like a breeding ground where the "eight" all came to multiply. (Gee, I wonder where he got all the stuff?) And all of it adds to entropy.

This is the word scientists came up with to describe the force behind the mayhem I was overtaken by that significant morning. It is the scientifically proven universal constant that all things move from relative order to disorder. *Everything.* The more things you have, in any "closed system" the more disorder there will be.

Two things have always struck me about this universal constant. First, I see it as irrefutable evidence of a Higher Intelligence. The universe started from a massive explosion (possibly in my son's room) called the Big Bang. The evidence of a higher power, then, can be seen in all life on Earth and in the incomprehensible balance of the cosmos.

Imagine it. Complete chaos from an explosion more powerful than billions and billions of our most destructive atomic bombs somehow moved in total opposition to the universal constant of entropy. Chaos, left to its own devices should become more chaotic, just as an anvil dropped off the top of the Sears Tower should quite rapidly move in a downward direction. Entropy is just as present and reliable as gravity. I don't see any other logical explanation for our existence than to say an Intelligence beyond our comprehension guided this unfathomable amount of scattered energy into balance and order.

Second, the existence of this law should be enough in and of itself to stave off our impulse to continually add more stuff into the "systems" of our life. For each and every thing we add, there is a corresponding increase in chaos. The Czech writer and former president Václav Havel wrote: "Just as the constant increase of entropy is the basic law of the universe, so it is the basic law of life to be ever more highly structured and to struggle against entropy."

This "law of life" he is referring to I think has something to do with the Intelligence that was carefully "sculpting" the energy of the Big Bang, creating quite a masterpiece. That Intelligence is still with us, in the balance of the stars and in the ever-increasing order of life. Evolution itself moves in complete contradiction to entropy. All life forms have moved from simplicity and relative disorder to higher and higher degrees of complexity. It's as if someone stepped off the Empire State Building and fell up despite the law of gravity. It's a miracle that's happening all around us all the time. You and I, as the highest point of evolution, have "fallen up" the highest. This is an indication that the Higher Intelligence that moved through the Big Bang is still expanding in and through us. We are It. The Challenge is to awaken to who and what we really are and be about the work, as it was in the beginning, of creating greater order.

However, I do not think Havel or the Higher Intelligence that created the universe desires us to continually struggle against the incessant entropy of Chotchky that we bring upon ourselves. Rather, the next stage in our evolution will be reached as we bring greater order to our thoughts, our actions, and, as a result, our world. Let's not waste another ounce of the miracle that is us. Instead, let's keep "falling up."

Besides, it is our struggle against the ever-present forces of entropy combined with all our Chotchky that creates . . .

### The Chotchky Effect

Whether we are consciously aware of it or not, we all grapple with it. A feeling of stress combined with ambiguity, tension, and immobilization. My son CJ was feeling the Chotchky Effect that morning curled up on the floor of his closet. The principle of the Chotchky Effect is this:

> *The conscious, waking mind is a kind of Sacred Shelf. It can hold only so much and should support only what truly matters. When we put too much on this shelf, it starts to bend. There is also a direct correlation between how useless and trivial a thing is and its weight. As we allow our Sacred Shelf to hold more and more weighty, unimportant contents, we unconsciously shove aside what truly matters, and eventually our Sacred Shelf starts to crack.*

Hence the term *nervous breakdown*. Most of us, however, don't have one of those. Instead, we experience something much worse: a *subtle takedown*.

Nervous breakdowns can actually be good, as they serve to get our attention, but subtle takedowns are sneaky. They slowly wear us out, lingering under the radar of our awareness as the Chotchky slowly fills our sacred shelf.

One Fourth of July, I experienced a kind of subtle takedown that illustrates quite vividly the elusive power of the Chotchky Effect. My family and I went to a little beach town in Oregon to celebrate the holiday. Everyone in the city and neighboring towns gather this time of year to watch the fireworks display and explode their own stash of pyrotechnics, which makes the official display seem like sparklers. When it was all over and the last of our gigantic Costco-sized box of fireworks had fizzed out, we gathered the burned shells and put them back into the box. Along the way, we probably picked up at least a dozen stray shells others had left behind.

My wife, Heather, told me to make sure they were "all the way out" before I put the box back in the minivan.

Well, duh!

Then we all loaded up and began what felt like a 5 o'clock, downtown Los Angeles commute back toward our accommodations. As we crept along the side streets, which ever-so-slowly poured into the highway, we smelled smoke. Teens on bikes were doing circles around the cars while throwing smoke bombs at each other. Others kids in bushes shot off an assortment of high-flying mini-explosions into the air.

"The smell must be from smoke entering in through the open windows," I remember saying.

Logically, we rolled up our windows, but somehow it didn't help. In fact, it seemed to get worse. I figured enough smoke had entered the minivan that by rolling up the windows, we were simply trapping the smoke inside, so we tried rolling down the windows again. Up and down we rolled, becoming more and more asphyxiated. Wherever the smoke was coming from, the effect was so subtle, it was baffling.

Heather said, "Maybe the burned shells in the cardboard box in the back have caught on fire. *Maybe the smoke is coming from inside.*"

"No, sweetheart. I'm sure it's not."

We continued driving despite the cloud of smog in front of my face. It did, however, seem better with the windows down, our heads sticking out like Scooby-Doo in the Mystery Machine. Soon, however, even with the windows down, we were close to gasping for air. Our minivan must have looked like a yuppie version of Cheech and Chong's vehicle in *Up in Smoke*. I wondered silently, *Is something on fire in the van, or is it coming from outside?* But it was just passive wondering . . . it didn't occur to me to actually find out.

Finally, Heather said very patiently, as if speaking to a four-year-old after he had too much birthday cake, "Honey, maybe we should pull over and just *see if the van is on fire.*"

But I was like, "Sweetheart, if we get out of line, we will never get back in." We had earned our place in line. I didn't want to have to try to wiggle my way back. The fact that our van now must have looked more like a barbecue when smoke is seeping out of the edges because several pieces of hamburger have broken off and fallen into the flames didn't seem to matter.

After about 20 minutes, we finally came to our exit. I drove as fast as I could around the twisty beach-lined road, I'm sure leaving behind a trail of swirling smoke all the way home. By this time, there was so much smoke in the van, the thought crossed my mind, *Maybe I should just drive straight into the ocean.* When we arrived and opened the back of the minivan, it was like sending a smoke signal to the next county, and where there's smoke . . .

There, in the back of the van, was a nice little campfire. Like at the tail end of a long evening of roasting s'mores. The embers glowed a beautiful red-orange. After a moment of staring, wondering if it was really happening, we grabbed the edges of the cardboard box, which were still somewhat intact, and yanked the fire pit to the pavement. Heather grabbed a hose conveniently located on the side of our lodging and quickly doused the embers. It sounded like steak sizzling as steam rose into the night air. Then when I looked at my wife, I couldn't be sure, but I thought maybe there was steam also exiting from her ears, adding to the mist. *Understandably.*

Heather took a deep breath and made a most astute suggestion. "Honey, the next time we think there's even the slightest chance at all that the van is on fire, let's just pull over and take a look."

I sheepishly grinned. "That's a good policy."

Folks, the minivan is on fire.

We don't know it because, as a culture, we've slowly become asphyxiated by our Chotchky. We're like the frog in a pot of water that is gradually coming to a boil. It's a phenomenon I call one-degree rationalization. The frog will just sit there, rationalizing away. "Oh well, it's just one degree warmer. What could it hurt? Okay, so one *more* degree. Big deal. Ribbit." *Frog Soup.* It's a subtle takedown. So subtle in fact that we don't want to "lose our place in line" because we so badly want to "get there" that we don't even notice *we're in the wrong line.* It's all so very confusing because the smoke (Chotchky) has gotten inside and is all around us. As a culture, we all need to pull over and put the fire out.

An interesting psychological observation regarding "The Case of Family in Burning Minivan" is the fact that it was my job to make sure the spent shells weren't smoldering. This only added to my denial, my unwillingness to acknowledge the burning van. We have done this with Chotchky. Who wants to admit they bought an exercise machine but never use it? So there it sits rapidly becoming obsolete. Or how about some powdered diet drink ordered off TV that has now taken up residency in the cupboard creeping closer and closer to its "use by" date? Who wants to have the tough conversation with that "friend" whose expiration date passed years ago? Who wants to acknowledge they went into credit-card debt paying for a get-rich-quick seminar? We simply do not wish to admit, even to ourselves, that we are continually feeding

Small Plastic Gophers. The only way, however, to put the fire out is to swallow our pride and humbly "pull the van over."

(*Note:* I am amazed by how quickly Heather forgave me for the whole Cheech and Chong shenanigans. I didn't even have to sleep on the couch that night. Thanks, honey. I love you.)

So, guess what? As the universe would have it, we have all been asked to pull the minivan over and put the fire out. The economy and the environment are just a couple of smoldering issues directly related to our Chotchky addictions. A daily dose of humility is in order.

The genesis of my outburst at CJ that fateful morning, I finally realized, was the result of the Chotchky Effect, which snapped my Sacred Shelf. It is very important that we make this connection. I was not angry with my son. He did not buy all the shampoos, gels, clothes, the Shelf Elf, or myriad cereals. He did not call me asking to borrow money he had no intention of paying back. He did not put all the e-mails in my in-box along with the endless celebrity gossip. He didn't even buy all the stuff that turned his bedroom into a graveyard where Chotchkies come to die. I did.

God help whoever happens to be on the receiving end of the Chotchky Effect and the subtle takedown or nervous breakdown that ensues. Unfortunately, it is usually the ones we love.

## Chotchky Challenge

Look around you. I bet if you are willing to really look, you can now begin to see some Small Plastic Gophers of your own.

In all eight areas that added to the Chotchky Effect in me that day, let's take a peek into your life. What percentage of your stuff is or has begun the transformation into Chotchky? As you take this Challenge, don't overthink it. It's very easy to rationalize any piece of junk into fool's gold. Instead, go with your soul. Feel it; let your soul rise to the surface. What percentage in each area has begun the transformation? Ready? Go!

1. Your bathroom. What percentage of your hair spray, hair gel, toothbrushes, hair colors, toothpastes, soaps, makeup, lotions, shampoos, pills, prescriptions, and so on is causing more confusion than it is helping?

2. What about gifts that have never been used, or ones that sit around taunting you with a twinge of guilt for not liking them? Or maybe those that live in one of your closets as part of a whole category of Chotchky called "storage"?

3. What about your garage, car, and closets? The shoes, scarves, belts, sweaters, T-shirts, socks, and God knows what else?

4. Your cupboards. How much food do you feel is truly beneficial, and what percentage is not?

5. The news you watch and read, from the TV to the newspaper, Internet, radio, and so forth. How much is feeding the drama of fear instead of helping?

6. Information from magazines, the Internet, e-mails, texts, and busybodies. Same question: How much is feeding the drama of fear instead of helping?

7. Items such as phones, cords, computers, headphones, chargers, DVD/CD/iPod players, TVs, speakers, remotes, keyboards, and so on. How much is actually useful to you and used regularly?

8. How about the people in your life—are there any Small Plastic Gophers disguised as friends?

Quickly now, taking all of this in, going with your gut, your soul, what percentage do you think just might be Chotchky? Circle below:

10%  20%  30%  40%  50%  60%  70%  80%  90%  100%

What did you get?

Whatever percentage it was for you, imagine what your life will be like a year from now as we begin the process of redirecting your time, energy, and money that were being wasted on Chotchky, toward building your Master Peace, the dreams of your soul, the very aspiration you wrote in the exercise in the "Backward." As we continue, you will probably begin to see your percentage go up. This is good. It means your Chotchky Vision is getting more powerful. As this happens, think of it as money being deposited in your bank account and as pure energy being given to your body and mind. Think of it as such not just because it's a lovely metaphor, but because these things will actually happen.

Do you see where we're going? The redirection of the life force in you toward what you really want is nothing short of miraculous. Do you remember the classic line from *Star Trek,* "Beam me up"? It was always followed by a most powerful response, "Energize!" It is proven through the laws of physics that energy cannot be created or destroyed. Instead, it is simply transferred, redirected from one expression to the next. What we are doing as we face the Chotchky Challenge is transferring all of our energy to our soul. In essence we are now saying, "Beam me up." And the universe's only response can be, as shown by the laws of physics, "Energize!"

To beam up now, go to the secret web page and click on the Scooby-Doo: **www.barryadennis.com/chotchkyvideos1.** When you return, we're going to see why God was a member of the '80s rock band ZZ Top and how your dog just might be the missing link.

# CHAPTER 2

# THE BIG BOX

### Truth or Fiction?

Approximately 70 percent of all nonfiction books are not read past the first chapter.

*Truth or Fiction?*

Fiction. It is actually estimated to be 90 percent! This means that 90 percent of all such publications are bookotchky. But, I'm guessing it's not the book. It's the Chotchky Mind's inability to be fully present, always in a hurry to get to the next book, thinking, *Maybe this one will have <u>all</u> the answers in the first 30 pages, or this one, or . . .*

This statistic also means that very soon, you will be among the top 10 percent! Congrats.

So where did all the Chotchky come from that was part of the "eight" that cluttered the Sacred Shelf of my mind, turning me into the Incredible Hulk? Here's a clue.

Christmas 2002 has become legendary in my family. My youngest son, CJ, was interested in only one present. Can you guess which one? The one in the Big Box. Some things never change.

When we finally gave him the green light to open "the Big Box" he attacked it, ripping the paper and tossing it in the air. Feeling his energy, the dog joined in, running and barking around the box as the scraps of paper floated down. Soon, there was nothing between him and the holy grail but the box itself. Finally, he slowly pulled back the cardboard flaps like it was some ancient archaeological find. You could almost hear rusty hinges creak. He was now Indiana Jones. However, when he finally pulled the "doors" open, revealing the contents of the Big Box, no mystical light came shooting out. The ground did not shake. People's faces didn't even melt.

Several of us simply asked, "What is it?!"

After staring into the box, frozen, stunned, CJ raised his head toward his mother and me. He seemed to be looking right through us though, as if we were rice paper, the words in his mind trying to find their rightful order. He looked at my father and mother, his grandparents, the ones who brought the contents of the Big Box. Then, through clenched teeth, beady eyes, and a shade of red I have not seen before or since, the words came with a fury: "It's just what I *always never* wanted in my whole life!"

Stunning. How can anything reach such a status? How could anyone be consciously aware of the one thing—out of everything in the world—that you would never want? Maybe instead of creating a wish list each gift-giving holiday, one would thoughtfully craft a hate list, in order from the most dreaded to the least despised.

Ultimately, I think "It's just what I *always never* wanted in my whole life!" was CJ's attempt at expressing something that cannot really fit into any earthly language. Maybe something closer to speaking in tongues. Something we have all felt and continue to feel with some regularity but have never attempted to convey. Something referencing the futility inherent in trying to find our soul, even God, in something, somewhere, out there. At age four, his journey had just begun. One foot still in innocence and wholeness, one now firmly planted in the world of Things—opposites, in separation. He just experienced, possibly for the first time, *projectionotchky: the projection of one's own natural state of joy and peace onto the world of things.*

It is a learned behavior. Nothing in the world, no matter how big the box, could ever contain the miracle that lies within us. It is a tale as old as time. Adam and Eve walked right out of paradise to see if there was something better somewhere else. I'm fairly certain now of what Adam said to Eve after biting the apple: "It's just what I *always never* wanted in my whole life!"

In the throes of projectionotchky, no matter where we go, there it is not.

What would happen if we were watching, say, *Avatar* in 3D and we got up out of our seats to go join the Na'vi in a round of chanting on the planet of Pandora under the Tree of Souls? We would go "bonk" right into the screen, wrinkling the image for those who still chose to participate in the illusion and yet knew better. Think of that screen as the screen of truth. There's nothing really there. It's a projection.

When we are projecting, we regularly go bonk into the screen of truth. "It" is not in this relationship, this job, this toy, this food, this drug, or this latitude and longitude. We never get to Pandora because we have forgotten that it's inside the projector. All the romance, the action and adventure, and even the happy ending.

Tag, you're "It."

A few hours later, CJ went up to the playroom. There it sat: the thing from the Big Box. Lifeless. Alone. It was a puppet theater with a marionette, not too dissimilar from Pinocchio. ("I want to be a real boy.")

And like Pinocchio, something began to change. Not the thing, of course. Things don't change. Something inside the real boy—inside the only "box" whose content really matters. Whose content is so miraculous it ultimately creates the experience of everything.

CJ began to play with it. Create characters. A whole world was given birth. A real love story. Now my son was living in the truth that all he ever really wanted, he always had. Returning to this truth, the contents of the Big Box transformed into something joyful simply matching his state of being. You see, the thing is neutral. All things are. This is big, like the box. _Things are neutral!_ Like a movie screen, they simply exist to reflect back to us our projections in the form of our thoughts. That's how powerful we all are.

CJ soon came to Heather and me in a way that I can only describe as "meek." Humble, peaceful, loving, true.

In this way, he said, "Daddy, can I call Grandma and Grandpa? I want to tell them something."

"Sure," I replied. "What do you want to tell them?"

"It's special, Daddy. A surprise."

He picked up the phone, which looked quite large in his 4-year-old hands, and, as I fed him the numbers, he dialed. "Grandma," he said, "I have something to tell you and Grandpa, too."

My father got on another line. CJ continued, "Grandma, Grandpa, I'm so sorry. It's my favorite! I didn't mean what I said. I love you."

He enjoyed the puppet theater on and off for three years, which is quite exceptional. Most Christmas gifts turn into Chotchky within days, if not hours. Many are Chotchky even before the unwrapping. God help us.

So three years later, the puppet theater made its transition into Chotchky. Little did we know that the puppet theater was part of a select assortment of Chotchky that sat under the constant influence of entropy, creating stress that would one day be a part of _my_ meltdown. Chotchky is like a time bomb ticking away quietly.

Recently, we finally gave it to another child to enjoy. One of the greatest superpowers that comes with Chotchky Vision is the ability to see when something has made that transition from useful, enjoyable, and life-enhancing, to a Small Plastic gopher. The sooner this is recognized, the sooner we are free to release, let go, and make room for something better. And the clearer our Chotchky Vision becomes, that something better is often . . . nothing at all.

## Chotchky Challenge

Consider the following: "Every 'thing' is neutral, therefore, all that I encounter is a projection of my internal experience."

What have you gone *bonk* into recently? For your soul, consider this carefully for a moment. Can you begin to accept the truth that it was your projection that created the drama? Whether it was a relationship, a traffic jam, a conversation, a computer, or a bowl of chocolate gelato. Every *thing* is neutral, simply a screen for your experience.

Choose one area where you forgot that you are the projector, and this forgetfulness has brought confusion or even suffering. Place it here:

_____

_____

_____

_____

_____

Now begin to see it for what it is. A screen for this movie you came to experience with all of its ups and downs, tension, and resolution. Understanding this is freedom.

One of the biggest reasons we project, look, and reach "out there" in things is because the Chotchky World has tried to convince us that God is out there somewhere. This often creates *spiritual practiceotchky: the practice of changing spiritual disciplines so much it becomes a habit motivated by the delusion that It is out there somewhere, if only you can find the right guru, retreat, church, drug, CD series, meditation, mantra, or yoga position and then hold it until you pass out.*

Spiritual practiceothcky is actually the practice of running away from God. It's not out there. A great teacher who wore a robe and sandals once said, "The Kingdom of Heaven is within." Nailed it.

It seems that all great wisdom teachers wore a robe and sandals. Think about it. The question is, which came first? The robe and sandals or the wisdom? There actually is a profound and enlightening connection between their chosen attire and exceptional wisdom. The reason for this is illuminating and soon will be discussed. First, however, it's important to recognize we took that image and projected it onto God. We put a robe and sandals on the Almighty. Then we gave him a cane and put him on a cloud with a beard so long he looks like a member of ZZ Top.

At times we've created a judgmental, even angry, vengeful "wrath of God." This is *Godotchky.* We have projected our own neuroses onto the Holy Spirit. In our mind, God needs a therapist, anger-management classes, a razor, and a nostalgic comeback tour with Rick Springfield as the second billing.

We've got it all backward.

I cannot claim to know exactly what God is, but I do know what God is not. God is not a flesh-and-bone human being with grooming issues. God is the opposite of this image. God is Spirit, Energy, Consciousness, Light. God is the absence of Chotchky. Therefore, as we eliminate it from our lives, we begin to find "God."

Atheist, agnostic, religious, or Trekkie, when it comes to the search for meaning, for God, we generally have it backward, which may be why God in reverse, is Dog. In Hinduism, it is said that dogs are the only animals capable of reaching divine perfection just as they are. A dog, it is said, does not need to go through the stages of being human in order to reach the evolutionary end point of Pure Love. Unencumbered by an overcerebrated brain and opposable thumbs, a dog is capable of reaching complete, selfless devotion and love. Anyone who has a dog knows this is true.

So maybe instead of seeing God as a member of ZZ Top, we should see God in our dog. This might just help us to see God as

God really is. Unconditionally loving. In fact, we do often say a dog is man's best friend. This way, when we call for our dog, we could see it as God running to us, overjoyed just to be asked to be a part of our life.

Yes, I think I'll see my dog as an expression of God. It's better than some hippie dude on a cloud far, far away. Well, all this writing has made me a little stiff. I think I'll go for a walk with my God.

## Truth or Fiction?

Recently in Shelton, Washington, a man called the police to report his wife missing. When police arrived at their home, they were aghast. Clothing, dishes, and boxes were crammed from floor to ceiling in every room. Police chief Terry Davenport reported: "In some areas, clothes and debris were piled 6 feet high. Officers were having to climb over the top on their hands and knees. In some areas, their heads were touching the ceiling while they were standing on top of piles of debris."

After ten hours of searching, the officers discovered the woman's body. She had suffocated under piles of thingotchky. The woman's husband told reporters that she may have been looking for the phone when she died.

*Truth or Fiction?*

Truth, sadly.

Yes, this really happened. I guess you could say the Grim Reaper called. This kind of horror is becoming commonplace. My heart goes out to this woman's family.

Now, I know what you might be thinking: *That's not me. I don't need an oxygen tank to answer my phone or climbing gear to get from one room to the next.* (At least I hope that's what you're thinking.)

Extreme examples such as this exist as a warning to us all; they point out a much bigger, yet subtler problem. Like a chain-smoker who has a lung removed, the bigger problem is the millions of more casual smokers who think they don't have a problem but are slowly getting cancer. The woman found under her junk is a "Chotchky" chain-smoker. The bigger, yet harder to see issue is, then, the countless millions of us who really don't think there is an issue here. This woman's fate is the consequence of a society of excess. Somehow we have convinced ourselves that excess is good. Excess is defined as an overindulgence or intemperance in eating, drinking, collecting, buying, and so on. Excess marks the line when anything can transition from useful to Chotchky. Eric Hoffer captured the conundrum quite masterfully with this astute observation: "We can never have enough of that which we really do not want."

## Chotchky Challenge

Circle your answer to the following questions:

- Do you agree there is a fair chance that we live in a society of excess? Yes or No

- Do you think it is likely that excess is extremely problematic in a great variety of ways? Yes or No

- If you answered yes, can you see how we might be totally oblivious to much of the excess in our own lives because we have accepted it as "normal"? Yes or No

Okay then, let's change the norm!

We might begin by asking how and why we became this way. When something has gone over the line into excess, it is now serving to numb us, to flatten our lives, and to alter our emotional state so we don't have to deal with the reality of our very messy and magnificent existence. In other words, "excess" is a drug. Paradoxically, of course, every time we "use" it by acquiring more, it makes life messier. It's a voracious cycle. Overdoing anything has the same effect: overeating, over-shopping, over-sexing, over-drinking, over-phoning, over-exercising, over-chatting (gossip), over-Internetting, over-movie/TV-ing, etc., ad nauseam. It's an attempt to avoid, to escape, and it has a profound numbing effect. And, to make matters worse, this drug is not only legal, it's encouraged. The addiction supports our current dysfunction. It creates a never-ending demand that must be filled while, at the same time, our suppliers keep creating a greater demand by pushing the "excess" through every conceivable outlet.

All the gorging is a misguided attempt to make a divine connection. But, like trying to fit a puzzle piece that goes with a picture of a desert into a puzzle that is a picture of an ocean, *it will never fit*. And yet, we keep trying as if somehow, someday, the excess will fix all of our problems and even bring spiritual fulfillment.

Albert Einstein said, "Insanity is doing the same thing over and over again expecting different results." So, why all the insanity? There are, of course, many contributing factors for which we all must take our part of the responsibility. However, travel back with me in time to the year 1929. It was a pivotal moment when our government decided to be the drug cartel of this highly addictive substance. It was then that economist and retail analyst Victor Lebow gave the following report to the President's Council of Economic Advisors: "Our enormously productive economy . . . demands that we make consumption our way of life, that we convert the buying and use of goods into rituals, that we seek our spiritual satisfaction, our ego satisfaction, in consumption . . . we need things consumed, burned up, replaced and discarded at an ever-accelerating rate."

And they took his advice. The Chairman of President Eisenhower's Council of Economic Advisors stated: "The American economy's ultimate purpose is to produce more consumer goods." That's our ultimate purpose? To produce more consumer goods so that we can find "spiritual satisfaction in consumption"?

Yes, this is what we have been taught, and it is constantly reinforced by the Chotchky Campaign. Excess is king. Think about that economic strategy in 1929; then consider our world today. They said they would convert the buying of goods into "rituals." Hasn't that occurred? They said we would seek "spiritual satisfaction" and "ego satisfaction" in consumption. Isn't our entire society set up now to both create and meet our demands to do this very thing? Here is the great confusion. They lumped two opposing human elements into the same category: Spirit and Ego. The spirit cannot find satisfaction in consumption. The ego, or lower vibrational aspect of our being, can . . . for only a fleeting moment, of course, which played right into the plan: "We need things consumed, burned up, replaced, and discarded at an ever-accelerating rate." We too, consciously or not, often lump the ego and spirit into the same category. Our spirit cries out from under all the excess.

We are going to take a closer look at these areas, where we tend to go "over," and begin to break the addiction to acquisition. We're going to perform a miracle. A paradigm shift. Freedom, joy, and peace are there, waiting patiently. Let's begin with . . .

### Stepford Wives

Even if your stuff is pristinely kept, you could still be surrounded by excess. In fact, it is often the people whose lives appear immaculate who are actually overcompensating for a profoundly disabling strain of the Chotchky Effect. I call it *Stepford Wifeotchky: a robotic existence, motivated by the desire to live up to an unattainable ideal, making all those in the general vicinity feel as if they are walking on eggshells.*

Think of couples who appeared outlandishly happy and then without warning, they're signing divorce papers. Chotchky, in one form or another, very likely eradicated the relationship. In many cases it's the Chotchky Mind's unconscious assumption that the grass is always greener on the other side of the fence, but the soul knows this is ludicrous. It's not greener. It's just that you are always farther away from the grass on the other side; therefore, you can't see the brown patches and weeds. The grass on the other side might be different, but it is not likely greener.

Regardless, the soul wants healthy grass because it knows that being close enough to someone that you can see the "weeds" is a blessing. Then with patient loving care, the weeds are slowly overtaken by thick, soft, beautiful green grass. That's what we do for each other: we weed each other's lawns (thanks, honey).

✳

A few houses down from my parents' place, there is an estate. Actually, it's more like a kingdom. I envied these people and their "castle," giant pool, horse arena, river, servants' quarters, and massive tree house for their kids (fully furnished, including a satellite dish).

Then one day I met the woman of the house. She was very gracious and took me on a guided tour. Afterward, a deep sadness fell over her face. Under her breath she said, "This is the hell that is my life." Suddenly, like through a subtle form of telepathy, I felt her pain. All the stuff to take care of. To worry about. To stay on top of. *Never* being alone with the constant supervising of crews, servants, and repairmen to fix the truly unfathomable amount of stuff. Excess? Giant bills to pay in an uncertain economy. A husband who was rarely in town, and when he was, he worked in his office a few acres away from the castle. (There was even an underground tunnel to his "lair.")

It *was* hell. I could see it in her eyes and feel it in my heart.

Could it be that she envied me? Was she now seeing the "greener grass" of my life? When I left, the misguided notion called envy was no longer with me. Something in me had changed. A *shift* occurred. Somehow, my grass got a lot greener that day.

## Chotchky Challenge

Can you identify a specific moment or an area of your life where you may be falling for the illusion of greener grass? The bigger house down the road? An attractive stranger? A different job? Place it here:

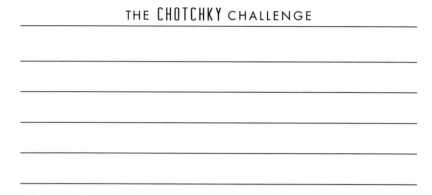

Now, before doing any fence jumping, get in touch with your heart. Do you have a history of making poor decisions based on the illusion of "greener grass"? It just *might* be time for a change, or it could be the Chotchky Mind creating confusion, always looking away from its blessings. With awareness, begin discerning between the two. This alone makes all the "grass" outside velvet green because inside, on the only lawn that truly matters, this thoughtful introspection is like a gardener removing the weeds of your perception.

### Your Ship Has Come In

It is said that when large sailing ships first arrived in the Americas, the native people literally could not see them coming. They had no concept of "ship." There was no place for it in their minds; therefore, their eyes were blind.

The first white men to see the Grand Canyon actually thought they could throw a stone across it. (And I'm quite sure they thought the grass was greener on the other side.) They were blind to the existence of something so grand. It took a long time for their minds to adjust to reality. It was a complete and total Paradigm Shift.

*The American Heritage Dictionary of the English Language* defines the word *paradigm* as "a set of assumptions, concepts, values, and practices that constitutes a way of viewing reality for the community that shares them."

Once a community has accepted and created a paradigm, giant sailing ships go unnoticed and grand canyons appear as creeks. I have even heard of entire communities who have accept-ed the practice of spending money they don't have, using pieces of plastic, for things they don't need or even really want. Can you imagine?

A paradigm is kind of like an old "para-glasses" that we never take off. Most of these glasses are quite filthy and scratched with prejudice, beliefs, and opinions. The quickest way to begin to see reality as it is, is to get a new para-glasses. This is called a . . .

*Paradigm Shift: a fundamental*
*change in approach or assumptions*

For the most part, this is not easy to do. But if we want to "see our ship come in," it is a necessary part of the journey. We must undo the thinking that Victor Lebow and so many others have planted in our mind. In fact, one could say it is the Challenge: to shift from the Paradigm of Chotchky to the Paradigm of the Soul.

*"You must unlearn all you have learned."*

—YODA (A LITTLE GREEN GUY IN A ROBE AND SANDALS)

### The Chotchky Paradigm

The Chotchky Paradigm is the current set of assumptions and values that constitute our culture's way of viewing reality. In this way, we are all standing on the shore, oblivious to the incoming ships (full of Chotchky).

Through this paradigm, we think that more is always better. And that bigger is always better. And don't forget faster. Imme-diate gratification is paramount since through this scratched up para-glasses, happiness appears to come from outside of us. There-fore, the faster we accumulate our Chotchky, the happier we will be. Through this paradigm, we are very attached to things, which eventually brings much suffering.

The Chotchky Mind lives in fear. Fear of not enough. Fear of commitment. Fear of success and failure. Fear of stillness. Ultimately, it is the genesis of all the dysfunction we currently experience as a human race.

It is a construct of our ego. An ego is a lot like an Eggo. It's true. Freedom is found in the ancient spiritual practice known as "Leggo my *Ego*." Every time we have the awareness to "leggo" of the Chotchky Paradigm's wayward impulses, we move closer to the soul. "Ego" refers to the aspect of our consciousness that experiences itself as "less than" and separate. This is why the ego created the Chotchky Paradigm. It puts us in a constant state of feeding our insecurities and fears. More stuff, more food, more admiration, more validation . . . more, bigger, faster, now!

The ego measures its success through Chotchky, and has now successfully made most of humanity a hive of worker bees. We're all buzzing around, working our lives away feeding queen bee Ego. The Soul's Paradigm, on the other hand, is a construct of Spirit, Higher Power, and Love. As our understanding deepens, more of our energy is diverted to the spirit, leaving us free to once and for all, "Leggo my Ego."

### *The Soul Paradigm*

Through the Soul Paradigm, we see a vastly different reality. This para-glasses is clear. More and bigger are not always better. In fact, less and smaller are sometimes more. Not always of course, but sometimes. The soul lives in these paradoxes and is quite comfortable with them.

The Soul Paradigm is patient—in fact, the "journey" is enjoyable because through these clear lenses, we see that the work, the creative process, is the destination. So why then, in the name of peace, would we want to go so fast that we miss the experience?

The soul is more than happy to slow down in order to speed up and knows that we can also be moving rapidly on the outside and yet be still on the inside.

With such clarity, we see that all emotions arise from within. They cannot come from someplace else. It is a silly notion to think they ever could, and yet we live our lives much of the time controlled by what lies "out there," emotionally subservient to "people, places, and things." (All my fears have been realized: *we are controlled by . . . nouns!*) Through the Soul Paradigm, compassion arises as we begin to recognize the level of suffering so many of us are experiencing from all the "nouns." This suffering is seen everywhere, whether it is a child overwhelmed by an excess of toys, a couple who unconsciously try to take happiness from each other, or a junk-food junkie trying to scoop contentment from Ben & Jerry's Chunky Monkey. (I tried that once; I just got chunky.)

Through the Soul Paradigm, we can deeply enjoy all of our nouns without being attached.

## Chotchky Challenge

There is a Zen teaching about a cup. In the Buddhist tradition, these teachings are known as koans. They are often in the form of questions and are designed to help us shift our paradigm. I'm sure you're familiar with the first half of this koan: "Do you see the cup as half empty or half full?"

A cup whose content is at exactly 50 percent is both half empty and half full at the same time. How you see it will create your emotional experience. The "cup koan" goes much deeper. There is a twist most people have never heard, as it is designed for advanced students and requires a genuine readiness to shift. Are you ready? When asking the question, "Do you see the cup as half empty or half full?" the master is waiting for the student to respond, "Neither, for I see the cup . . . already broken."

Challenging, isn't it? You might be asking, "How can this be liberating?" In the eternal existence of the materials that make up the cup (atoms), they will only be in their current form for a relative wink of an eye. When you become attached to its "cupness," you are holding it back from its greater expressions. Those same atoms will undoubtedly be, at some time, part of a blade of grass blanketing Mother Earth; a leaf on a tree reaching for the sky; feathers of a bird soaring in the air; the eye of a whale breaching in the ocean; and even the nose of a human being who, in all probability, will someday be asked, "Is this cup half empty or half full?"

And if they are truly awake, the answer will be right under their nose. "Neither," they will say. "I see it as already broken."

This koan is designed to reveal the freedom that lives in non-attachment. Everything breaks. Being in denial of this creates suffering and keeps us, and the rest of existence, from evolving into greater expressions of life. When we can see the cup, not only as it is now but also as "already broken," then when it does break, it is simply a release, a celebration of greater things to come. We can say, "Okay, there it goes," because just as nothing lasts forever, the opposite is true as well: Nothing stays broken forever. It simply transitions—transforms into what will be. This is true for every-thing. Including you. Needless to say, the Chotchky Mind suffers when things break, but the Soul celebrates.

### The Truth

As a construct of the Spirit, it is only through the Soul Paradigm that we are able to see reality as it truly is. The mission of all wisdom teachers has been *to assist in humanity's shift from the Paradigm of Chotchky to the Paradigm of the Soul.* The process begins by simply acknowledging that we have a paradigm, and that it is flawed. Knowing this we can begin to observe how our own beliefs create our pain. For example, to judge people based on their clothing is shallow. We know this. And yet consciously or not, we regularly participate even though such judgments create pain and suffering in the world. Underneath an Armani suit or a dirty pair of coveralls, priestly robes or gangster bling, we're all wearing the same designer "garment": the human body. Miraculous and beautiful. This garment is connected to our soul.

Beliefs and opinions are clothes, too, that we have put on over our brain. Underneath the beliefs of a Christian and a Muslim, a Republican and a Democrat, a priest and a gangster, we are again wearing the same designer garment: the human mind. It does not matter what culture or continent a child is born into. At the moment of birth, there are no clothes on the body or the mind. Later, slowly, this innocent child is dressed by the culture in which they are born. They are told they are what they wear. This becomes a belief, and we deeply believe that we are our beliefs. Out of this misguided notion comes great conflict, globally and internally, because we feel we must defend our beliefs.

Recently while doing an exercise that involved examining my own beliefs, I gazed out the window as the wind whisked through the fall-colored trees, and leaves gently fell to the ground. I felt as though nature itself was telling me to allow my beliefs to "be leafs": Let them drop so the seasons could change in my mind. In this way, we can begin to change the most unflattering of garments, those of prejudice and judgment.

## Chotchky Challenge

Is there someone in your life right now who is driving you nuts? Getting under your skin? The answer is an unequivocal *yes*.
You!

Consider someone you think is driving you cuckoo. Bring them to mind. See them. This is important. Use the power of your imagination. What do they look like? What clothes do they wear? What bugs you about them? Can you feel some stress, anxiety, or anxiousness rising within? Maybe anger?

Unless the person is in the room right now, repeatedly slapping you in the face, there's no way he or she can be hurting you. You are hurting yourself.

Realize what's bugging you is your paradigm. It wants to be right. The other person is most likely experiencing the same angst thinking about you. And therefore they are also blind. The simple awareness that we have a paradigm and it is flawed is boundless within its implications. Therein lies the seed of miracles. It has been said that the first step is admitting that we have a problem. Unless you are consistently at peace regardless of circumstance, your perception is flawed. You are regularly handing over your free will to nouns.

Let's admit it. We have a problem. There should be a 12-step group for Chotchky paradigms. The only problem is, where would we fit all the people? Wait a minute. Planet Earth, that's where.

### Snodia and the Man in the Wheelbarrow

To further assist us in understanding the Paradigm of the Soul, I'd like you to meet a couple of people who made quite an impression on me.

I found myself asking, "What does it mean to be blessed?" The Chotchky Seduction has us convinced that there is a direct correlation between how many things we have and how blessed we are. I used to subscribe to this notion. That is, until I met Snodia. I know, it's a strange name, but she's also a strange woman. So strange, in fact, she just might be living from the soul.

Snodia resides in one of the countless obscure spots scattered about this earth that, to us, would appear to be the opposite of blessed—maybe even cursed. There, she grows peanuts. With pride, she explained the process of planting the seeds, harvesting the nuts, roasting them over a fire, and adding just a touch of salt. She, and a little girl in need of medical assistance, had just made a very difficult trek to meet the medical team with whom I was serving.

Snodia came with a smile and a whole bunch of bags filled with peanuts fresh from Mother Earth. When she wasn't giving them away, she sold them for a dollar. She eventually sold out, probably amassing something in the neighborhood of 20 bucks. I was there when she sold the last bag. After the transaction was complete, she sat down, lowered her head, put her hands in her lap, and began to cry.

"What's wrong?" I asked.

"Nothing," Snodia replied. "I am so blessed."

This from a woman whose great-grandmother had to sell their herd of goats so a girl could have the money to travel across the country for a potentially life-saving surgery. This from a woman who used her own money to pay for the transportation to accompany this girl on her journey. After selling her bags of peanuts, her response is, "I am so blessed." It was a moment that pushed the reset button of my soul.

*What does it mean to be blessed?* I asked myself, struggling to accept a new paradigm. Is there a direct correlation between the amount of stuff we collect and how blessed we are? Or maybe "blessed" is a state of mind completely separate from and unrelated to things.

I realized then there are two ways of living, and whichever one we choose, at any given moment, determines the quality of our experience. To varying degrees it seems we are either living our life "for granted" or living "for gratitude."

Who is more blessed? The one in a penthouse suite overlooking Central Park with a six-figure bank account living "for granted"? Or a woman with "nothing," overjoyed by the sale of a few bags of peanuts living "for gratitude"? I have come to believe there are very few people on the planet as blessed as Snodia, for I now know that . . .

*Being blessed has little to do with the number of gifts we have been given, but everything to do with how our gifts have been received.*

## Chotchky Challenge

Begin the shift today. Allow yourself to reach this profound state of living "for gratitude." Snodia did it for what you and I would consider "peanuts."

List just three things you are blessed by:

1. _____

2. _____

3. _____

Can you feel the gratitude rising in you? You are now touching on one of the highest states of mind there is: the Latitude of Gratitude. It places us on mountains from which we can see our life as it truly is. *Blessed.*

I have often played a little came called "water or light." I pretend, each time I either turn on the faucet or flick on the light, that it's a bona fide miracle. And really, I think it is. How is this happening? Just imagine all the people involved in conjuring up this wonder. Each one blessing us.

Would you like to join me now? "Water or light." The turn of a knob or flick of a switch? Pause and give thanks for all the mystery in it. Let that simple act we so take for granted lift you up to this most blessed place—the Latitude of Gratitude.

Stay in this openhearted space and think of one person who casts a light upon your life. Hold this person in your heart and say, "I am so blessed to have you in my life. My heart overflows."

Now call, text, e-mail, or write the person you just thought of and repeat the previous statement. They may find this act of love shocking. Simply explain that it's a part of a Challenge from this crazy book you're reading. Let them know that they were the first one to come to mind. It makes for a great excuse to be loving. The vulnerability and honesty you're expressing will open a place for the miraculous to come and play.

Please do this for yourself, for this person, and for the world. The repercussions of such an act can be astounding, like the first light turned on with the simple flick of a switch.

### Truth or Fiction?

In 1957, a monastery in Thailand was to be relocated. Among the monks' prized possessions was a giant clay statue of the Buddha.

As they began to move it, they noticed a crack on its surface. One of the monks got a flashlight and shone it slowly, consciously, over the entire Buddha, looking to see if there was any other damage. When he reached the crack, he was astonished to see light reflecting back into his eyes almost as if there was someone inside, shining a light back at him. Carefully, he chipped away at it with a chisel and hammer. After hours of work, he stepped back, looked up, and to his utter amazement, there before him was a priceless, solid gold statue of the Buddha.

*Truth or Fiction?*

Truth!

Historians believe that the monks had covered the statue with clay hundreds of years earlier to make it appear worthless just before they were attacked by the Burmese army.

We, too, in fear, have covered our most valuable possession. The clay we have used is all the forms of Chotchky; the gold Buddha is our soul.

Right now, however, you are the concerned monk shining a light into the opening. The light is shining back. With each turn of the page, with each "moment" and every Challenge, another piece of clay is chipped away. Let's take a big piece out now. Our friend Snodia has prepared us well.

### Getting Down to the Needy Greedy

*Need: to require out of necessity, as in*
*"water is a necessity for all living things"*

I did not consider myself a greedy person. I don't think many of us do. It's also true that over 90 percent of people consider themselves above-average drivers. Statistically speaking, it's impossible for 90 percent to be above average. After some painful self-inquiry causing a minor tremor in my paradigm, I came to the conclusion that I am not the best driver on the road, and I am greedy at times.

I now define *greedy* as having way more than one actually needs and yet still using the word *need* with some regularity when referring to things like clothes, pizza, sunglasses, cars, art, electronics, and so on. This use of "need" has no relationship to the actual definition of the word. When I use the word in this way then I have become greedy in my neediness, hence the term *needy greedy.*

There is another word I have often misused: *starving.* When I say "I'm starving" when referring to food, it's like saying "I need" when referring to a pair of pants when there's a closet full at home.

I was co-facilitating a spiritual pilgrimage in the strange, powerful, and perplexing country of India when the significance of such a shift was brought to my awareness. We had gotten up at the crack of dawn to experience the sunrise over the River Ganges. There was a thick fog as we wandered through the dirt roads and skinny alleyways in the old city of Varanasi. As the sun pushed through, it appeared that the fog itself was emitting a golden light from within. This light reflected off the old walls and temples that make up most of the cities in India. The only sound was that of our footsteps on dirt as we meandered toward the river.

There were 40 or so of us tourists who had donned fanny packs, Nikes, and sunblock. I hadn't had much to eat for several days because, when in India, you eat pretty much the same food every day: Indian food. And I, unfortunately, was no longer feeling very grateful for my meals. I had even skipped breakfast that morning. As we neared the Mother Ganga, an affectionate way locals refer to the river, I thought several times to myself, *I'm starving!* I had said this more than once out loud over the last few days.

Then many yards in front of me, from out of the golden light, a person entered my view pushing an old wheelbarrow. The dark, silhouetted figure looked more like a skeleton whose ragged clothes draped over like a hanger. There was something in the wheelbarrow, but I couldn't make it out; maybe it was wood for one of the many cremation ceremonies that occur daily.

Whatever it was, we were headed right for one another. I wanted to change trajectory, but my efforts were thwarted by something bigger than my own will. Just feet from the man and wheelbarrow now, I strained to see what its contents were. As I glanced downward, it moved. A man who looked older than life itself struggled to lift his head and open his eyes. *He was starving to death,* with less skin and bones than the skeletal one who pushed him. As we passed, just inches from each other, our eyes met. I saw death in his eyes, pain and pleading. Suddenly a pang of hunger entered me that was so powerful it sucked the life force right out of my body. I felt faint and dizzy as tunnel vision filled my eyes, accompanied by a humming in my ears. I stumbled five steps while my left hand reached for the nearest wall to lean on.

*What's happening to me?* I thought. *God, please help me.*

And I believe God had done just that, but not in any way I could have known at the time. For a moment, *I was starving.* This is one of the greatest gifts I have ever received. Then, as soon as it came, it was gone. Simple hunger once again. Since that day I do not say "I'm starving" or "I need." To say so is untrue. When I feel those words coming, I replace them with the truth: "I'm hungry," or "I would like." This changes me. Then I take a moment for self-inquiry. I try to understand what my motivation is behind the "wanting." Half the time, the truth is, I don't really want anything. I say a quick prayer for the millions of those on the planet who are actually in need and truly starving.

The gift I received from the man in the wheelbarrow that day was, maybe, the most precious gift of all: compassion. Through it, we can heal ourselves and that's the start to healing the world.

## Deep Thought

When we say "I'm starving" or "I need," we are giving a powerful message to our subconscious mind. The subconscious does not discern between exaggeration and truth. It takes what we think and say at face value and manifests it into our life as it sees fit, taking great liberties with interpretation. "Starving" and "need" denote lack. They point to the experience of desperateness, emptiness, drama, and loss. One way or another, to the degree that we say and think such things, they will play themselves out in our lives in many and various disguises.

## Chotchky Challenge

In becoming more real now with this state of being called "need," what percentage of the stuff in your life do you think you actually do need? Really! Circle one:

2%   10%  30%   50%   70%   80%   90%   98%

Challenging, isn't it?

Through the Chotchky Paradigm, we often think we need 98 percent of it and even more! That's greedy and makes us "needy."

So much that we have us is extra. Blessings "runneth over." The question is, at what point do "blessings" become burdens? A wall between us and compassion, depth, and soul.

That day, I made a promise to myself to never use those two words again. Will you give it a try? When you feel those words coming, allow your heart to be filled with compassion for all beings who may actually be starving and in need. Then speak the truth: "I'm hungry" or "I would like." For me, it has begun to eradicate one of the most detrimental streams of *wordotchky:* complaining. What would happen if we stopped? Would the things we complain about disappear? Well . . . *yes!* Contrary to Chotchky belief, complaints are all in our head! I would be honored if you would accept this Challenge with me. It just might "change" our mind. In fact it might even be the remedy for a . . .

### *Brain Freeze*

While under the influence of a "brain freeze," "slush rush," or "milk-shake mind melt," do not operate heavy machinery! Quickly rub your tongue against the top of your mouth. It helps. Then make a commitment to your soul to slow down. Brain freezes, slush rushes, and milk-shake mind melts are a consequence of the Chotchky Paradigm since, when living through it, we are unable to be present and simply enjoy life now. We want to finish, to get "there," to be done and onto the next thing, quick. So we chug drinks; wolf down food; impulse buy; and rush into relationships, jobs, hobbies, and spiritual practices. This is what causes the excruciating pain that often accompanies an icy beverage. It is not the coldness of the beverage; it's the "hurry up and chug" of the Chotchky Mind.

## Chotchky Challenge

How would you rate yourself in the following "Slush Rush of the Soul" areas? After each question, insert a number from 1 to 10, where 1 means "That's not me at all!" and 10 means "How did you know? Have you been stalking me?"

- When I'm "starving," I scarf my food down like a prisoner of war who has had nothing but scraps of bread for months. ___

- Once I am full, I continue to eat until I'm stuffed. ___

- When I see a "half-off" or "going-out-of-business sale" sign while on vacation or at an outlet mall, I whip out the plastic faster than you can say *Chotchky.* ___

- In new relationships, I've had the tendency to jump in like Greg Louganis off the high dive. If it's romantic in nature, I begin imagining what our children will look like after the first date. ___

- When I hear about a new remedy guaranteed to cure the common cold, or a new kind of diet or exercise plan that just "melts the fat away," I take it as gospel. ___

- I believe most everything I see on the Internet and in magazines. ___

- When a new minister, spiritual teacher, or "mystical" guru enters the scene, especially from a foreign country, I tend to think everything they say is deeply profound (they do have an accent), even though others have said the same things for thousands of years. ___

Place your total here: ___

If you scored a seven or less, you probably weren't being honest. However, if you were, you may now give this book away to the next person you see spending hard-earned cash at an outlet mall next to a half-off sign, wolfing down chicken teriyaki, and on the verge of proposing marriage on the first date.

For the rest of us, if you scored an eight or higher, there is work to do. (I got an 18.) Pay close attention to any area where you scored a three or more.

## Deep Thought

*The impulse to rush into everything—whether it be a dessert, a relationship, or a clothing store having a fire sale—causes a slush rush of the soul. Can you conceive of the possibility that by building in a pause every time you feel the urge to rush, you actually speed up? This magical pause brings wisdom to your decisions, delivering you more quickly to what the heart truly desires. Build in a pause, and begin to feel a quickening of the spirit.*

The next link will help. Go to the secret web page and click on the leaf: **www.barryadennis.com/chotchkyvideos1**. You won't "be leaf" it. And when you return, we will discover why the robot from the 1960s TV show *Lost in Space* was always yelling "Intruder alert! Intruder alert!" It's downright illuminating.

# CHAPTER 3

# LOST IN SPACE

As a child, my favorite show was *Star Trek* in reruns. It's quite amazing to me that one of my children's favorite shows is also *Star Trek*. I was watching an episode with my kids when it hit me. Space *is* the "final frontier"! But it's not just out there in "outer space"; it's much closer. We don't need Scotty to beam us anywhere. It's the space in which we live, and most assuredly, it's "inner space"!

*"The world cannot be discovered by a journey of miles, no matter how long, but only by a spiritual journey, a journey of one inch, very arduous and humbling and joyful, by which we arrive at the ground of our feet and learn to be home."*

— WENDELL BERRY

In another classic '60s TV show *Lost in Space,* there was the robot that looked like a washing machine with accordions for arms. The accordions would start windmilling in the air as he yelled, "Intruder alert! Intruder alert!" whenever anything unsupportive entered the space in which they were lost. The area where they lived was precious; it needed protection or they would not survive. That robot had great Chotchky Awareness.

As our awareness expands, we see that all space, as it pertains to our lives, is a kind of profoundly precious "storage" space that needs protection. Every Small Plastic Gopher that gets into our space adds to entropy (those little rascals). When we recognize how valuable our space is, we will no longer take it for granted by cluttering it up, lowering its inherent value.

Some "storage space" is obvious, others not so much. Closets, drawers, garages, shelves, cabinets, and attics: obvious. What about the bedroom, kitchen, and *living* room? They store our body, mind, and soul. And what about our body and mind? Possibly the most precious storage space of all. What we put into our mind creates our reality; what we surround ourselves with we put into our mind.

"Intruder alert, intruder alert!" To help illustrate, I give you . . .

### *The Case of the DVD*

I realize that DVDs, CDs, and the like are slowly slipping into oblivion. In fact, if you found this book on some shelf somewhere in the future, then these archaic devices may already be history. However, in my time, this "format" is still around. Much of it is Chotchky. No matter what century you are in, future or past, the "Case of the DVD" has all the parallels necessary to shed light upon the Chotchky Challenge.

I once purchased a DVD because it cost less than renting one. How could I pass that up? I could take it home; it could be *mine*. The Chotchky Mind rolls over, flips, shakes, and plays dead like a dog begging for a treat when it sees such "deals." Not only did this DVD add to other piles of video and DVDotchky, it was a terrible movie. I was appalled with myself and with the Hollywood machine that made that piece of *sin-ema*. I decided I did not want to live under the same roof as this disc that had captured in its grooves a lame excuse for art. I did not want my children to be influenced by its lack of imagination. I didn't even want my dog to see it.

What I had actually done was taken DVDotchky out of the vendor's precious, valuable storage space and put it into my precious, valuable storage space. They no longer wanted it on the relatively endless shelves at the video store. They were selling it for one reason: no one wanted to rent it anymore, which meant the demand for watching the movie was just about gone. So why did I think it was worth keeping on the limited shelves in my home and ultimately in my mind?

We are paying storage fees for everything we put in our home. We do this every time we write a check for the rent or mortgage. Empty space is more valuable than we are often capable of seeing because, through the Chotchky Paradigm, we err on the side of "fill it up, put things in it." This goes for the storage space of the body, mind, and home. The soul knows emptiness is a *thing* itself. A very precious thing.

*The soul wants more nothing.*

It is a shift to acknowledge that most things we purchase will cost more in storage space and "shipping and handling" *than we would have ever actually paid for the item*. If, at some outlet mall, the price of everything suddenly, magically, reflected its total actual, eventual cost, customers would run screaming like extras in an old black-and-white Godzilla movie.

## The Chotchky Factor

Factoring in the time and energy it will take to get it home, put it away or find a place for it, take care of it, pack it up when you move, unpack it, find another place for it, finally sell it, give it away, recycle it, or throw it out—plus the cost its continual production and disposal may have for our shared home, Earth—is sobering. Paradigm shifting. (Remember, all of that energy could have gone to creating your Master Peace.) This awareness is called the Chotchky Factor. When we factor in the actual cost of even the cheapest doodad, we begin to see we are trading our true treasure for Chotchky.

*Everything* we bring into our lives, we will eventually have to get rid of. And that is much, much harder to do than bringing it in. In the buzz of accumulation, we forget this. Unless, of course, we decide to leave it to our children. Then the prophecy is fulfilled: "The sinotchky of the father becomes the sinotchky of the son."

So unless you really need something or you are very clear its presence *supports your soul's expression,* where is the best place to store it? The store! That's why they're called "stores." Let them store it. Otherwise, your life slowly becomes a warehouse, which by definition, wears you out.

Let the stores keep *all* the Chotchky. This will radically transform the system of supply and demand. Currently it is mostly our Chotchky *demands* that are creating the *supply.* By demanding only soulful things, the supply will be very different. It doesn't matter how wonderful a thing is, how useful it might be, or how beautiful it looks. If we don't have the space for it in our lives, it is Chotchky.

In the case of DVDs, part of the seduction of buying them was to avoid the dreaded *late fee.* Oh, how we hated the late fee. But the truth is, our soul does not hate late fees. The soul knows that like an overdue DVD, *everything has a late fee.* There is a deep truth here that the one-dimensional Chotchky Mind is incapable of comprehending. For everything we put off until tomorrow, our soul pays the dues.

## Chotchky Challenge

Imagine all the DVDs and videos you have in "storage," including your hard drive. Circle the percentages below. This will bring you face-to-face with the Chotchky Mind.

- What percentage of your DVDs/videos do you really think you are ever going to watch again?

10% 20% 30% 40% 50% 60% 70% 80% 90% 100%

- What percentage have you never seen and likely never will?

10%  20%  30%  40%  50%  60%  70%  80%  90%  100%

As our awareness grows, we see that *everything* we surround ourselves with and spend our energy on has a direct effect on our soul. Everything.

Once I realized the *true* cost of that video, even though I had bought and paid for it, I got on my bike, rode five miles to the video store, and slipped it into the return slot. I'm not joking. I gave it back to them. Wasn't that nice of me? I felt the weight of the world lift off my shoulders. As I rode away, I laughed, intoxicated with the knowledge that I had exercised a choice. I wasn't just taking the video back . . . I was taking my *life* back.

In that liberating moment, I realized how powerful I am. I could return it all. All the confusion, manipulation, distraction. All the lost dreams. It was quite an exchange: a DVD for my soul.

I had *exorcised* a piece of Chotchky from my life like the priest exorcised the demon from the girl in *The Exorcist*—my head no longer spinning around looking for some *thing* to fill my time and provide a false sense of purpose.

Then I said a few words I call the Divine Vision and Destiny Prayer, or The DVD.

### Let's Take a Moment . . .

Take a breath of life now. In through your nose and out through your mouth. Read the following from your soul:

> *Destiny is calling. I have a new Vision for my life, and it is Divine. This life is too precious to waste. Time is too valuable. Money is too powerful to spend without consciousness, for I am Divine, this is my Vision, and therefore my Destiny.*

DVDs, CDs, and the like *are* fading into oblivion. The digital world *could* be a great help in eliminating DVD *and* CDotchky. The problem is that we're bringing our Chotchky Mind into the digital world. In what we once thought was endless storage space, we've created *gigabyte-otchky*. We just keep putting more stuff in there because, well, we have the space. Soon however, we have to buy *more gadgets* because we are incapable of using the little trash icon. We think we need something like a million songs in our music players, most of which we never listen to.

Can you hear that? It's the sound of Big, Floppy, Flowered Sun Hats flapping in the wind. I call it . . .

### The FedEx Syndrome

When FedEx first came out, it was a great tool when you "absolutely, positively had to have it there overnight." At first, people used it only when something really did need to be there the next day. But then the Chotchky Mind took over, and soon *everything* absolutley positively had to be there overnight. Everybody was suddenly more stressed, trying to get everything "there" while lying awake, worrying that it might not arrive by morning.

As long as we live through the Chotchky Paradigm, *no matter how advanced our technologies become (which should relieve our stress), we will use them to create more stress.*

I, for one, am Fed Up. Why, it's an outrage! No, it's much worse. It's . . .

#### Store-Rage!

Case in point: Here's a story from my friend Mary, who told me about her friend Becky. The following is quite a storage soap opera. Please pay close attention. Mary and Becky both lived in Bakersfield, California, but eventually moved to Oregon.

Moving is a time we all end up facing our addiction to our things. It can be overwhelming! *Where did all this stuff come from? What was I thinking?*

When Becky moved, she was confronted with the arduous, yet potentially freeing and blessed task of deciding what was truly important and what she needed to let go of. She took time to separate it out and agonized over everything. She just couldn't release. So she got a storage unit down in Bakersfield for $50 per month. Stuff she decided she didn't need, want, or even like sat in this unit for five years as she dutifully wrote a check month after month. If you're doing the math, after five years that's $3,000!

Then one glorious day, Becky forgot about her Chotchky. No check was written. No ink wasted. No postage stamp licked. The heavens rejoiced!

Guess what happens when someone doesn't pay their rent? The company that's taking your Chotchky money holds a storage sale. Everything must go! And do you know who comes to such a sale? The neighboring storage-unit renters. Guess where they end up putting all the junk they have just liberated from someone else's soul? In their own storage units! It gets better. Often they have to rent another unit to contain it all, and this means there's a good chance they will end up putting your junk back in the unit it was sitting in, in the first place.

Oh, the humanity.

Becky was this close to being free from it all, but then Mary, Becky's friend who also moved to Oregon, spoke to her grandfather who still lives in Bakersfield. He was reading the Bakersfield newspaper and saw Becky's name under "storage-unit content sales." He then called his sister there in Bakersfield and asked, "What's up with Becky? I just read that her storage-unit contents are for sale." So Mary's grandfather's sister called Mary up in Oregon and said, "What's up with Becky? We just read her storage unit is being sold off." So Mary called Becky directly and told her what she heard through the Chotchky grapevine.

Becky then immediately wrote a check to Save the Chotchky. So she saved the junk that she had already decided she did not need nor even want, which she had finally forgotten about because she hadn't been within 400 miles of it for five years.

The heavens mourned.

She had already spent more money storing her Chotchky than her Chotchky is worth and she doesn't even really want it. What do you think would have been the best thing that could have happened to her and her stored possessions?

If it had gotten sold off and she never found out.

You can't pay enough to get rid of Chotchky! They were going to sell it all for her, for free! And there she was writing another $50 check. And another and another. Someday, Becky is going to have to get rid of that storage. And it's going to cost her time, energy, and yes, more money.

And maybe in the process, she will come face-to-face with the Chotchky Paradigm. She may start the profound journey toward *liberotchky*. It could happen. Stranger things have. Like, for example, I once saw a seagull fly off the roof of a restaurant, take a piece of someone's fish and chips, dip it in tartar sauce, eat it, and fly back to the roof, waiting for the next unsuspecting victim! For real. And yet, even though I witnessed this most incredible fish appropriation by a lowly birdbrain, I still seriously doubt the whole storage-unit incident was enough to change Becky's mind. I say this not because Becky is different from the rest of us. I say this because, when it comes to our Chotchky, we forget what's truly important.

Two thousand years ago, a carpenter-turned-prophet said, "Look to the birds of the air, they do not sow nor do they reap, nor gather into barns [storage units] and yet your heavenly father feeds them [fish and chips with tartar sauce]. Do not be anxious then, saying 'what shall we eat or what shall we wear' [a robe and sandals]. Seek first the kingdom of God and all these things shall be added unto you."

His point was that we live with less trust and more fear than actual birdbrains.

## Chotchky Challenge

If you are currently paying for a storage unit, stop. Have a storage-unit sale. Don't worry about your junk. It will all end up in the same storage unit it's already in. And the next time you move, allow it to be a time of complete and total freedom from the past. Let it all go. Don't take all your junk from one storage place in your home and move it to the next. You're paying for all that square footage while your soul waits on the sidelines. Your time, your money, and your life are worth more than that.

Check it out, there is a paradigm shift occurring now. Wow. Go to the secret page at my site, and click on the brown mail envelope: **www.barryadennis.com/chotchkyvideos1**.

When you return, we will take a close look at an evil dictator and how Chotchky not only created the evil, but also the actual dictator!

# CHAPTER 4

# MUFASA

Once after speaking about the Chotchky Challenge, a friend asked me to lunch. We met at a floating restaurant on the Willamette River in Portland. It was a beautiful summer day. Occasionally, the restaurant rocks when a considerably sized boat cruises by.

I didn't know why my friend called the meeting. She just said it was important. Her son and her granddaughter, who was four at the time, sat across from us. While her granddaughter colored away on the children's menu, she told me the purpose for our gathering was to see if I would be available to perform a funeral ceremony. She had already given the event much thought. There would be a horse-drawn carriage for the casket. She had music selections in mind and a specific reading. All the while her son and granddaughter worked on the menu art, characters from *The Little Mermaid.*

After about 20 minutes of planning the service, I finally asked, "Who is the funeral for?"

She glanced at her son and granddaughter. With tears slowly welling in her eyes, she returned her gaze my way and softly said, "It's for me."

I thought I felt the restaurant rock, but I couldn't be sure. "I'm so sorry," I said.

She flashed a faint smile of acceptance. "I have cancer. The doctors give me a month or two."

I took her hand. We began to talk about the beautiful life that she had lived. She was so grateful to have had this human experience. Her acceptance and gratitude were humbling and inspiring. As we talked, her son and granddaughter got up and went for a walk to feed the ducks just outside the window. I watched them, wondering, and my friend must have known what I was thinking. She explained that her granddaughter was aware of the situation. They had told her that Grandma would soon be like Mufasa from *The Lion King,* up in the clouds.

As we watched them feeding the ducks, she began to cry. And so did I. Through the tears, she said, "Barry, there's one thing I want you to understand. Something that at this time in my life is so clear. Something I wish I had known my whole life." She paused, squeezed my hand, and continued: "It's all Chotchky—all of it. With two very important exceptions: the ones you love, and your soul's purpose. Those two things are all that matters."

The tears flowed as she stared directly and unflinchingly in my eyes, as if trying to tell whether or not her words had reached me. They had.

Why wait until we have a month left to live to get this? We know it's true. Our soul resonates with the raw authenticity and undeniable accuracy of her observation. Let's see through my friend's eyes now. From that perspective. In so many ways, we have been living backward.

I asked her if there was one thing she could say to the world, what would it be? She replied, "Don't let all the Chotchky fog your vision. Don't let it distract you. Live your passions."

She looked out the window. "And love with all your heart."

It was not much longer after that day that my friend passed away. I sat with her granddaughter in the grass next to her final resting place. She pointed up at the sky. "Grandma's in the clouds now, like Mufasa."

The song she requested at our meeting that day, which we did play at her funeral, was "Another One Bites the Dust" by Queen.

### *"There Your Heart Will Be Also"*

That carpenter truly urged us to live from the soul. He also said . . .

> *Do not lay up for yourselves treasures upon earth, where moss and rust destroy and where thieves break in and steal. Lay up for yourselves treasures in heaven where neither moth nor rust destroys, where thieves cannot break in, for where your treasure is, there your heart will be also.*

Isn't this what my friend was saying before she left this world for the next? She was telling us how to live in the world and, at the same time, place our heart in heaven.

## Chotchky Challenge

Live each day as if it could be your last.

That's what we're doing here, at your next link. Go to the secret page and click on the "live" lion: **www.barryadennis.com/chotchkyvideos1**.

# THINGS

The previous section was designed to convey a comprehensive understanding, the full breadth of the Chotchky Challenge philosophy. It is not so much about removing the excess as it is about getting in touch with our soul, living from the inside out. The thing is, we can't really do that until we deal with our "stuff."

Ah, what a great word. It means our physical junk, but so much more. Our "stuff" is also the psychological "baggage" we carry that must be dealt with. To "stuff" something is to fill it to the point that it is cumbersome, near the breaking point. As we awaken to our Master Peace, we are beginning to deal with all aspects of this wonderful concept.

It might get a little rough from here, but you know, I think you have the right stuff.

At this first level, physical Things, the Chotchky Challenge can be reduced to three simple steps.

- Step 1: **Gather and release.** This is the task soon to be taken.

- Step 2: **Stop bringing it in.** This is even more important than Step 1.

- Step 3: **Energize!** Transfer the energy once wasted on Chotchky into the dreams of your soul.

# CHAPTER 5

# GLAD BAG

Soon you will be getting a Glad Bag and facing your *thing-otchkies,* but it's not going to be easy. Remember, you are seeing through a flawed paradigm. Shifting is hard. We love our hooey.

Before I would dare ask you to do such a thing, let me tell you about my first attempt.

As my Chotchky Vision grew stronger, suddenly, like Dan Aykroyd and John Belushi in *The Blues Brothers,* I was on a "mission from God." I had to share this insight with the world, so I began putting together a presentation. I went around the house with the goal of filling up two big white Glad Bags. I wasn't sure I had enough to actually fill two bags.

I could have filled two U-Hauls!

And yet, it was one of the hardest things I have ever done. We're so attached to our Chotchky that as soon as we allow ourselves to call it like it is, our minds counter with *Justificationotchky: the ability to justify the presence of any thing, no matter how useless, outdated, or unpractical.*

Through the Chotchky Paradigm, we are so psychologically identified with our stuff that we actually believe our value is tied up in it and that to part with it is to part with a piece of ourselves.

This shows how much work we have to do in self-love: You are not an outdated, useless piece of junk!

The first thing I grabbed was something I hadn't thought about for perhaps a decade: a little cassette recorder. But as soon as I tried to put it in the bag, I began to feel paralyzed, like my fingers lost the ability to release. My Chotchky Mind said, "Barry, come on, you could use this. How have you lived for the last decade with this in that drawer? You could record your voice . . . and then listen to it!" *Seductionotchky!*

I have several digital dictators. This cassette version could now be placed prominently in a museum of '80s memorabilia next to a Wham record and *The Preppy Handbook.*

Still, I just couldn't put it in the bag. I finally pressed the record button and said to the thing, "You are Chotchky." I thought it was a good idea, but when I played back the message, I heard what amounts to as possibly the worst affirmation in the universe. My own voice telling me that . . . *I* am Chotchky.

It was now an Evil Dictator.

I changed the recording to "This is Chotchky" and pressed "play" every time I had difficulty letting go of my stuff as my hand hovered over the Glad Bag. The problem with these dinosaur gadgets is that you have to rewind and listen to that high-pitched mousey squeak sound. Each time I rewound, I would start to think, *I don't know . . . maybe this thing I'm grabbing isn't Chotchky.*

That's because I was hearing my message in reverse. It's called back-masking. They did it a lot on records in the '70s, like *The Dark Side of the Moon* by Pink Floyd. Every time I rewound my recording, because of the inflection with which I recorded, instead of hearing "This is Chotchky," subliminally, I was hearing something close to "Chotchky, is this." Not only did it make me question everything, but that's how Yoda speaks. Now I'm Luke Skywalker in the jungle of Chotchky being manipulated by Jedi mind tricks!

Somehow, I was able to use the Force to remember that squeak sound happens only if you press "play" and "rewind" at the same time. So I carried the Chotchky dictator with me as I continued on my mission. Each time I came across something that I knew was

Chotchky but my hand wouldn't release it, I would press "play" on the Chotchky dictator and there was my own voice saying, "This is Chotchky." As Justificationotchky would rear its ugly head, I would play it again until I could override the old programming, allowing the truth to reach my fingers so I could let go.

The contents of my bag eventually included a basketball. How could a basketball be Chotchky? I had seven of them. Seven! The one I put in my bag couldn't even hold air! (Just like all of our justification.)

That ball had been sitting around for years. Countless times I had grabbed it on my way to play basketball only to be hoodwinked once again as I tried to dribble, left with the deflating sound of "splat" instead of "boing."

I found a Frisbee that I had used to spend many wonderful hours playing fetch with my dog. She taught me unconditional love with it and proved to me that she would always return. This again is why I see God in my dog and vice versa. But now, that Frisbee has so many holes in it you could use it as a colander. But I already have a colander. A stack of them, of which I use maybe one. I don't need a Frisbee colander that doesn't even fly anymore. I was feeling *sentimentalotchky*. Still, I held it over my Glad Bag, pressed play, and released.

There were also books. Can a book be Chotchky? We all have books that we bought through the Chotchky Paradigm but never really intended to read. The Chotchky Mind was simply playing tricks on us when we saw the book. It made us think, *Now this book, this one will change my life. I will actually read this one.*

Remember, approximately *90 percent* of all nonfiction books purchased become *bookotchky*. They clutter our shelves and confuse our minds. I could have grabbed several boxes full. The one I put in my bag after playing the ancient cassette dictator several times to remind me "This is Chotchky" is called *Are You the One for Me?* by Barbara De Angelis. It's a great book. So how could it be Chotchky? Because I found the one for me. My wife! That book became Chotchky the day Heather and I met. I don't want that book in my space. Its very presence can plant a seed of doubt and confusion. *The grass is always greener, right?* That's the Chotchky Mind messing with our Master Peace! It's time to get that book back into circulation to someone who actually needs it. That book represents the person I was, not who I am becoming.

I also put a logo-embossed water bottle in the bag. You know, the reusable kind. I didn't even have to press play on my dictator. When I speak publicly about Chotchky and I pull a water bottle out of the bag and ask, "Is this Chotchky?" there is always an overwhelming *yes.* That's interesting because one water bottle is not necessarily Chotchky. And yet all I do is pull one bottle out of the bag. The reason I believe audiences instantly see it as such is that they have begun to remove the Big, Floppy, Flowered Sun Hat and are having hippie-like flashbacks of all the times they were given some promotional item for "free" that ends up causing angst as it clutters their lives until they come to their senses and throw it away with a twinge of guilt for all the waste in the world. So when people instantly say, "Yes, that's Chotchky," I assure them that it is not.

One reusable water bottle is in no way Chotchky. Heck, maybe even four or five could be useful. Once my point has been made, I turn the bag upside down and out drop 16 water bottles. Sixteen! I found an entire kitchen drawer devoted to water bottles. That's some very valuable storage space.

Because we are so attached to our Chotchky, eliminating it can cause tension between people who cohabitate. Heather knew what I was up to. As I began collecting Chotchky from around the house, she got a little nervous. She began sneaking peeks into my Glad Bags.

Later, she said to me, "I saw your bag of water bottles. You don't even know the half of it. That's after I cleaned out all the ones I don't like."

Where I live in Oregon, we are blessed to have good drinking water. Buying cases of water that has been flown across the planet is nonsensical. It's right there on your bottle of Evian. Look, it's "Naïve" backward. If you're buying Evian water, you're buying water that was bottled in the mountains of France, trucked across many miles to harbors, sailed across oceans of water, trucked across more miles of land, and then stored in a supermarket where you have to drive to pick up those heavy cases at physical risk to your lower back, bring it home, unload it, and then put it in your precious storage places like your refrigerator and cupboards.

And remember, you actually spent money on that water. To add insult to injury, we don't even finish drinking much of it—that water, which was bottled on the other side of the world. We throw it out the window of our car, in the grass, the driveway, or dump it in the sink.

It is estimated that recyclable plastic water bottles use 17 million barrels of oil each year just in transport. Because of this and the cost of recycling, the town of Concord, Massachusetts, recently passed a city ordinance that bans the selling of bottled water. What will they do? They're going to have to drink out of drinking fountains for free. Forced to save money and the environment. They're going to have to push a knob, bend over, and slurp.

Hey, I remember that. It was fun.

But then the Chotchky Paradigm made us think it was crazy.

At my house, the water goes through a battery of filters before it reaches the faucet. We had to actually remove one of the filters. I think by the time it reached the sink, it was no longer "$H_2O$". It was just "O." *It seems we filtered the "H" out of it.*

Doesn't it make more sense to get a good reusable water bottle and just turn on the faucet? The Chotchky Mind says, *But Evian is from France—this is designer water. It must be better than the water we have here.*

All the water in the world slowly but surely circulates around the earth. What's dumped over France today will someday be dumped over the hills of Oregon. If you must buy bottled water, make sure it's local. However, I highly recommend saving all that time, money, and energy and getting one reusable water bottle and a good filter. Then turn on the faucet and truly enjoy this nectar of the Gods.

So the question is, how did we end up with 16 water bottles after my wife had already sorted out a bunch of logo-embossed bottles she didn't like? Well, we all know how it happened. That's why, as soon as I show one water bottle, everyone knows Chotchky is near. I went to an event at some point and they were "giving them away." What does the Chotchky Mind think? *Oh, it's free! I must have it!* Then my wife went to a different event and they were "giving them away." Then my children went to some event and they were "giving them away," and on and on it goes. The Chotchky Paradigm feeding the ego. Pretty soon we've dedicated an entire drawer to water bottles we don't use, forced to one day deal with it.

Nothing is "free"! No "thing" is free! Understanding this changes everything.

### *The Dumpster*

A funny thing happened to me and my Chotchky the day after I filled my Glad Bags. I started examining everything I had painstakingly "severed" from my life so that I could speak intelligently about each thing and how completely ludicrous it was that I felt so attached.

At the time, we had a huge red Dumpster in the front yard of our house. We were getting rid of a bunch of junk from our old barn and then building a new one. We actually recycled our old barn. People came, took it apart, transported it, and rebuilt it in their own yard. Cool. They did not, however, want to take our Chotchky. Wise.

Every few months, I have professional cleaning people come to my studio whether it needs it or not. Okay, it always needs it. Entropy!

So there I was. My Chotchky and me. I took one piece out of the Glad Bag at a time, examined it, considered it, made notes for my presentation, and then put it back in the bag. Time flew as I reveled in all the whatnot. When 12:30 rolled around and the cleaning people arrived, I excused myself and went to town to run some errands, have lunch, and begin putting my thoughts to paper.

I often lose track of time in the throes of creativity. When we allow all the random *thoughtotchkies* to settle, something magnificent happens. For me, it feels as though I have a direct connection to "The Information." Some would call it a Higher Intelligence. Maybe that which was behind the explosion of pure energy "in the Beginning." And since energy cannot be created or destroyed, that same essence moves through us now. So when I'm in that place deep in thought, I wonder, *Whose thought is it?* It seems as if the lines begin to blur between the individual known as "me" and the One eternal essence that started it all, often referred to as "I am."

So there "I" was in a restaurant, sipping tea and nibbling on sourdough while the information poured from my pen. As it appeared on the paper, a part of me was truly surprised and wondered what this scribe would conjure up next. I began to feel as if I were divinely led to each piece of Chotchky I so arduously had released into the bag. Like each thing was chosen not by me, but by divine appointment. Each one had a story to tell and that story was being written before my very eyes.

And then suddenly, from that deep place like a lightning strike, it popped into my head. "Oh no . . . my bags of Chotchky!" The cleaning ladies had no idea those trash bags were for my presentation. I left the money on the table and ran. When I got back to my office, the cleaning ladies were gone.

And so was my Chotchky.

It also happened to be trash day. Had they picked it up already?

We have a big green plastic trash container. I threw open the top and there were five large white Glad Bags crammed inside. I pulled them out and began wading through them with a kind of urgency that, today, seems quite mad. Sure, they were full of Chotchky, but not the chosen ones! Then in an act of desperation, I peered into the recycling bin. Nada. I began plodding through the house, knowing full well that Chotchky has a tendency to gravitate back from whence it came. While in a zombie-like state of desperate searching I looked in the refrigerator. I guess, for my bags of Chotchky. *What am I doing, standing here with the refrigerator door open, looking for trash?* (This tendency we have to stand there, unconsciously looking in the refrigerator, are moments the Chotchky Mind has achieved a full takeover.)

Then another lightning strike . . . the giant Dumpster!

I first skimmed the top perimeter by pulling myself up and shimmying around with my toes on a kind of welded fissure like a mountain climber on the crack of a rock wall. There, in the far left corner, was a white Glad Bag. My heart raced. I quickly made my way to it, but like a mirage in a desert, it was not as it appeared. I climbed around until my legs and toes were spent, reaching, hoping. Finally, as a last and final act of despondency, I sunk to the lowest depths of Chotchky despair.

I climbed into the giant trash receptacle and began wading through Chotchky Hell! Oh, the humanity!

Each piece tugging on my psyche. Thoughts scattered. Logic on hiatus. Things that had sat in our garage or barn for years, driving me crazy, that I had finally released, suddenly had an irresistible appeal. And since it had been removed from my space, through the Chotchky Paradigm, that oversized trashcan was now a giant bin full of "free stuff."

The madness lies in the fact that Chotchky itself is always a distraction from our purpose. This moment, however, reached unprecedented levels of diversion. The Dumpster Chotchky was so distracting I kept forgetting that my purpose was to find my bags of Chotchky. The irony!

I happened upon an old badminton racket. Now the Chotchky was speaking directly to me: "Come on Barry, remember all the good times we had that one time you used me nine years ago? Remember how the birdie would fly through the air? You would swing and miss? We could have it all again. Never mind the broken strings."

If only I had my dictator, I could play "This is Chotchky" and silence the rambling in my mind. The problem was that my little tape recorder was in one of my trash bags.

The relationship we have with our junk is similar to an old romantic flame. We run into them and begin romanticizing about how good it was. This is selective memory, a sneaky device of the Chotchky Paradigm that blinds us through half-truths. We don't see the "broken strings." We think that this time it will be different. Then one day, a month later, we wake up in the wee hours of the morning, wipe the sleep out of our eyes, and turn to see a harsh reality. We've been shacked up with a badminton racket.

I later realized that crawling through all the Chotchky is a perfect metaphor. The more Chotchky, the more energy we expend just trying to move through each day. There's a kind of invisible attachment, a string that links us to everything in our environment. Every string has a vibration like a note played on a guitar. That vibration can lift us up, bring us joy like the "Hallelujah Chorus," or it can bring sadness, like, say, most country songs written before '98.

I did eventually find my bags of Chotchky. They were in the bottom of the first bags I looked in. That's how it works. Always covering what we actually want. The challenging thing now was to get out of the Dumpster. I was trapped. That's how big it was. I felt like Luke Skywalker in the trash compactor scene. Luckily a friend, who sometimes borrows stuff, dropped by.

I began yelling, "Help, help! I'm in the Dumpster."

My friend "experimented" with a lot of controlled substances from about '68 to the present. He may have thought he was having a relapse. He started yelling, "What? Who said that?"

"Me, in here."

"In where?"

"The Dumpster."

"Huh?"

He finally came over, pulled himself up, and saw me standing there among the carnage.

"Wow, Dude. What are you doing there?"

"Please," I said, "just help me get out of here."

And that is what our soul has been calling out from behind all the Chotchky: *Please, help me get out of here.*

## Truth or Fiction?

*Staging* is a term Realtors use to describe the process of setting up furniture in a house to make it more appealing to potential buyers. The idea is to put lots of furniture in a home so that people feel they are getting more.

*Truth or Fiction?*

Fiction! It has been shown that people feel a greater sense of peace and tranquility, like this could be the "home" they have always dreamed of, when they experience a relatively empty space. That is staging, and it resonates with our very soul.

✳

Okay, you're almost ready. Soon it will be time for your Glad Bag junket, but first a fair warning. . . .

> *The author is sympathetic to the potential bedlam that can occur as a result of the soon-to-be-taken Challenge because of the potential involvement with the most fretted form of Chotchky, which is* <u>spousalotchky:</u> *territorial items that create tension between once blissful couples, as one partner deems the item "precious" while the other simply sees "junk."*

Spousalotchky is not limited to spouses. It can exist between any two or more people in the act of cohabitation. No matter your race, religion, color, creed, size, or shape, spousalotchky binds us all together in a childish psychological display of "Mine, Mine, Mine!"

My mom and dad were recently at a gar(b)age sale where they found a box full of cassettes (which are now Chotchky by definition). They were a collection of lessons by a great teacher named Jack Boland. My parents had followed his work most of their life.

When my dad saw those tapes, his coverall high waters transformed into the Big, Floppy, Flowered Sun Hat.

He called to my mother from across the garage, "Sweetheart, we should get all these cassettes," to which my mother retorted, "But honey, I'm sure we have two copies of every one of those at home."

To which Dad countered, "But we'll never find them!"

Here's the thing. If they had bought that box of cassettes, it would have ended up with the other two copies of those same cassettes: in Chotchky limbo.

My parents have a wonderful marriage. The closest they ever came to getting a divorce was rooted in spousalotchky. It's very powerful. Within it hides all of our "stuff": attachments, insecurities, defensiveness, fears, and cassettes.

My wife recently looked at one of my bookshelves and said, "I think there's some bookotchky building up in there."

"There is no such thing," I responded. "I read my books. I enjoy my books and reread them. I resent that." The truth is, I resemble that. I do love books and I do read them; however, it is very true that my bookshelf is slowly becoming the place where old books come to retire. The Florida of bookshelves.

I will probably never read a quarter of those books again, and many of them I don't even like. Heather was right. I'm getting them back into circulation. In fact, I recently gave one away. As a friend was admiring one, I simply took it off the shelf and said, "Here, keep it."

I have read it and enjoyed it, but I will never read it again. Sitting on my shelf was a gift, something that might assist another person in their search for peace and joy.

Imagine a "joy meter." What a wonderful thing it would be. When my friend held the book in her hand, it would have gone "beep-beep-beep" right off the scale. Conversely, when I held it in my hand, it would have gone "ribbit, ribbit, ribbit" down to zero. By virtue of the joy factor alone, the book is rightfully hers. The only way left for me to get anything more out of the book was to give it away. To freely say, "Keep it; it's yours." Truthfully, I may have received a greater gift in that moment than my friend did. Not only did I get the joy of giving it away, but I got the bonus gift of free and clear empty space, making room for something better.

From my wife's unattached perspective, she was able to help me get back in touch with my soul by pointing out an area of my life that had slowly begun to overwhelm me. In doing so, she was being a loving spouse. The soulful purpose of relationships is to heal each other. To assist each other through the painstaking process of identifying our *characterotchkies: excess characteristics that impede progress toward one's Master Peace.*

Here's how it works. When we meet someone, there is a chemical release in our body. We mistake it for love, but it is actually infatuation. It blinds us to all of the person's "flaws." If we weren't blind to them, we would never get "into it." (In fact, we might be repulsed.)

As infatuation blinds us, any Characterotchky Vision we may have had is gone, AWOL. For a while, he doesn't notice the women's magazines on every bathroom rack, counter, and bedside stand. She doesn't notice his dirty underwear piling up on the floor, nor has it really sunk in yet that he rarely puts the toilet seat down. Be assured, however, that these things are slowly creeping up (especially the toilet seat). At some point, the pendulum swings, and pretty soon we're not only seeing the flaws our partner may have, but just to add a little extra something, we begin projecting our flaws onto them.

Our worst nightmares are realized as we are forced to come face-to-face with our own abominable traits. This is the greatest gift our partner gives us. With awareness, we begin to see and recognize our own shortcomings as we project them and reflect them upon each other in the dance of love. In this way, like Michelangelo, we can consciously chip away at that which is not the masterpiece in ourselves and each other so that, with time and patience, our true Master Peace is known.

## Let's Take a Moment . . .

Let's take a moment to own our reflection. Hold in your heart and mind someone you are currently in a relationship with—romantic or friendship. Feel gratitude rising within as you realize the profound gift he or she is giving to you, and recite the following:

*Thank you for helping me become a better person by being a mirror for me. I'm sorry for the times I have not been aware that it was me, not you, I was frustrated with. I am so blessed to have you in my life.*

Think of the qualities you love in this person, and let them flood your heart. Feel it? Now also realize that these qualities are in you.

## Chotchky Challenge

Tell the one in your life how grateful you are to him or her for helping you wake up. Pick up the phone, send an e-mail or text, buy a card, or write it in the sky or on a Goodyear blimp. It's like magic. You will be amazed by how this simple act can be the impetus for healing and peace. I recommend that you do this now.

### *The Case of The Big Freeze*

When I was 11, my mother went out of town for a week. This was not a common occurrence. In fact, I don't think it ever happened again. With my father at the helm, things got a little strange. We ate cereal for breakfast and dinner, there was no longer a bedtime; and with each day that passed, the groceries that three growing boys continuously devoured no longer magically replaced themselves. Food became scarce. This inconvenience, however, was offset by the fact that we no longer had to bathe, nor was there any reason whatsoever to "mind our manners."

The day before my mother returned, my father became visibly distressed. Like a drill sergeant before the colonel inspects the barracks, he began shouting things like, "Do the dishes!" "Pick up the dog poop!" and "Clean up your room!"

As my brothers and I bumped into each other like Larry, Mo, and Curly, my father began to notice things he had never seen before. Things that didn't seem to "belong," like one of those very disturbing segments on *Sesame Street*. These things, of course, were all my mother's. Remember with spousalotchky, one person's Chotchky may be another person's "precious." When one partner is attached to something that the other views as Chotchky, it often is the latter.

This is another gift your relationships bring. However, you must tread lightly. Very lightly. And if your spouse is out of town, unless you want a divorce, don't touch it. If you do want a divorce, touch it a lot. That is one of the fastest ways to get those papers signed.

My father systematically went through all of my mom's stuff and discarded everything he deemed as junk. He seemed to be in some kind of altered state. You couldn't rattle him. He actually thought he was doing my mother a favor. And he was—kind of. There are just more conscious ways of dealing with spousalotchky. Safer ways. More humane ways.

When Mom came home, my father was as proud as a peacock. The place was almost as clean as it was before she left. This was shocking to my mother, which is probably why it took a while for her to notice what he had done. That and, of course, it was Chotchky.

In time, though, she wondered where the piles of magazines that she never read went. Maybe certain articles of clothing that she didn't wear walked right out of her closet. Observations such as this began to weigh heavy on her mind. A part of her knew my dad had done it, but she just didn't want to believe that the man she loved would be capable of such a sacrilegious act.

She finally brought it up almost in passing: "And by the way, did you throw out a bunch of my things while I was gone?"

Dad launched into his explanation like it was a surprise gift he couldn't wait to give her. Like maybe a new vacuum cleaner.

My mother is a kind woman. She endeavors to be a good Christian. Understanding. Forgiving. Accepting. She gives to charity and is a hospice volunteer. Which is why what happened next is irrefutable evidence that when it comes to Chotchky, all evolutionary strides that may have occurred over the course of billions of years are circumnavigated in the brain. My father may have been standing there in high water pants, but suddenly my mother was a lizard.

It seemed her higher consciousness, which is generally situated in one's frontal lobe, no longer received any blood. No life there whatsoever. Dark. All flow rerouted to the ancient, reptilian, fight-or-flight almond section of her brain. Compassion and logic left to fend for themselves as a zombie-like creature appeared. This was not the woman who bore me.

They didn't speak to each other for seven days. And around the house, it really did feel like the length of time it took to create the universe. Not a word or peep. Cold. As if somebody turned the heat off and left the freezer door open. By the sixth day, the mercury dropped so low I was afraid to take a shower for fear snow would come from the shower head.

We actually thought my parents might get a divorce. Over Chotchky!

So why was my mother so distraught because the man she loves, with the best intentions in the world, threw away some magazines and a few other assorted items that had been sitting around collecting dust since they said "I do"? (There should probably be an amendment to the wedding vows, something like: "I promise to honor your Chotchky.") We want to get rid of our excess. All great masters said so. So why was there steam escaping from her ears making a whistling sound while the top of her head started bobbing up and down like a tea kettle? Because, the bottom line, in this case—the "Case of the Big Freeze"—is *identificationotchky: the feeling that one's identity, actual essence, is in one's things.*

My mother was suffering from this deception. She actually felt a part of her soul was thrown away, tossed in the trash by the one she loved. It was deeply confusing to her. These are the moments when paradigms can shift if we are capable, through the process of summoning keen self-awareness.

That week was scary. Our house felt like a Buddhist monk meditation retreat in "opposite world," where the point of the silence was to feel as much tension as possible. That time for my mother, however, was a kind of chrysalis. She was changing. We must all detach if we wish for a peaceful transition from this life to the great beyond. However, our Master Peace is found in letting go now. Why not beat the rush?

A word to the wise: As your Chotchky Vision continues to improve, do not assume that everyone else, especially your loved ones, have this superpower. If you do, you may end up being their *peoplotchky.*

## Deep Thought

You are not your things. They do not make you worthy. You see things, but how much meaning do they really hold? Zero. *All the meaning is in you.*

### *The Chotchky Test*

As we begin the blessed work of removing the "debris" from our lives, it's very helpful to use the Chotchky Test. It's like a lie detector that reveals whether or not we are lying . . . to ourselves.

As we become objective observers, we realize that just about anything in our own habitat could be Chotchky. The way to be sure is to give it this test. But first, a short treatise on Love.

We cannot actually "love" things. At least not in the same way we might love our children, our "lover," God, or Mother Earth. This is an illusion created by the Chotchky Paradigm. To use the same word to describe my feelings for my wife and children as I do, say, for a shirt, is actually jarring to my soul. If my house caught on fire, I would not give a thought to the material things that I, at times, have professed love for. My heart would be concerned with only one thing: family. My wife and children, then our pets. Anything else is a distant second. The carelessness with which we use the word *love* waters down its power.

In the original Greek language, there are four distinct words for love: *Agape, Eros, Philia,* and *Storge.* Each refers to different aspects of the love between people and, in the case of Agape and Eros, it could also be used to describe a kind of love for "God," divinity, and life in general. This is very telling. Not one of them has anything to do with any kind of "love" between a person and his toga and sandals or any inanimate object.

Clearly, they understood that love is a sacred and holy thing that exists only between two or more living entities. I have a Challenge for us all. Let's bring sacredness back to this highest of ideals. When we use the word *love* associated with things, let's define it appropriately. Let's define this lesser kind of love as "an appreciation for something that is useful to one's soul purpose." (Coincidently, our collective soul purpose just might be to know true love.) I, for example, "love" my piano. Playing it is a soulful experience. It's not the same as the love I have for my wife and children, but it's still a good and wonderful thing.

Okay, now that we've put things in perspective, to perform the test, when considering some thing, ask yourself: *Do I really "love" it? Is it truly useful to my soul's purpose?*

If it doesn't pass this test, release. Give it to someone who really will enjoy it or find it useful. It's time to free up some of your precious, valuable storage space for something better.

Until you make room for your better good, your better good has no room in your life.

And guess what might be the better good that is waiting all around you right now, straining, all set to automatically flow into your life? It just might be clear, stress-free, easy, emptiness. Empty space to find yourself in, to be at peace within—empty space to stop hiding from yourself.

Imagine the feeling. Imagine getting to a place where everything that surrounds you nourishes your soul. That's "staging."

Whenever some thing fails the Chotchky test but you still can't let go, you can try this ancient cure. Find the most authentic Chinese herbal store in your town and purchase two containers of this most rare herb grown only in the Far East province of China known as Sofre. The people there truly know that it is better to give than receive. Every evening the villagers gather, make tea from the herb, and share stories of the day. Many say that Sofre is the happiest place on Earth (even more so than Disney Land). The ancient herb is called "Giv-Eeng."

Make a Giv-Eeng pot of tea. Sip it slowly and you will find great ease and joy in the process of gathering and releasing that which is not in service of your soul. Like the villagers in China you too will then be . . . *So Free.*

### *The Journey Begins*

Life is not a spectator sport. Get a Glad Bag. You may want to get three: one for stuff to give away/donate, one for recycling, and one for the dump. Simply begin walking around your living spaces. Or you may want to choose one troublesome area—a place that has been weighing down your spirit.

As we eliminate what has become meaningless from our surroundings, it begins to clear our mind. Eventually, it will lead us face-to-face with our soul. "Nice to see you; sorry it's been awhile."

Ultimately, the rewards of this Challenge have more to do with a freeing of the mind than the clearing of your space. Hands-on experience with our dysfunctional relationship to things is the first step to finding and honoring our soul. And so, get started. Go now. Be strong. You can do it.

To see my bags of Chotchky, go to the secret web page and click on the bag: **www.barryadennis.com/chotchkyvideos1**. This is embarrassing. But do this task! Accept the Challenge.

Afterward, we're off to Niketown followed by a trip to an orphanage in Africa with some shoes and a soccer ball. I think you're going to need some tissue for this one!

✳ ✳ ✳

# CHAPTER 6

# NIKETOWN

Well done! If you didn't take the last Challenge, your Chotchky awaits.

Did you put any shoes in your bag?

*Shoeotchky: (a) When the number of shoes one owns actually trips one up, often making it stressful and time consuming to simply "choose your shoes"; (b) An excess of shoes*

I often do, literally, trip on my shoes and others' shoes that are strewn about the house. There is much irony in tripping on something designed to help one walk. Not only do my kids and I leave our shoes around like little land mines, but my dog makes great sport out of carrying one of a pair into unseen corners of the house, creating a game of "find the matching shoe." It's her way of playing fetch with us.

At the back door of my house, we have two floor cabinets, almost like toy boxes, approximately 2 square feet and 18 inches deep. They are full of shoes. The ones on the bottom rarely see the light of day. There is a rotation, however, kind of like crops. When I'm desperate to find a shoe, I will reach in and mix them up. On the wall next to the boxes are seven shelves that are two and a half feet long. These shelves are generally also full of shoes. I am often very confused by this.

My wife is amazing. She doesn't seem to have this problem. Maybe for women, choosing shoes is as natural as childbirth—one more thing a man will never understand. In the process of writing this book, which has been over a period of about four years, I decided *not* to get rid of my Chotchky. I wanted to feel the tension and confusion, the Chotchky Effect, so it would truly be alive in me. I must tell you, at this point, it's beginning to feel as if I'm suffocating. *I want to give away all of my shoes and go barefoot for a year.*

A great master from India who lived about 2,500 years ago and who became known as the Awakened One, said, "Any possession that increases one's selfishness or does nothing to confirm one's wish to renounce what one has, is nothing but a drawback in disguise."

How many of our possessions actually increase our selfishness? It would appear to me that many do. We often seem to get one thing and then after having it, we later "need" to get more. A newer style, version, or update and yet we still have a hard time letting go of the old. That wise teacher also made a powerful observation: that all of us ultimately want to "renounce" what we have. I believe he is speaking from the Soul Paradigm.

## The Best Investment

I try regularly to have special days with my boys. Just me and my two sons, or just one of them, doing father-son stuff. Once we happened to drive by a "Niketown" retail store. CJ has become something of a shoe collector. He had never seen a Niketown before, so it caught his eye. What am I saying? *He flipped out.* Niketown? A town called Nike? *Can we move there, Dad?!*

As we entered this shrine to shoes, there came a kind of nervous pacing. CJ wanted to try on every sport shoe he could see, like an addict who needed a fix. After drooling over the names of several endorsed high-tech, air-sole *Back to the Future*–type basketball shoes, he finally found *the* shoes. With this $119 pair marked down 20 percent he could, maybe, enter the NBA draft now at age ten.

He was clear about this. He told me several times, "I really, really, really, want these." He had been saving his money for months for just such an occasion. Wondering where he might spend it. However, when he started saving, he didn't even know about Niketown. Clearly, it was a *shoe-in*.

Allowing him to buy them would have been like giving an addict a fix. However, his puppy-dog eyes and protruding lower lip were having their intended effect. He was wearing me down. I turned away in an effort to disconnect from the power of his forlorn furrow.

As parents, we are greatly challenged by the developing Chotchky Paradigm in our children. We don't want them to become slaves to it, even though we know we are. "Do as I say, not as I do" drips from our demeanor. We want their love so badly we fall for the illusion, drilled into our mind by the Chotchky Campaign, that we can buy it. We do this not just with our children, but they are often the greatest casualties. The giving of stuff for affection is *loveotchky: a plastic emotion based on power struggles and control leading to despair and often fostering in children a most debilitating effect known as entitlement.*

It's an epidemic in our country and all developed nations, which goes to show you we've got it backward. A truly developed nation would not ever allow its children to develop entitlement. What shows our children real love, of course, are boundaries, structure, discipline, and a lot of fun, heart-to-heart connections.

It took everything I had to *give* him love. I took a breath, opened my mouth, unsure myself of what might come out, when into the room came . . . "No." I was as cool, calm, and collected as a stockbroker shifting investments on a hunch, going with the gut on a long shot.

"But why, Dad?"

"Because we're just *looking*. We are not *buying* anything today."

Talk about dejected! You'd have thought I just took away his breathing rights.

"But, Dad, I've been saving my money. It's *my* money."

"Not today, Son."

"But all of my friends have them."

"No."

"But why?"

"No."

"Come on."

"No."

"Bu—"

"No."

"B—"

"No."

When we finally left, CJ was pretty dejected.

That night after dinner, once he had some time to digest it all, he came to me. There was a kind of lightness about him. He gave me a hug. And then with those same puppy-dog eyes, he said, "Thank you, Dad. Thank you for saving me from those shoes."

I believe that says it all.

Then he confessed, "I didn't really want them. I just *thought* I did."

Who put that thought in his mind?

It was a beautiful moment. I had made the right stock option. I invested in my son instead of Niketown.

## Let's Take a Moment . . .

Let's take a moment for the SHOE affirmation: the Soul's Hope Of Evolution. Take a deep breath and then . . .

*Starting today, in no way will I allow the Chotchky Campaign to manipulate me into purchasing things in an effort to try to buy my children's love or anyone else's. My soul cries out from under this false practice. Instead, I give my children all of my love by saying no when it is the most loving thing to do. I*

*know that buying them things may create an "I love you" re-
sponse, but that isn't real.*

*Always giving in to their demands takes away their Soul's
Hope Of Evolving. The soul knows that a yes now may be a big
no later. A no to a life filled with true happiness and fulfillment.
By my giving in, as my children's bodies grow, I fail to help their
character grow. Giving in grows an adult ill-equipped to fully
step into the adventure of life. And so, I love my children. I love
them enough to listen to my soul instead of the wayward plans
of the Chotchky Campaign. For my children and me, I commit
to this truth like a favorite pair of old shoes that truly have soul.*

I was blown away by my son's awareness and willingness to
share his process with me and to thank me for really loving him
when he was "strung out." Together we faced the Chotchky Challenge and emerged victoriously. Through self-inquiry, CJ began
the shift. No small feat for anyone of any age. If we are honest
with ourselves, how often could we say, "I didn't really want it,
I just *thought* I did?" The difference between us and my son, of
course, is that we don't have an authoritative voice following us
around.

Or do we?

A still, small voice resides at the center of us all. The voice
of the soul. It's just buried under so much Chotchky it's muffled.
Let's remove that muffler.

### Love More

When CJ was 12, Heather and I took him on a medical mission
in Zimbabwe. We served as nonmedical support for a team of doctors performing delicate surgeries on children with birth defects,
burns from village fires, and myriad other injuries.

CJ wore one of his favorite pair of Nikes.

We also brought some soccer balls that a friend gave us to
give to the children after surgery. One afternoon, I noticed one of
those soccer balls under a gurney and thought, *I wonder how much*

*joy we could spread with that soccer ball?* I went to the head nurse, Go-Go, which means "Great Mother." She couldn't be more aptly named. She's a fireball of positive juju. I once asked her, "Go-Go, how do you stay so positive surrounded by such oppression? How do you show up for work with a smile and a song every day when I know they pay you next to nothing?"

She jumped up off her chair like she had been sitting on a coiled-up spring. The way she began to move, you would think James Brown's "I Feel Good" just came on through the old rusty PA system dangling from the ceiling.

Then she began to preach: "Barry, I say to them, 'You don't pay me enough, you don't give me any benefits, but I don't care . . . because I don't work for you. I work for God! I work for Love!' Every day, when I wake up, I ask, 'God, what would you have me do today? Where would you have me go today, Love? How would you have me be today?' And then everything is good, good, good and I am happy, happy, happy."

That's Go-Go. So, I came to her with the soccer ball in hand and said, "How much joy can I spread with this soccer ball today?"

She replied, "Ah, Lovemore."

"Yes, I want to love more, with this soccer ball."

Like a fortuneteller, she leaned in. "You must go to Lovemore."

"It's a place?"

"Yes, Lovemore is a school for homeless boys. Go there and you will *love more*." And so we did.

The broken windows and rusty door handles of Lovemore were quite deceiving. I had to push through the fear just to knock twice. As the door squeaked open, you could almost feel the love pouring out from within as two women, who could have been Go-Go's sisters, welcomed us.

"We have gifts for the children," we announced. Along with the soccer ball, we had brought a suitcase filled with shoes and clothes that had also been donated.

As we entered the living room of Lovemore, there on the floor, writing with broken pencils on crumpled papers, were 12 scrawny, barefoot, shirtless boys. They had been found wandering the streets and taken here. Some had lost their parents to AIDS, as it's estimated that one-third of all adults in Zimbabwe are HIV positive. As the two women introduced us, the kids all sat up as polite as can be and took turns telling us their names and ages. Then we told them we had gifts. CJ slowly reached into the bag, revealing its contents as their eyes lit up. Then their hands shot to the sky as they began jumping up and down, singing a song of thanks.

Then we opened the suitcase full of shoes. I don't know who was happier, the children of Lovemore or CJ. Suddenly he was like a shoe salesman at Nordstrom. He could size those kids up with one glance at their feet. In no time, he had all but one fitted and ready to run. Then came the last boy. At 14 he was the oldest and tall for his age with feet to match. CJ looked at his own feet and then at the suitcase. There were still several pairs of shoes in there but I think he somehow knew none would fit the boy. He looked deeply disturbed.

He said to him, concerned, "I'm sure there's a pair in here somewhere for you. Just let me see." Then he opened the other side of the case where there were several more shoes. He grabbed them one at a time, looking back and forth at the boy's feet.

"There's got to be a pair in here." He kept looking, as if by doing so the right-size shoes might materialize.

I had to intervene. "CJ, we don't have shoes for him."

Looking to the older boy now, my heart broken, I said, "I'm sorry, we just don't have any that fit you."

He simply replied, "It's okay."

As the boy walked away, CJ collapsed on the suitcase. The tears came silently. He didn't understand. Why is there a place where children don't have shoes? This reality did not fit into his privileged American upbringing.

Moments later, while I was talking to the women who ran the home, I saw CJ and the older boy disappear down the hall. When they returned, they were both wearing huge grins but guess who was wearing the shoes? Not only had CJ given the boy his precious Nikes, but he had also given him the shirt off his back. Literally. Barefoot and shirtless, CJ couldn't have looked happier. CJ and his new Zimbabwean pack of friends ran outside to play. He was home.

He may have been down two articles of clothing, but he now possessed something much more valuable. He was wearing *Love More* right on his heart.

✳

We have been bamboozled, hoodwinked, swindled, and duped into thinking we work for Chotchky: things, excess, recognition, false friends, and so on. It's the biggest con job in the universe. The truth is, and we all know it: *we work for love!* Always have and always will. Anything else is an illusion created by the Chotchky Campaign.

Like my son collapsing on a suitcase full of shoes that don't fit, let's surrender now and allow the change to come. Love More isn't just a home somewhere in a developing country; it's a place that is developing in our hearts. Our soul and the soul of humanity is counting on it.

## Chotchky Challenge

- Do you even know how many shoes you own? Yes or no? What percentage do you wear with any real consistency?

10% 20% 30% 40% 50% 60% 70% 80% 90% 100%

- Do you really think the money you spent buying all those shoes was put to its highest and best use in the world?

- Is it possible the number of shoes in your closets, on your shelves, in storage, and on the floor causes you at least a little confusion, even stress, from time to time?

- Is it possible that having all those shoes was not your idea in the first place but placed there by the Chotchky Campaign?

Is it possible that we have all been conned? Remember: *I didn't really want them. I just thought I did.*

## Truth or Fiction?

The most popular tourist attraction in the state of Oregon is an amazing waterfall called Multnomah Falls.
*Truth or Fiction?*
Fiction.
Multnomah Falls is breathtaking, and it is less than 30 minutes from downtown Portland. Right on the edges of the city are countless miles of hiking trails and one of the most beautiful rose gardens in the world. There is also the Oregon coast and its endless rocky beaches. And don't forget the white-peaked mountains like Mt. Hood with its world-famous Timberline Lodge. Just over the mountain lie endless desert canyons and heart-stopping white-water river rafting. Truly there are very few places on Earth as beautiful and diverse as Oregon.

So what is the number one tourist attraction in the state? The Woodburn Outlet Mall. May God have mercy on our souls.

Now click on "Go-Go" on the secret web page: **www .barryadennis.com/chotchkyvideos1**. Her spirit is in the house! Then read on and find out how my favorite tie walks the streets of Harlem at night . . . without me wearing it. Spooky.

# CHAPTER 7

# "WHAT TO WEAR?"

While standing in front of our closets, we have all muttered, "What to wear?" *That's how blessed we are.* We have so many clothes that at times, we just don't know which ones to put on.

*Shoeotchky,* of course, is just a footnote of *apparelotchky.* We stand there frozen, staring at all the shoes, shirts, pants, ties, belts, Large Floppy Sun Hats, muumuus, dresses, shawls, coats, boots, and scarves. When the question of "What to wear?" comes, we've just been *apparelyzed.* And when the thought *I've got nothing to wear* follows, all perspective has left the closet.

Can you now see why all the great sages of the ages from Jesus to Buddha, Gandhi, Mohammed, Moses, Lao-tzu, Yoda, Splinter, the Dalai Lama, Mother Teresa, and all the way to Paramahansa Yogananda all made the same fashion choice? Isn't it clear? *They never had to worry about or waste an ounce of energy wondering what to wear.* Nor would the thought, *I've got nothing to wear,* ever cross their minds, because they were profoundly grateful for their simple robe and sandals. In each of these beings simplicity was a choice, a detachment from the overwhelming world of things, allowing for a clear channel through which great wisdom flows. When the worries of the world are simply and gracefully discarded, it leaves much time to contemplate truth.

I do not suggest that we swap our entire bulging wardrobes for a robe and sandals. I do, however, encourage us all to take a closer look in the closet of our minds so that we may more humbly and consciously choose our garb.

Let's find that holy ensemble now. What percentage of your clothes do you actually wear with any regularity?

10% 20% 30% 40% 50% 60% 70% 80% 90% 100%

During the course of a lifetime, did you know that the average person in America spends 3.4 months trying to figure out what to wear, standing and feeling trace amounts of anxiety and confusion in front of the closet? Okay, so there has not been an actual scientific study of apparelization. But there *was* a study with jam that will be sufficient for our purposes.

At an upscale grocery store named Draeger's Market in Menlo Park, California, Columbia business school professor Sheena Iyengar set up a booth with exotic and very tasty jams. Sometimes she had six different jams, sometimes 24. She wanted to see if the number of jams presented would affect sales. Conventional Chotchky Economics dictates that the more jam choices, the more jam sales, since individuals would be able to find the jam that fits their taste. The results, however, were enlightening. While she displayed six jams, 30 percent of those in the market for a tasty spread bought at least one jar. By contrast, with 24 to choose from, only 3 percent purchased. Why? The answer is simple. *They got jammed.*

This, of course, is the tack the Chotchky Campaign takes on everything. Just look, let's say, at the dressings aisle of the grocery store. With all due respect to Paul Newman, how does one choose? Whether it be the supermarket down the road or the closet down the hall, one thing is clear: we're overdressed! Everywhere we go, there is more than our conscious mind can process in peace. We wonder, *Why was I short with my spouse and children today? Why was I irritable at work? Why was I so anxious in line at Starbucks?*

Because we've been jammed. It ties us up in knots. But with a little help from my friend in Harlem, we can get . . .

## *Untied*

Once, after I had just finished giving a concert, a stranger approached me with the most beautiful tie I had ever seen. It was pure silk with piano keys and musical notes dancing about.

The man simply said, "I love your music. I saw this tie the other day and felt I had to get it for you."

He handed it to me and then walked away, never to be seen again. Before that moment, I never had a favorite tie, but after that all ties paled in comparison.

Soon after 9/11, I wanted to go to New York to try to make sense of it all, to learn from it and to help out, if there was anything I could do. From this yearning, I was inspired to create a spiritual pilgrimage to the city. Twenty-two people joined me for what turned out to be a life-changing experience. Since I had never been to New York before, I decided to go ahead of time with two co-facilitators, Mat and Nola, to lay the groundwork.

I wanted to truly experience the heart of this most famous of cities. After much research, one of the places we wanted to check out was an African American church in Harlem called the Abyssinian Baptist Church. Before leaving for this information-gathering trip, I put a lot of thought into what to wear. I figured this Baptist church would be more formal than what I'm used to, so I packed a suit jacket, nice slacks, and a dress shirt. Then I looked at my rack of ties. There it hung: the silk one from the guy I don't know. I hesitated because the last thing I would want to do was lose my favorite tie. That's fear for you. What's the point in having a favorite tie if you're afraid to wear it? Then that soft voice that speaks to us from under all the Chotchky, the one that tries to get us to live from love and trust, found its way to my heart. "Don't be a silly nilly," it said. "Take your favorite tie. Enjoy it." So I packed it up and left for my very first trip to the Big Apple.

When Sunday morning came around, somehow we got a little behind. That night I had a hard time getting to sleep. The hotel bed was lumpy, the pillow too thick, and now my back had a knot in it I couldn't get untied. By the time we arrived at the Abyssinian Baptist church, it was packed. An usher showed us to the top balcony where the three of us were separated and led to a few of the only isolated seats left.

My spot was in the middle of a long row in the old-style pews. There was very little space between the knees of the people sitting and the back of the pew in front of them. It became one of those awkward moments like in a movie theater when you have to shimmy down the row to find your seat, but this was worse because the preacher was preaching! The first guy in my row was about 6'8" and upwards of 300 pounds. His legs were so long, his knees hit midway up the back of the pew. Getting past him was like trying to hop a fence. He shifted his knees this way and that as I attempted to proceed. He finally stood up, towering over me, still taking up the entire space allotted. I stepped toward him as we now commenced with what must have looked like a couple of awkward teenagers on their first date on the dance floor. Rocking to the left and then to the right, sticking one foot forward and then pulling it out, slowly spinning, belly to belly, hands held stiffly at our sides as his relatively petite wife looked on in amazement. After doing the Hokey Pokey in front of God and everyone else, I finally slipped past. All the while the preacher preached on.

I continued down the row past at least a dozen other people, whispering, "Excuse me, pardon me," until I finally got to my little allocated space. Someone from the stage said, "Please turn to hymnal number 89, 'The Old Rugged Cross.'" They began singing. I tried my best to join in, vaguely remembering the melody from when I was four years old, forced by my parents to put on a brown polyester suit every Sunday to go to the early service at the Church of God. (For a four-year-old kid, *it was hell*.)

I opened my mouth, finding about every third word. The rest that came out was akin to speaking in tongues. After the singing, everyone quickly sat. It was like a huge game of musical chairs, everyone knowing that if they didn't sit down fast, their spot on the pew might be absorbed. There are no dividers in pews and the ushers packed 'em in like a suitcase—*there's always room for one more.* Hearing approximately 800 people simultaneously sit in pews so old they should probably be decommissioned creates a creaking sound not unlike the musical score from the Alfred Hitchcock classic *Psycho. Screech!*

Then the preacher caught on fire—his sermon so powerful that *people fainted in the aisles below.* I soon started to hear this "pssst, psst" sound. I ignored it at first; it couldn't be directed at me. However, the "psst" continued. I finally looked down toward the end of the row and there he was, all 6 feet, 8 inches and 300 pounds, staring right at me down the long pew. I mouthed, "Me?" He nodded a very slow, clear *yes.* Now I was scared. Did my massacring of "The Old Rugged Cross" offend? Had I stepped on his toe during our little promenade? Eyebrows up, I mouthed, "What?" He responded in a whisper that was somehow also a scream that smacked me right between the eyes:

"I . . . want . . . your . . . tie."

Frightened, my first thought was, *I want my tie, too.*

That's the Chotchky Mind responding out of lack. Typical. There is not enough in the world, therefore, I must cling. But then somehow, my soul made a crack in the thick plastic Chotchky armor and whispered, *A miracle is here; step up to it.*

With an overwhelming sense of joy, I almost laughed out loud. I was having what some might call a "religious" experience, and yet, at the moment I had absolutely no idea what the preacher was saying. With a deep sense of gratitude, I began untying my favorite tie that was given to me by a guy I'll never know. Then I handed it to the person on my right, saying, "Pass it on." As the tie began its journey down the pew, each person looked back at me with an expression of "Really?" I just smiled, nodding.

He didn't even see it coming. My initial expression of "Are you crazy?" had turned his attention back to the podium where words of brotherly love now poured into the aisles. The tie finally reached his wife, who tapped him on the knee and then pointed at me, about 12 people down. He was taken aback, as if the things the preacher was saying were more than just empty platitudes but actually had some basis in reality. He looked at the tie in his hand. Then he smiled and shook his head "no" as he tried to send it back down the row through the now fully enrolled participants. They all watched, wondering what would happen next.

"No, really, I want you to keep it," I shout/whispered back.

After the service was over, as I made my way down the pew, I didn't know what to expect. When I reached him, he stood, reached down, wrapped his arms around my back and *picked me up two feet off the ground.* Shook me like a rag doll. The pop in my back was audible. The knot that was there from the lump in my bed had just been untied. It was the best adjustment I've ever received because it was more than just a realignment of the spine. I was realigned with my soul. When he put me down, he looked me right in the eyes and said, "I will never forget you. Ever."

Now whenever I look in my closet and see the empty spot where my favorite tie used to hang out, I put that musical tie on my heart, as a reminder of how I wish to be in the world. Peace and contentment come when I think of my tie walking around New York City without me, knowing that whenever he, whoever he is, puts it on, he too feels a kind of simple yet profound hope because some guy he doesn't know gave him a beautiful tie. Not only that, but I am sure it is quite the conversation starter. And each time he tells the story, the Chotchky Paradigm's grip on those who really listen is lessened, allowing a little more wiggle room for the soul.

Now I actively look for ways to give people "the tie off my neck" whenever the opportunity arises. That tie was *not* Chotchky as we have known it thus far. But we are going deeper now. As the soul rises, possession of things becomes less and less important compared to the joy of being in the flow: giving, receiving, and staying open to the miracle moments all around us. As much as I loved that tie, when you put it in perspective, compared to the soul of that moment, for *me* the tie became Chotchky. It now had a higher purpose than to hang around my neck. It had become something to be passed along to create an invisible tie between myself and another human being, between me and my soul and all of humanity.

Mat, Nola, and I walked from there to a restaurant in Harlem called Sylvia's. We were served the best fried chicken and greens possibly available anywhere this side of the Milky Way. As we slightly strayed from our normal diet under the heading of "when in Rome," we debriefed all of our amazing experiences in the Big Apple thus far. Sylvia's was quickly becoming one of them. They have incredible live gospel music, and a kind of soulful hospitality that makes you feel like part of the family.

Three years later, I received a gift in the mail in a long skinny box with a note that read:

*Hello, Barry,*

*I was in New York last week and went to Sylvia's. I saw this for sale there and it made me think of you.*

*Love,*
*Nola*

Under the note was a tie. The design had the name "Sylvia's" scattered about with chicken and greens and hot sauce. Now *that* tie became my favorite.

There is a flow to life. The Chotchky Mind chokes the flow off, smothers it by clinging and hoarding and grabbing and worrying. The soul yearns to let go in the *flow*. It's part and parcel in the creation of our Master Peace.

A few months later, while teaching a lesson on giving I told the tie story and I wore my new favorite tie. Toward the end of my talk, I took it off and walked down the middle aisle, looking for the right person to "pass the baton." I was just trusting my intuition to find someone who would carry on the tradition and give it away at the right time and place. Somewhere in the middle, I saw a man humbly beaming. That's the only way for me to describe it. "Humbly beaming." I had never met him before. I knew nothing about him. It turns out that he and his wife were visiting from out of town.

Afterward, his wife came to me and said, "You have no idea. I can't believe you chose him. He is the most giving person you will ever meet. Really. In fact, he recently gave one of his kidneys to a friend in need."

I chatted with her for quite some time, inspired by the stories she told me of this man's generous heart.

Later, the Sylvia's tie found its way back to me with this sentiment:

*Thank you so much for the tie; it is wonderful. Now I return it back to you to pass along again.*

It was quite a joy to receive it back, especially from him. I wonder who the next receiver will be as my Sylvia's tie awaits on my tie rack (clearly non-Chotchky).

I haven't spoken of the tie for about five years now and yet the stories keep coming. I received an e-mail just a few weeks ago. A woman named Kate, who was there when I told the story, explained that she had recently been on a Lawrence Welk cruise to Alaska. Kate was with her 85-year-old grandmother. At dinners, they were seated next to a couple they found difficult to be with. The grumpy woman, let's call her Ellen, after griping on and on about the eternal unfairness of everything one evening, noticed Kate's necklace and commented on it. Kate "loved" her necklace but the tie story came welling up in her memory and she suddenly knew just what to do. She took it off from around her neck and gave it to Ellen.

Kate received this e-mail from her a little while after the cruise:

*I have been thinking of you and wanted you to know that I am celebrating my 85th birthday today. Some of my cohorts are taking me to lunch. I am celebrating by dressing up a little and wanted you to know I am wearing "our" necklace. I had a friend take a picture of me to send to you. My life has changed for the better after knowing you and your grandmother. I am more thoughtful of other people and try harder to be a good friend to those I am in contact with. You have truly improved my attitude in life.*

> *Thank you and bless you,*
> *Ellen*

There are Miracle Moments dancing around us all the time. I call them "M and M's." What's great about these is they have no calories. In fact, *they make you lighter.* They appear every time you transcend the fear and greediness of the Chotchky Mind, let go, and fall into the flow.

A new kind of living is waiting. A life of true abundance. Once, the Chotchky Paradigm had us all in knots, but we just got "un-tied."

## Chotchky Challenge

Let's take our "Glad Bag" exercise directly to the closet. In a moment, go into your closet(s) and, in the spirit of the tie, gather everything you haven't worn *more than once* in the last 12 months and give it away. Think of people you know who would not only love the article, but would be touched and inspired like Ellen. Or just give it to Goodwill!

I guarantee you will feel lighter and freer, not only because your soul longs for spaciousness and because you will no longer experience apparelization, but because *there are people who actually need those clothes.* Our existence should make others' lives better. Much of the Chotchky that is only stressing us out could actually be relieving someone else's stress. Once you eliminate the excess baggage, make a pact with yourself that for every new piece of clothing you bring into your closet, you will give one away. Ah . . . the flow. How sweet it is. Find that sweet spot, the "clothes line" where all of your attire is authentically you and your closet *never exceeds 80 percent capacity.* After that point, even things we truly "love" become Chotchky because of the stress caused by overcrowding.

When my family moved from a large house to a lesser-big house, my closet size was cut in half. After I crammed all my socks into my new sock drawer and shut it, the next day I couldn't get it open. My drawers had become jammed. My first thought, of course, was that I needed bigger drawers, a bigger closet. Then I began yanking the socks out of the drawer one at a time. I had a total of 27 pairs of athletic socks. This is not including the ones in the dirty clothes or my dress socks, which I almost never wear.

Then the revelation came: I do not need a bigger drawer, *I need fewer socks.* I do not need a bigger closet; *I need less clothing.* We do laundry about twice a week. With all the athletic socks I have, probably totaling somewhere in the neighborhood 40 pairs, I would have to wear approximately 8½ pairs *per day* to actually run out of clean socks before the next wash. This is ludicrous. I'm giving away two-thirds of my socks . . . now.

## Challenge Continued . . .

In your closet, have a giving bag at the ready at all times. Once it's full, feel the joy of generosity. At first it might take a little adjustment, but trust me, it's in alignment with your soul.

Helpful hint: simply by measuring the width or your closet you can keep your mind from being jammed. For every foot of hanging space, six shirts can be hung without inducing overload, also known as the Chotchky Effect. One hanger for every two inches. Oh so easy.

*

Go to the secret page now and click on the tie: **www .barryadennis.com/chotchkyvideos1**. I've got some "M and M's" for you! After that, we move to Level II, where you will discover why some scientists are saying that God lives in our fat!

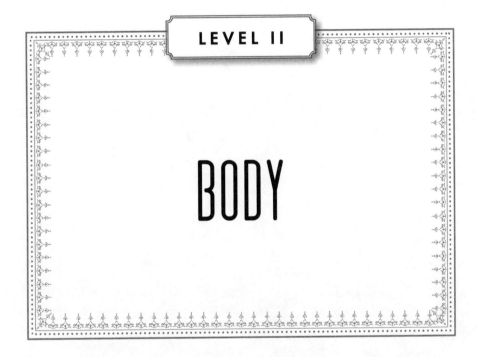

## LEVEL II

# BODY

We now delve directly into the "storage space" called our bodies. I only put one chapter here simply because as we move on to the next two levels, the Mind and the Soul, it becomes increasingly clear that Chotchky at these higher levels also impact the body. They envelop one another.

In the following pages, be aware that the same Chotchky Effect that's created from putting too much junk in your home—stress, confusion, anxiety, lethargy, and so on—is also created by putting too much junk in your body. Like the ancient philosophy says, "As within, so without."

# CHAPTER 8

# THE ARMOUR HOT-DOG BOY

## Truth or Fiction?

Our children are the first generation in human history predicted to have a shorter life span than the previous generation.

*Truth or Fiction?*

Sad, but true.

Even with all the miracles of modern medicine—tiny instruments that can actually clear clogged arteries and medicines that counteract some of the damage we have done to our bodies—it's true. The kinds and the amounts of food we are giving our children, combined with a lack of exercise, is killing them. And the Chotchky Campaign relentlessly supports our behavior. Taco Bell, for example, has had a campaign called "Fourthmeal." That's *mealotchky.* Through the Chotchky Paradigm, however, it sounds like heaven because . . . more is always better, right?

*Foodotchky: (a) Any food consumed after the body is already full; (b) food that has little or no nutritional value to the body, mind, and spirit, which is generally labeled as "processed" or "refined"*

"Processed" and "refined" are the Chotchky Campaign's way of saying, "We took all the healthy stuff out."

While recently at a water park, I saw a mother duckling and her eight little chicks appear out of the bushes and begin waddling through the lounge chairs and the sea of people who "oohed" and "awed" at their incredible cuteness. One man began breaking off pieces of his funnel cake and feeding it to the baby chicks.

Do you know what funnel cake is? It's cake batter "funneled" into a vat of fat, fried, and then doused in sugar. The manager of the park came out running.

"Please stop feeding them! It creates bad habits. They're supposed to learn to feed on their natural food sources," she said.

Then she noticed what it was he was feeding the chicks. With urgency and compassion, she said, "My God, and you're feeding them funnel cake. Don't you know? That will kill them. Please stop."

She was not joking. The baby chicks became ill, and I don't know if they survived. The man was not only feeding the baby chicks funnel cake, but he was also feeding it to his own offspring. Needless to say, he and his children . . . waddled.

The only difference between the baby chicks and us is that the Foodotchky Effect takes longer. Just like the baby chicks, we too need to learn to eat from our natural food sources because our body—just like our home, our car, and our mind—is a storage space. What we put in it, we become. The old cliché "You are what you eat" is truer than we'd like to admit, and . . . I don't want to be a funnel cake!

Also, most spiritual practices teach that the body is a temple: the temple of our very soul. That is some pretty precious storage space.

### Free Cookie Day, Yeah!

Subway is by far my favorite fast-food restaurant. You can actually eat a very healthy lunch quicker than many fast-food joints fry up a "Happy Meal." Subway also gave us Jared, who has become an inspiration to the world. In fact, I recently had dinner with Jared. Crazy, I know. He is as he seems. A really nice guy who is helping us shift our paradigm so that we can begin turning the tide to a more healthy future. Thanks, Jared.

*That said, I do have one "beef" with Subway . . . Free Cookie Day.*

Yeah, free cookies! I mean, what's not to like? It's free. First of all, of course it's just amortized into the cost of the meal. I mean, you can't just walk in and say, "Give me a free cookie." But truthfully, the money is the easiest part of the payment for that cookie. When the "sandwich artist" says, "It's free-cookie Tuesday; what kind would you like?" almost everyone they ask pauses for a moment. I recognize the confusion. We all know there is a very fine line between a cookie and foodotchky. After all, how much junk food does one need to ingest before the rest becomes Chotchky? One could argue, none. We, as a culture, have already named it what it is: junk. However, Chotchky is subjective, so we all must be our own judge.

Almost every person asked the question "Would you like a free cookie?" experiences confusion and other aspects of the Chotchky Effect. This is brought on by the fact that most people who come to Subway are there to eat more healthfully. If they take the free cookie, they know they have pretty much taken the "healthy" right out of the meal. Most end up taking it, though. It's what we have been trained to do. What follows is almost always justificationotchky: "Well, I did choose whole-wheat bread; I think I've earned a few hundred empty calories."

Unless you are going for a two-mile jaunt around the parking lot after lunch, that cookie, over the next 24 hours, is slowly going to become *buttotchky: disproportionately large cheeks eventually making airplane travel twice as expensive as one is forced into purchasing two seats, one for each cheek.*

The cookie can just as easily become thighotchky, waistotchky, or double chinotchky. I don't mean to make light of the situation; however, the Chotchky Campaign has created a heavy contradiction. We want to be healthy. We join clubs and pay fees to rid ourselves of buttotchky. We feel good, maybe even a little inflated, being a member of a health club because we can say . . . we're members of the health club. On the other hand, we feel guilty about not going, especially each month as we pay for our membership with money that could be going to Love More.

We want to eat healthy for our body, mind, and spirit; and yet as a culture, we put impulse-buy junk food next to the impulse-buy gossip magazines at nearly every checkout stand in the modernized world. This is the most prominent retail space available!

We're working against ourselves. We're doing it to each other.

As it said in the classic comic strip *Pogo:* "We have met the enemy, and he is us."

We are "The Campaign"!

When I was a kid, my mother and father made us cut everything in half. I remember whenever we had a soda, we could never actually have an entire can, ever. We would have to split one can between the two of us . . . or the three of us! After my younger brother came along, my portions got proportionately smaller.

I'll never forget the day when my older brother and I had a cookie to split. After analyzing the knife display in the kitchen, he made his choice and cut the cookie. I studied the two pieces sitting there, making quick geometric calculations and, pointing to the portion on the right, I exclaimed, "I want the big half." My brother retaliated, "There's no such thing as the big half. If one is bigger than the other, it's more than half."

*Bang! Kapow!* A true "Aha!" moment. There's no such thing as a big half. There comes a moment, a coming-of-age, when we get it. It's part of growing up, evolving.

And yet, even so, there are times when I enter a Subway sandwich shop that I seem to "de-evolve." There's a point where I become Zug, Neanderthal Man in a fast-food sandwich shop. It happens soon after the sandwich artist asks the all-important question: "Would you like a 6 inch or 12 inch?" I often respond, "Six inch, please." Then they cut the bread. That's when the transformation occurs because as soon as they make the cut, I want the big half.

I do! I don't care if it makes sense or not. "Zug want big half." And the guy behind me in line, who may, during the day, be a professor of mathematics, is thinking the same thing. Master's degree and all, he knows if I get the big half, he's getting the small half.

But why? Why do we "de-evolve," always thinking bigger is better? Because the Chotchky Paradigm is stuck in the past. It's Neanderthal. There was logic to this a very, very long time ago, kind of. Logic, however, dictates that we use current information to reach sound conclusions. There is nothing "sound" in "Me not care if me is stuffed now. Could be Zug's last meal."

Currently, I'd like to lose six or seven pounds. Wanting the bigger half makes no sense. I'm actually working against myself. Through the Chotchky Paradigm, we are all working against ourselves, but the soul knows better. Through the Paradigm of the Soul, we would not want the "big half" simply because the soul wants the healthy half. Whatever that may be.

## Deep Thought

Recognize that our culture is trying to make us overweight in body, mind, and spirit. See it as a challenge to overcome. Accept it because as we lead by example, our children become lighter.

## Chotchky Challenge

The next time someone is cutting a cake at a wedding or party and putting the pieces on little plates and offers you one from the table, take the smaller half. Apply this illogic to all areas of your life and begin to feel oh so much lighter.

When I was a kid, Armour hot dogs had a popular commercial driven by a very catchy jingle. Do you remember it? It talked about fat kids and thin kids and kids who ride bikes—all loving to eat hot dogs! They actually showed an overweight kid eating a hot dog. The commercial would not make it on the air today. It would not be PC, I suppose because of the challenge we face with obesity and now share with all Westernized countries. This struggle is just one effect of the Chotchky Paradigm's insistence that more is always better. We've become heavy in every conceivable way. We are overweight in thought, which is weighing down our mind; overweight in stuff, weighing down our homes; and overweight in emotion, putting a heavy burden on our soul.

However, there is a liberating paradox moving throughout the cells in our body that are designed to carry the weight.

### Fat Is Not Bad!

Like most things, fat only becomes Chotchky after a point. In fact, fat is extremely helpful. The body needs quite a lot of it for optimum health. Around 15 to 20 percent body fat is considered good. That's a lot of girth. Another word for fat is *energy,* which is stored in the body. Many quantum physicist/spiritual gurus today say God is energy. Hmm . . . think about it. That should change how you see your fat! And changing how you see this growing concern, in each area of your life, changes everything. To further assist you in fostering the shift, it is helpful to know: *What you resist persists.*

I wasn't sure if I believed this somewhat clichéd "New Age" notion. Then one day, a fly showed up on my computer screen. He would not go away. He flew into my face and landed on my head several times. I don't like to kill anything, even a fly. I tried to shoo it out the door and window, but he would have none of it. Finally after hours of irritated, unfocused work, I rolled up a newspaper and began swatting away. I worked up a bit of a lather, actually getting angry with the fly. Then I remembered the saying "What you resist persists."

But how does one not resist?

Tolerate? That didn't seem enough. I needed to go to the opposite end of the spectrum. What is the opposite of resistance? Love, I supposed. So I sat down in my chair and, to the best of my ability, loved the fly. I thought how difficult his life must be at times and how short-lived (especially with swatters like me around). Then it landed on my arm.

*Okay,* I thought, *Now what?* I looked at the fly up close as he rubbed his front legs together in that sinister manner. But suddenly, it didn't seem so sinister. In fact, it was as if he were trying to tell me something. "Get up and walk outside. You sure are slow for a human." Finally, it sunk in. I stood and carefully walked my fly out of doors. And that was the end of it. All that time lost in resistance. Frustrated. And here's the Paradigm Shift. Once he flew away, I missed my fly!

So, the more we push against something, the harder it pushes back. This happened to our entire culture regarding fat sometime after the Armour hot-dog boy. Fat has created a whole new subcategory of our "shadow." There is so much shame and guilt around it, how can we possibly love ourselves if we consider ourselves fat? How can we stop accumulating Chotchky in general if we do not like ourselves? The whole "addiction to acquisition" is a misguided attempt at loving ourselves. And there is a direct correlation; the more we truly love ourselves as we are, the less stuff we need to try and validate our existence.

## Chotchky Challenge

On a scale from 1 to 100, how much do you love you? This will reveal much in the way of the work that needs to be done to create your Master Peace. Circle the number on the scale that represents the degree to which you have learned to love and accept yourself just as you are. Then simply draw a vertical line straight down connecting the upper and lower scales.

## Self-Love and Acceptance Scale

*I love and accept myself just as I am:*

| 0 | 10 | 20 | 30 | 40 | 50 | 60 | 70 | 80 | 90 | 100 |
|---|----|----|----|----|----|----|----|----|----|-----|
| 100 | 90 | 80 | 70 | 60 | 50 | 40 | 30 | 20 | 10 | 0 |

*The corresponding amount of Chotchky in my life*

The goal is to unabashedly draw a line from 100 (unconditional self-love) to 0 (zero Chotchky). When we can do this, we will have reached liberotchky: total and complete freedom from all things Chotchky! There is no higher state of being. However, it is not likely that any of us reaches 100. (If you did, please run for President!)

As you can see, there is a direct correlation between the number we chose on the self-love scale and how much Chotchky needs to be chipped away to create our Master Peace. This is made clear by the corresponding, opposite scale. I, for example, after no small amount of contemplation, circled the number 70 on the self-love and acceptance scale. This reveals that approximately 30 percent of everything in my life, including food, thoughts, things and emotions, is Chotchky. I am using it to try to fill the emptiness where love is missing in me. This attempt is futile. As much as the Campaign would like us to believe it, Chotchky cannot give us love. So, one could say, attaining complete and total self-love and acceptance is the final Chotchky Challenge. But how can we do this? How can we reach this enlightened state?

Look at the scale again; the answer is right there. There are two opposite ways. One, we can attempt the difficult task of directly learning how to fully love ourselves. Part of the difficulty here is that the Chotchky Mind sees this effort as an assault and counters with feelings of unworthiness, guilt, shame, and a warehouse of other emotionalotchky. Countless modern-day "gurus" from Leo Buscaglia to Deepak Chopra, from Marianne Williamson to Eckhart Tolle, have done good work at shedding light on the process.

However, there is a second way. A back door, if you will, to self-love. It is the tangible, measurable work of identifying and releasing all forms of Chotchky. And it just so happens that doing so is the most loving thing you can do, for you. Either way, the end result is the same. When complete self love and acceptance is attained, all Chotchky does simply fall away. You have no desire for it anymore. No desire for relationships that aren't real in an attempt at validation. No desire for food when you aren't hungry. For things you don't really need. You would no longer even desire acknowledgment for anything. Why would you? You would be motivated to do that which you do for one reason only. For you, and the betterment of humanity and all life. Accolades are not needed when the ego's Chotchky Paradigm has been let go, for you are overflowing with love. And the good news is as you do the visible work of letting go of Chotchky, you inadvertently and relatively easily reach the graceful state of self-love and acceptance. All enlightened teachers are evidence of these truths.

Based on the scale, what is the current percentage of Chotchky you need to release? As we continue, that number will drop; and each time it does, you are, one increment at a time, remembering your true worth. As this happens, you can't help but be in love with you.

### "I Love My Hot-Dog Fat!"

In that Armour commercial, there was no shame associated with the fat kid; he was loved and accepted just as much as every other kid in the commercial. That's why, in part, there were relatively few obese kids around. The level of shame associated with fat today had not yet arrived. Over time, however, we slowly began to shove the Armour hot-dog boy away in the closet of our mind as we were told by every image given to us by the Chotchky Campaign that we are supposed to look like toothpicks—to the point where the image in our mind of "perfection" needed a fattening.

Skin-and-bones models were paraded around on stages wearing bizarre, sometimes "fashionably" tattered clothing. At times I wasn't sure if I was watching a fashion show or a special to raise money for the starving people who walk runways. The Chotchky Campaign has so messed with our self-image that there are teens and even children all over the world starving themselves in an attempt to look like the rails they see on magazine covers. The absurdity plays itself out right there at the checkout stand. Prominently placed next to the images of toothpicks in magazines are what? Giant candy bars! Should I go on a binge or starve myself?

These impulse-buy sections, like the checkout stands, feed right into the Chotchky Campaign. As we compare ourselves to the images on the magazines, we fall into the trap: I am just a carbon-based, separate, flawed, sinful, less-than, screwed-up individual; therefore, the magazine is "gospel." I really should look like the models and movie stars on the cover. Fame, fortune, and looks are all that matter. *I am so flawed!*

It's clear we have given these "stands" the appropriate name. Every time we approach them, the Challenge is on. As they tantalize our lower impulses, we tend to completely "check out." Instead, think of them as "check in" stands. Breathe and remind yourself of what is real and important because what is placed before you there as you purchase your groceries is mostly a lie. The models and movie stars on the front of the magazines have all been airbrushed! The Chotchky Campaign is presenting an ideal that doesn't exist. *They* are not even that beautiful! It's altogether unattainable. The premise is off. They remove all those funny little imperfections that make us so perfectly, gorgeously human.

When we see through the Soul Paradigm, we already are perfect, airbrushed by God. It's a different way of seeing. That which the Chotchky Campaign deems as imperfections and wishes to airbrush out are most often unique expressions of our soul reflected in our physical form. Why would we wish to airbrush out the soul?

Along with the photos, these "idols'" entire lives have been airbrushed to look like nirvana to perpetuate the Chotchky Campaign. The "stars" who have actually attempted to attain the image the Campaign has created of them often become distressed, mentally unstable. Cases in point: Michael Jackson, Britney Spears, Elvis Presley, Lindsay Lohan, and Marilyn Monroe. The pain, anguish, and sorrow these and so many like them have experienced is tragic. They had all the fame and fortune that the world tells us is the "answer," even our "purpose." And yet they lived or are living in a kind of despondency from which there seems no escape.

As a musician, I have great respect for Elvis Presley and Michael Jackson. I also believe their hearts were true. Their fate saddens me. So much beautiful music left unsung. The Chotchky Mind created a tragic life for them and we bought into and perpetuated the illusion. Now, I hope Britney Spears, Lindsay Lohan, and the countless others like them, find peace. These "icons" chose very difficult incarnations. Their lives are a profound lesson to us all.

## Chotchky Challenge

When you see a magazine cover of a "glamorous" movie star with their movie-star lover in their movie-star car and with their movie-star paycheck, what percentage of you feels: "If only I could have their life, then I'd really be happy. I'd have it all!"

0% 10% 20% 30% 40% 50% 60% 70% 80% 90% 100%

Whatever percentage you chose is the degree to which the Campaign has persuaded you into accepting its agenda, and therefore, it is the amount of your thinking that is in opposition to your soul. You cannot have their life, and, anyway, what you think it is, it isn't. You can, however, have your life. And your life is altogether miraculous. Read the line again with one word change: "If only I could have my life, then I'd really be happy. I'd have it all!"

What if we yearned for and idolized our own lives with the same curiosity and envy we often give movie stars, models, the extremely wealthy, sports heroes, and the guy in the corner office? What a shift that would create.

Now you might be thinking, *But I already have my own life, so how can I be envious of it?* Well, you don't have it, not fully. To some degree, we are all living somebody else's life. Someone else's idea of what it means to be successful and happy. Instead, *yearn for your* life, your unique, perfect expression of this one life. Push through the Chotchky Paradigm and there your masterpiece will be. Vibrant, alive, unafraid, and glorious. You will love this life. This life will love you back. And that, my co-adventurers on this sacred sojourn, is *self-love.*

## Deep Thought

The fundamental Challenge resides in an underlying current that moves throughout the Chotchky Campaign. It is opposed to the idea that we might one day reach complete self-acceptance and love. For if we do, I would venture to say, over half of the world's businesses would go under. We would no longer feel the need to give them our money.

Can you see how motivated we are by our lack of self-acceptance? It's quite the trigger for Chotchky. However, the shift is under way. Slowly. We are evolving. A holy "retooling" is afoot. For each venture that does not fit into the emerging paradigm, a transition will occur. A business about the work of spirit will arise in its place.

I know some people live in fear that if we don't buy whatever is pushed by our society, and buy lots of it, the economy will collapse. The feeling is that it's better to buy lots of stuff we don't really need or may not even be good for us than let the economy fall. Let's question that thinking now. What if living by this belief eventually ravishes Mother Earth of her beauty and resources? What if living this way makes us physically unhealthy? I, however, believe there is nothing to fear. When I was a kid, there were cigarette dispensers everywhere. Cigarette dispensers were a huge enterprise. Now, not so much. Yes, many people have lost their jobs as cigarette smoking has become less and less popular. Do you think we should bring cigarette smoking back to gain those lost jobs? That of course is crazy. As we shift our paradigm, things must die so better things can be born. I predict there will be fewer doughnut shops and more health-food stores 20 years from now than there are today. Not only am I *not* worried about the ones who work at the doughnut shop, I delight in the vision that there will be jobs available for those same people, if they wish, in an environment that supports their body, mind, and soul—working for a company that is environmentally conscious.

The underlying purpose of every business venture will eventually be to assist the soul's expression on Earth. In the meantime, polarization will be seen and felt.

Luckily for us all, what you resist persists. As those in fear push against a more authentic, peaceful way, a more authentic, peaceful way must eventually push its way right into their hearts.

### Enjoy the Fat

As I mentioned, I am currently about six or seven pounds over my ideal weight. And just like too many shirts in my closet, I am enjoying the process of giving my fat away. It's stored energy, which makes it potential expressions of God. As I choose to use that energy in a heartfelt way, God is expressing through me. Whether it be playing basketball with my kids, leading a talk on the Chotchky Challenge, giving a concert, or going for a bike ride with my wife, with each act of passion and joy my spirit is moving in and through me. The more in touch with this we become, the more we wish for our body, mind, and environment to be in optimum working order, makes it possible for us to truly shine.

So, let's love our hot-dog fat, or any part of us we think should be airbrushed. Stop resisting and let it melt away in joyful expressions of life. Thank the fat for the energy it gives. No more shame. The pendulum is swinging back now to balance, and while it does, let's put the Armour hot-dog kid on it. Swinging is good exercise. It's also very joyful. And there's no shame in joy!

## Let's Take a Moment . . .

. . . for the FAT affirmation: the Fun Airbrushed Truth.

Become centered. Take a breath into this *fun* storage space called the body.

> *Right now, I accept myself just as I am. There is nothing I need to change, for I am a miracle of life itself. The imperfections that a backward world may see are not real, for they do not see the truth.*

Who do you consider to be a great master, a truly loving being?

> *Visualize that person gazing into your eyes. There is nothing there but perfect love and acceptance. This individual sees the divine being you are. So who do you believe, this being or the Chotchky Campaign? The master you envision is right of course. You are beautiful. It is from this place that you can create change if you wish. It is not required, nor is it needed in order to be deeply loved. Isn't that Fun? You have just been Airbrushed by the Truth.*

## Chotchky Challenge

Begin to genuinely love this most precious storage space called your body. Allow that God energy to come out and play. For at least 20 minutes, five days a week, do something joyful with this miraculous instrument of expression. Go swing on a swing, dance, walk, run, or play. Your body, mind, and spirit will thank you.

What physical activity brings you joy? Place it here and begin doing it regularly:

_____

_____

_____

At the next link, anything could happen. I may take you on a trip to a strange and magical café where I end up transforming into a chicken. Click on the chicken at the secret web page: **www .barryadennis.com/chotchkyvideos1.**

Next we're off to the South Pacific where I completely lose touch with reality and run screaming mad all over a cruise ship, all because of Chotchky.

## LEVEL III

# MIND

The human mind—more mysterious than the cosmos itself. We are just now beginning to understand its true power and potential. The storage space that rests on our shoulders, oh, how vitally precious it is.

At this level we can see the Chotchky Challenge is, ultimately, an invitation to begin breaking the habit of seeking fulfillment from "out there."

# CHAPTER 9

# WHONE! (TECHNOTCHKY)

### Truth or Fiction?

While meandering the streets of New York, a woman named Sue walked right into an open manhole as she was texting. After climbing out of the sewer, she actually tried to sue the City of New York.

*Truth or Fiction?*

Truth.

This is called "sue-age." It's a new low and occurs when the preoccupied Chotchky Mind has become incapable of taking any responsibility for its own lack of awareness. (Okay, so I don't know what her actual name was, but if the Sue fits, wear it.)

*Technotchky: (a) what technology is when we unconsciously allow it to interfere with our relationships, our safety, our aware-ness of the present moment, and our general peace of mind; (b) the overwhelming onslaught of "outdated" or newly released technological paraphernalia slowly creeping out of our drawers and closets, spilling into our lives, homes, and landfills*

### *"Instant Karma"*

Misplacing my wallet has not been an uncommon event in my life. I have often wished that my wallet had some kind of beeper or GPS system so I could locate it when it was lost among all the Chotchky.

Another classic root of stress is the misplacing of one's cell phone. However, when you misplace your cell phone, you can at least call yourself. After a year of thoughtful introspection, I made the leap to an iPhone. Replacing technology is not something I take lightly. One of the most disturbing aspects of the Chotchky Paradigm is the feeling that we must constantly upgrade anything that uses electricity, even things we rarely used that were full of options we never knew they had. Our landfills are overflowing with tons of perfectly good electronics that we seem to think are disposable: "Tissue Technology."

Used appropriately, technology is wonderful, even miraculous. The "appropriate" line, however, is becoming very blurred. Sometimes it seems as though cell phones have been superglued directly to the face. Sometimes we walk around talking on the phone when we are already with people. These people are actually there. In the flesh. No chance of losing bars. They came . . . in *person!* There is the option of speaking directly to their *faces*. And if they have not had too much *Botoxotchky,* communication can take place *with expressions*.

And then there are the compulsive "texters" running into lampposts, doors, parked cars, and each other like pinballs in a pinball machine. People are wandering right into the street getting hit by other people who are texting behind the wheel. Wouldn't it be something if you were texting someone and got hit by the one you were texting because that person was reading your text? I think John Lennon knew "smart" phones were coming when he wrote the song "Instant Karma." Text messaging and other technology-based distractions *have* become one of the main causes of personal injury.

And what about the ones who are texting in the middle of the movie? Are we so addicted to distraction that we are no longer capable of focusing on a gigantic screen in 3D with surround sound, popcorn, and Sour Patch Kids?

Technology is supposed to make our lives *less* stressful. It should be a tool in support of our purpose. As we go unconscious, however, the opposite occurs: it stresses us out. We go overboard. Way overboard.

So, I got an iPhone. I committed myself to understanding it and using it to simplify and assist my life, my soul, and yes, my purpose. And I must say it proved to be a wonderful tool. Right away I thought there must be a "case" for the iPhone that was also a wallet. To have my wallet and my cell phone in one place together would be, well, *science fiction.* If I could find such a thing, I could call my wallet. I was shocked to discover that the Apple Store had no such wallets available. I was convinced they must exist, so I began searching on the Web and, lo and behold, there it was, being manufactured someplace south of the border.

I don't buy much off the Internet, but I took a leap of faith. And miracle of miracles, my iPhone wallet showed up a couple of weeks later. I no longer have a wallet or a phone. I am the proud owner of a *whone,* a wallet/phone. Yes, the future has arrived.

I was so excited I could hardly contain myself. Not only had I simplified my life by morphing my wallet and phone into one thing, but this was the fruition of a dream. I could now *call* my wallet.

That night, several friends came over. As I munched on a few squares of Life cereal as a snack, I waxed poetic about the improved quality of life of which I had become the recipient of as a result of my whone. At one point I placed it on the kitchen counter, left for just a moment, but when I returned, it was gone. Everyone tried to act innocent. I could almost see mouse tails sticking out of their mouths.

I knew what was up. They wanted to see if my "invention," the great whone, was legit. I lurked around the kitchen for a couple minutes looking for clues. Then like a proud papa, I picked up the house phone and called myself. I heard a ringing. It was distant. Muffled somehow. I tried to follow the stifled ringtone. It reminded me of when I used to play "Find the Thimble" with my grandma when I was five. (She once said she hid it, but I think she just wanted a break from me. I wandered around the kitchen for hours! Oh, the therapy.)

It seemed to be coming from the kitchen table. Near it, the ringing would get louder, yet it was still muted. For the life of me, I couldn't tell where it was coming from. I had to call myself several times. When the ringing would stop I knew what my message was saying: "Hi, it's Barry. My whone and I are busy. Leave us a message and we'll get back to you ASAP—as soon as practical. *Beep.*" The irony is that at the moment, I *was* busy . . . looking for my whone!

Finally, I looked at the kitchen table and "heard the bells ringing." I grabbed my "Life" by the horns. I ripped it open and there, tucked in with a hundred brown square bites of cereal, lay my whone. The bite-sized pieces spilled as I turned to this group of vagabonds who were trying to keep straight faces; and like a B actor in a black-and-white whodunit, I said, "Aha! I knew it. You can't hide my whone from me." And then I commenced with what must have looked like a Native American rain dance as I celebrated, smashing pieces of Life underfoot.

So, the very first day with my whone, my wife put it in a box of Life. Leave it to my wife to mess with my *life.*


### *"So Happy Together"*

Me and my whone—yes, it was a match made in heaven. A true love affair. We went everywhere together. I learned how to take pictures with my whone and transferred my entire calendar into it. I could check the movie schedule, do my e-mail, whip out a credit card, and calculate the tip at the same time. It was like having a Siamese twin. It seemed to know what I wanted before I did.

And then one day the unthinkable occurred. I scratched the surface of the iPhone—half of my whone. *Nooo!*

## My Son, the Zen Master

My oldest son, Xander (Z), who has been known to wear a robe and sandals, is a true "wise guy." An enlightened being. He does not know it, which is the first sign of the real deal. We were having lunch together just after the scratch occurred. Being 18 years old and brilliant, Z would know what I could do to fix my whone. His generation knows everything about technology. I showed him the scratch like a patient shows a wound to a doctor.

"What can I do?"

He held his hand to his chin for a moment like the *The Thinker,* then looked at me with a sort of highbrow expression—two parts Spock, one part Yoda—and replied, "You can learn to live with it."

*Pow! Bang! Shazam!* Cue the theme to *Batman.* I was stunned. This is the kind of thing I attempt to teach. "You can learn to live with it." I was actually considering buying another one because of one little scratch. So let me see . . . I could spend $300, or I could learn to live with it.

Through the Chotchky Paradigm, the answer is simple. Spend $300. Throw the damaged item away. And do it again and again and again. A scratch is unacceptable. *I've got to do something with my money. Why not support the economy!*

That scratch represents, of course, an entire "aisle" of the Chotchky Mind. We have accepted the idea that "imperfections" are unacceptable. A little scratch, a tiny dent, a small stain, and it's "ruined." Trash. We can't "live with it." It stresses us out. We run around like plate jugglers trying to keep everything spinning. Exhausted. There are so many things we simply cannot change and things, like a small scratch on an iPhone, that just don't matter. In these areas, learning to live with it is a brilliant stroke in the creation of our Master Peace. There will always be another scratch, no matter how hard we try.

As we learn to be at peace with these "imperfections," we begin to see the perfection within them. It is no wonder we find relationships so challenging today. Not only are imperfections unacceptable, but we *look* for them. We seek them out. We even create them where they were not because of our Chotchky addiction to drama. We have allowed this mind-set to meddle with our marriages, as well as our relationships with our children and friends. Sometimes I wonder that if we could, we just might throw *them* away and buy new ones.

The iPhone worked perfectly. The scratch didn't impede my ability to see what was on the screen. It didn't affect the touch-sensitive technology whatsoever. The only thing that was truly scratched was my mind. If my brain were a record, it would have skipped.

If you are under 29½, you may not have understood that metaphor. A record was a thing that played music and you could use it as a Frisbee. Sometimes, they would melt. That was cool. They used to get scratched a lot, but we did not care. We would put a penny on top of the needle that played the record, and the extra weight would push it right through the scratch. I once put a penny on top of the needle that was playing the Beatles record that contained the song "Penny Lane." That was weird. But here is the truly strange thing. If the penny or even a stack of pennies did not work, we would actually get up, walk over to the record player, pick up the needle, and *move it by hand*. We would not buy a new record to replace it, not "buy" a long shot.

I am not a sentimentalist. I am all about progress. But sometimes what is disguised as progress is actually a step backward. And what appears to be a step backward . . . can sometimes be *progress*. What I am saying is that I think we should start putting "pennies" on top of things that are "scratched" again, instead of just throwing everything out.

The next time your wife or husband seems "scratched," get up, walk over, and lovingly put a penny on his or her head. It might fix their "groove." It will certainly be a pattern interrupt.

Or maybe your loved ones are not scratched at all. Maybe you are the one who is saying the same thing or doing the same thing over and over expecting different results. That is a scratch. That is insanity. Put a penny on your own head, and get out of the rut.

Do you realize the number of things that would instantly be "fixed" if we just fixed our perception? Everything. It's the Chotchky Mind that keeps skipping. Skipping right over our very lives: trying to keep up with the Joneses, maintaining appearances, fixing what is not broken.

Telling the difference between what is scratched and what is actually broken is enlightenment. It's liberotchky. Let us all "learn to live with it." And let the records play.

## Chotchky Challenge

What can you fix right now, without moving an inch? What "imperfections" are driving you crazy in yourself, in a loved one, or in some *thing?* Don't throw them out just yet. Cast a magic spell. Put a lucky penny in your hand and "learn to live with it." You may well begin to see that it was never really broken. Or, if you're ready for your master's degree—learn to love it!

Place it here and see its beauty, just as it is: _____

_____

_____.

### *Overboard*

So I learned to live with it. And every time I saw that little scratch on my phone, it actually brought a smile to my face. Little imperfections that did not affect the usefulness of a *thing* just did not matter anymore. Not only that, but instead of detracting from their look, the "imperfections" added character.

I once returned to my car after buying some Chotchky at the mall and discovered a new little door ding. I have a nice car, a BMW. I've had it for 13 years. Once upon a time, a door ding on the side of my BMW would have left a ding in my mind, too, as if my identity were somehow a part of this thing that I drive. When our identity becomes entangled with our stuff, that stuff actually begins to control our emotional state of being. Our happiness relies on the condition of our stuff. Quite insane, is it not?

So that day, I found a new ding in my car door. Thanks to the scratch on my whone, instead of losing my mind, I thought, *Hey, nice placement.* I got in my car and started driving, and made a phone call. This is not something I recommend. I've read that talking on the phone, even "hands free," is as dangerous as driving drunk.

Gradually, I began to notice that I was driving and talking more and more on my cell phone. I wondered if I was approaching the line that turns technology use into technotchky. Then one day, pulling out of the driveway while glancing at an e-mail, I swerved onto the grass. A few weeks later, while checking the movie listings, I walked into a Stop sign. Tell me that wasn't a sign!

Yes, the line had been crossed. I went *overboard.* My beloved whone was like a drug. I felt naked without it on my person, like Adam's fig leaf hiding his shame. My whone was the "apple," and I had taken a big bite. *Darn you, Steve Jobs.* All of your "i" this, and "i" that. It is no wonder I began to feel like it was part of me. And do not even get me started on the "apps." They're really cool and sometimes even helpful, but one too many and it's *Appotchky.* I bought so many apps for my iPhone that I had to scroll through seven or eight "pages" every time I wanted to get to one of the few I actually use.

And then one day my family was getting ready to go on vacation, a cruise around the islands of the South Pacific. While I was packing, I considered *not* bringing my whone. And then I thought about just bringing the wallet half. The iPhone slips in and out of the wallet with the greatest of ease. One second it is a whone; the next it is a wallet and phone. I have actually considered getting that "sticky substance" you can put on stuff to keep the iPhone from sliding. I never got around to it. In the end, I could not separate my iPhone, or myself, from the wallet part.

One day at breakfast, outside on the deck of the ship, CJ, who was ten at the time, picked up my whone and pushed the "light-saber" app. It turns your iPhone into a light saber from *Star Wars*. It glows red or green, and when you wave it around, it makes an ominous hum-wa sound just like in the movies. And what's more, if you wave it quickly and come to a sudden stop, it makes the "clashing" sound—replicating the classic battles in the *Star Wars* saga. So there we were at breakfast, enjoying a beautiful South Pacific morning just off the coast of Bora-Bora. CJ began waving my whone around, and it hummed and clashed. He waved it faster and faster as if he were Luke when angered while battling Darth Vader at the moment when Vader said, "Good, good. Feel the power of the Dark Side."

My wife said what moms generally say in such situations: "Not at the breakfast table." She said it several times. But he could not stop.

My son's pupils dilated. In his mind he was battling Darth Vader, Darth Maul, and every other Darth he could imagine. His back was to the ocean while Heather and I faced the sea so we could view the beautiful scenery from the sixth floor of the ship.

He whipped his arm in the direction of "up." The whone hummed. When his arm reached vertical, he brought it to a screeching halt, and the whone dutifully made the "clash" sound.

This is the part where the earth stopped on its axis.

The iPhone shot out of the top of the wallet, like a giant stone from an ancient trebuchet, or a rock from the sling that David used to slay Goliath. In slow motion, it took to the air, spinning and twisting, set free.

I yelled *"Noooo,"* as it went up and up. On its way down, I held my breath while it hit the top of the railing of the ship. On one side lay the endless depths of the ocean, and on the other side, the wooden deck. It felt like a free throw with one second left on the clock when the ball rolls around the rim in agonizing suspense. Is it going to go in?

It made a "ting" sound as it hit the rail, followed by a "clash-ing" light-saber effect. I jumped up from my chair and ran the seven feet between me and the railing. It seemed I was on a tread-mill, my legs spinning in place.

By the time I reached the railing, my iPhone was splashing down like *Apollo 11* when it returned to the earth from the moon. I am sure that when my iPhone hit the water, it made the "clashing" light-saber sound—although I couldn't hear it. Yes, my iPhone had literally gone overboard.

The water in the South Pacific is truly the most beautiful I have ever seen. It is so clear it is what air would look like if you could see it. Spectacular luminescent blues and greens. My iPhone was white. Like Gollum, I watched my "Precious" hit the ocean facedown, so that all the apps got a slap in the face, which left the white side facing up. We watched it drift back and forth in the water just like a piece of paper in the air as it slowly, oh so slowly, drifted out of sight . . . *twenty thousand leagues under the sea.*

It was one of those moments in which, for a while, you actually do not believe what you are seeing. We all stood there in shock. Then I took off running. This is how desperate I was. I ran and jumped down the stairs, willing myself to move faster than gravity could pull. On the third floor, at the back of the ship was a door that led to another door that went down to the second floor to a kind of landing where you could take kayaks out for a row or even scuba dive. This is where the dive masters hung out. They are like any other "masters"; I was never sure if they knew everything, or nothing at all. It is a fine line.

I was going to ask them to dive down and rescue my iPhone. I know what you are thinking, *Excuse me? Did I read that right?*

Yes, you did. I was going to ask them to dive down and rescue my iPhone.

Looking back now, I realize the idea was completely mental. It would be like looking for a needle in a haystack the size of Russia. I even had this passing daft thought that if I called myself, bubbles might come from the ocean floor, revealing its location.

*Bubbles from the ocean floor? Yeah, that crazy.*

Luckily, the dive masters were out on a dive. Otherwise, I would have actually requested this madness of them, and they would have had to try to think of something masterful to say. Maybe something like the Buddhist koan, "If a tree falls in the forest and there's no one there to hear it, does it make a sound?" In this case, they might have said, "If an iPhone falls into the ocean and there is no one there to hear it, does it have a ringtone?"

Yes, I am glad the dive masters were diving. The Chotchky Mind had completely overcome me. I would not want to subject any master in a robe and sandals, or a snorkeling mask and flippers, to the blithering idiot I had become.

I did, unfortunately, tell the tale to a Swedish woman at the receptionist desk. I actually asked her to see if the dive masters could rescue my iPhone when they got back from their dive. I do not think she ever mentioned this to them. As English was her second language, I'm hoping she simply figured that she did not accurately interpret my rambling. She just stood there for a moment, dumbfounded, searching her mind for a response. I think she did get the gist, but what do you say to someone who has lost all perspective?

The befuddled yet somewhat concerned look the Swedish counter lady held, frozen on her face for an excruciatingly long time, became like a bucket of ice water thrown on my face. Suddenly, I began to return to my senses. I bounded back up the steps to the sixth floor, the scene of the crime. Heather and CJ were gone. I almost expected to see an iPhone chalk outline on the deck next to the railing where it happened. I withdrew to our room, hoping they would be there. No such luck. Settling into the kind of smaller than average armchair that you find only on enormous cruise ships, I began to let it sink in. My iPhone was at the bottom of the ocean, and there was nothing I could do about it.

The honest realization that there was "nothing I could do about it" is deep. We struggle against reality. We push against the past. This effort is fruitless.

*It makes no sense to resist the past tense.*

We cannot touch it. We cannot "go there." We can only move forward or be stuck. It does not seem an accident we call it the "past tense." When we argue with it, we will lose, which will leave us quite tense. And then it comes with us into the present, making the *present tense.*

"There is nothing I can do about it." This is the mind of a Master. Robe and sandals or snorkel mask and flippers. The Chotchky Mind wants control of every "thing." And yet the only thing we ever have control over and, the only thing that really matters, is our response to what happens.

In this way no matter where you live, know that everything happens in the same state (and it's not California!). It all happens in your *state of mind.* Make sure it's a friendly place to live.

### I Love . . . You!

So there I sat in our cabin, slowly returning to a contented state. When CJ and Heather walked through the door, CJ was red in the face from crying. He looked at me for a split second and then disappeared into the bathroom where he fell to the floor and then crawled in the bathtub. He could not stop crying and couldn't look me in the face. He actually said to his mother through the tears, "I cannot imagine Dad without his whone. He *loves* his whone." Of this I am ashamed.

It is these moments when the Chotchky Mind is tempted to treat a human being like a thing, persuading us to damage the human by yelling, shaming, and punishing. All the while defending the importance of the thing as if it were a sentient being.

I crawled into the tub with CJ and wrapped my arms around him. I rocked him and whispered, "I love *you,* CJ. Not my whone. I love you more than you may ever know. The iPhone is just a thing. It is *nothing.*" The truth is, until I verbalized it, I'm not sure I believed it. But once it was said, once the truth was out, my insides changed. And then it came easy as I declared: "It's Chotchky. Compared to you, everything is Chotchky. It doesn't mean anything. I know it was an accident. It doesn't matter." I kept repeating these truths, over and over again like a mantra, while rocking my son in my arms. *It's just a thing. I love you. It doesn't matter. You are what matters.*

Many spiritual practices teach the power of chanting, repeating a word or two, over and over until the word is transcended into the truth it is pointing toward. Buddhists chant *"Om mani padme hum"* (translation: "Hail the jewel in the lotus") sometimes for hours. I have participated in this practice many times in my life, but never before had I experienced such holiness, sacredness, as I did sitting in a waterless bathtub, rocking my son on a cruise ship, somewhere in the middle of the ocean.

"It's just a thing. I love you. It doesn't matter. You are what matters," I repeated again and again. After five minutes of this, something shifted. The closest I can come to describing it is to say I felt myself become very light as if my body was no longer bothered with such trivial things as gravity. Or maybe separated from my body, now floating above the ship we were in.

I can only conclude that, at that moment, the sincerity with which I was speaking and the truth the words pointed to, transcended the Chotchky Paradigm and all of its trappings, setting me free to experience the deepest truth of all of us. I am Spirit! For a moment, all the Chotchky residue, like a thin layer of dirt on my skin, was just washed away by the truth, right down the drain of the bathtub.

Yes, when that iPhone sank to the bottom of the ocean, I lost a lot of unrecoverable information, a lot of valuable stuff: contacts, apps—even notes for this book, of which I can remember nothing. I'm just sure of one thing: Those notes were the best parts of this book! Oh well, there's nothing I can do about it. Sorry. There were notes from meetings, calendar events, and hundreds of pictures that are not backed up on any other devices. Even so, there was transcendent peace.

Suddenly, I was back in the tub. Back in my body but blessed by the experience forever. Later on, CJ and I considered all the things that might have happened if he had *not* thrown my iPhone overboard. These kinds of conjectures are possible only with a kid under the age of 13. Maybe, we thought, when it sank to the bottom, a shark ate it. And maybe if this shark had not been diverted from its original course by my iPhone, it would have attacked the two fishermen just now pulling in a catch a half mile off the bow of our ship. Or maybe it will be found at the bottom of the ocean in 6,000 years. And there, in the lost notes for this very book, they will discover an ancient wisdom that saves humanity (that's how good those notes were). Or maybe that little splash as my iPhone hit the sea rocked the ship just a tad, so a torpedo shot by the enemy missed us by "that much." We quickly came to the conclusion that *it sure is lucky my iPhone went overboard.*

As silly as this banter was, there is much truth there. The ripple effects of our actions reach out to the world in ways rarely seen. Responding with anger, rooted in a lack of perspective from a Chotchky-driven world, creates more anger through the people we come into contact with. As we infect them with our foul mood, they in turn pass it on. In this way, it spreads like ripples on water. Responding with love, from the soul, creates ripples of joy like a splash from a kid doing a cannonball into a lake on a warm summer day. Waves of laughter, peace, and light.

The news of my iPhone "disaster" spread throughout the ship like gossip in a church. We actually heard people talking about it among themselves, not knowing we were the ones they were talking about. How did this story affect their lives? Maybe some of them found a little reprieve from the Chotchky Mind as they considered what was truly important to them. And maybe some of them, *not so much.*

At one point, in a crowd of people, a guy next to me was telling his friend about the poor sap whose son threw his iPhone overboard. I smiled. "That was me."

His face divulged his terror, "Oh man, I *never* let my children come near my phone. If they threw my phone overboard, I'd kill 'em."

We say things like this, don't we?

I understood. I once felt that way, too. I responded with my best dive-master impression: "It doesn't *really* matter."

Toward the end of our vacation, over his lunch of pasta with Parmesan cheese and butter, my ten-year-old son, like a master in a towel and flip-flops said, "Dad, maybe I threw your iPhone overboard because you had become too attached to it."

Touché.

## Deep Thought
## (as Deep as the Ocean Where My iPhone Sits)

I learned a powerful, life-altering lesson from the "iPhone Incident," and the story itself has become a powerful tool illustrating the utter madness of the Chotchky Paradigm. I'm just saying . . .

*The worst things that happen to us are*
*usually the best things in disguise.*

The gifts of that disaster keep coming. That is the shift that occurs as we begin seeing through the eyes of the soul.

### *Starting Over*

When we got home, the first thing I did was buy another iPhone. Hey, don't throw the baby out with the saltwater! I now have a whone once again. I am very careful when I speak on it while driving. And when I do, I do so "hands free." I never walk anywhere with my head buried in the web, and I almost never talk on the phone when I am with others. And the light-saber app? I got it again. *I love that thing!*

What was once Chotchky, something that took my mind off what is *truly* important and diverted me from my purpose, has transformed back into something that is truly useful. I can now even go places without it, and I don't feel naked. When it comes to technology, be a user, not an abuser. The Chotchky Challenge is there on *every* glowing screen. *Thanks, Steve Jobs. Well done. Your example of living a soulful life will not be forgotten.*

## Truth or Fiction?

When texting while driving, you are twice as likely to crash. *Truth or Fiction?*

Fiction.

Studies have shown that you are approximately *23 times* more likely to have an accident.

## Chotchky Challenge

Circle the number that reflects the level of truth for you in each statement. The awareness gained could save a relationship, or even a life! A zero probably means you have never been online and you use an abacus for basic math; a ten means you probably don't understand the instructions because you were busy playing *Angry Birds* on your mobile device while trying to read this.

1. While driving, I text, dial, chat, check e-mail, and input GPS navigation, sometimes even while sipping coffee and eating a doughnut.

   0   1   2   3   4   5   6   7   8   9   10

2. During meals with people, I regularly take phone calls and send texts on the sly in an attempt to hide my active thumbs.

   0   1   2   3   4   5   6   7   8   9   10

3. While at movies, concerts, sporting events, and birthday parties, I am often preoccupied with my smartphone because, well, the future of the planet rests on my personal affairs.

   0   1   2   3   4   5   6   7   8   9   10

4. While walking, whether in town, on uneven ground, up and down stairs, or on the StairMaster, my attention is devoted to a handheld, illuminated

screen. I sometimes bump into others doing the same. (How rude!)

0   1   2   3   4   5   6   7   8   9   10

Add up your total here: ____.

If you scored more than a 7, as I did, there are times when you do go overboard. If you scored 20 or more, seek help.

Simply resisting the temptation to respond to every "ding" "ring" "buzz" or "squeak" that comes from our mobile devices has become a way of saying to those present: *I love you, I'm listening, I care.*

*"In the year 3000, YouTube, Twitter, and Facebook will merge to create one super time-wasting website called YouTwitFace."*

— CONAN O'BRIEN

The Internet is having a huge impact on humanity. The question is, is it making us more humane or less human? The scales could tip either way.

*E-mailotchky: the preposterous amount of never-ending, useless information received at the speed of light through which we spend our days wading, lost in a swamp of discourse*

We all know the overwhelming feeling of opening our e-mail account and seeing so many new messages that it feels as though they just spill out onto the floor. We wade through them, trying to decide which ones really need our attention and which ones are the latest life-suckers, such as: "Forward this to at least 27 friends now, and within the next 24 hours, something truly amazing will happen. If you do not do so, you are a bad person and will be struck by a plague of locusts."

E-mail is great for letters, directions, appreciation notes, announcements, and the like, but it does not take the place of conversation, and it never will. There is a synergy, a dance to the ancient art of talking, especially in person. As I became aware of *e-mailotchky,* I began to realize that I was involved in discussions that dragged on for days or weeks—ones that could have been over and more productive in one conversation.

With e-mails, misunderstandings run amuck. Without voice inflection or, even more powerful, facial expression, we are constantly misreading each other.

The most repugnant of all are the self-righteous, "blasting" e-mails people send to each other or, worse yet, copy to the whole Eastern seaboard, which are written in anger, judgment, and wrath. Such e-mails convey a false sense of righteous power. With no direct feedback from the receiver, we have begun to feel that the "send" button gives us the right to slam, judge, and disrespect each other. We often do not edit our reptilian brains when there is no one there to defend him- or herself.

It's a powerful shift to understand that "blasting" e-mails are actually a call for love, as is most anger. For example, a message that reads, "You're a complete loser," when read through the eyes of the soul, might translate into, "I feel like a loser. I'm reaching out from my pain in the only way I know how right now." Or "Jim and Carol are such flirts at work it's shameless. It makes me sick." This might translate into "I wish I had a boyfriend. I don't feel lovable." Or, say, e-mails about unsuspecting third parties that read something like: "As your friend, I just want you all to know that Joe is an insincere, arrogant liar, and is out of integrity. Do not trust him. I'm just saying this as your friend." Translation might be: "I'm out of integrity and can't see it. I feel insincere and I'm compensating with arrogance. Help."

As you can see, the rantings of the Chotchky Mind are generally the opposite of what the soul is crying out for. We must then consciously choose to respond through the Paradigm of the Soul in order to see the deeper truth and reply appropriately.

Here, try one yourself. Write your soulful interpretation on the following lines. If someone conveys to you in e-mail or in any other form of discourse "You are such a thoughtless jerk and you're always late," how might the soul translate this disguised call for love?

_____

_____

_____

_____

If you feel you must send a negative, feedback-oriented e-mail, consider the following guidelines first:

- Have an objective third party read your response before sending it.

- Let at least a day pass before you press a regretful "send."

- Erase the e-mail. Instead, pick up the phone and call the person (hands free)! Get together . . . so you can use all of the amazing facial muscles that evolution has spent thousands of years creating for the express purpose of expressing. Smile, listen with compassion, and respond with love.

### *A Technologically Updated Prayer*

What if before pushing the power button on our computers, we all said this 21st-century version of the Lord's Prayer?

> *Our Father, who art in The Cloud, hallowed be thy Password. Thy Updates come, thy Downloads be done, on Google Earth as it isn't on YouTube. And lead us not into Chat Sites, but deliver us from E-mail, for thine is the Keyboard and the PowerPoint and the Browser, forever and ever . . . Send.*

Imagine a world where everyone agreed that any time spent using the Internet should in some way raise our Inner Net. Every "search" a search for the soul. Every chat a dialogue of truth. What percentage of sites would you say are designed, in some small way, to improve humanity as compared to those designed to reinforce the Chotchky Paradigm? This is an important question because what we do online is a reflection of our consciousness, a mirror. In this way, the Internet can be a great tool for transformation.

Like someone trying to lose weight, by carefully selecting what we allow on our Internet "menu," we will become lighter. With such awareness, we can begin to monitor our thoughts. What comes first? The Internet site or the consciousness that Googled it? When the number of hits on sites that support the soul out-weigh the number of hits that distract from it, the shift will be . . . at our fingertips.

## Deep Thought

Every site is an affirmation, every search a meditation, every chat a prayer.

### Facebookotchky

I have a friend who told me she got involved in a conversation on Facebook with some relatives who were discussing their garden. My friend Jenni thought this was wonderful. She even commented a few times, telling them how much she, too, loves to garden. Then one day she spoke to one of them on the phone and asked how the gardening was going. To her utter amazement, all along, it had been a conversation about a cybergarden.

She replied, "But with all the time you spend on your cyber-garden, you could have an actual garden . . . with food." They could even bring their cell phones so they could eat healthy foods hands free!

It makes you wonder. Will there come a day when speaking of a garden, the given understanding will be that of "cyber"? I won-der what the soul enjoys more? Actually growing and planting healthy food to nourish the body . . . or pretending? What if the never-ending stream of food that pours into our supermarkets someday dries up? Will we all think, *Oh well, that's okay; I have my own garden.* Only to discover, to our bewilderment and dismay, there is no nourishment in there?

The Internet is a most amazing tool. However, we quite often go overboard. It is a seductress. *Just one more,* we think. One more quick text, one more YouTube video, one more minute "chatting" or "Facebooking," as we slowly alienate ourselves from those we love and even, at times, put them in real danger. *Just a minute, sweetheart. Daddy needs to make just one more quick phone call while I finish eating these French fries while driving hands free.* But just like an alcoholic, that "one more" becomes two, that two becomes three, and so on. Pretty soon we wonder, *Why should I ever leave the house and deal with all that reality? I have so many cyberfriends.*

Sometimes my kids pull out their iPads or what-have-you during dinner. This is against the house rules. When I tell them to turn it off, their response might be, "But why? We're not talking about anything."

If we don't leave an open space, an emptiness for meaningful conversation to arise, it can't. We have crowded out the spaciousness, the emptiness from which heartfelt connection is born. Sometimes that even means we need to leave room for that most dreaded of things in our technologically addicted society: stillness and silence. Ironically, often the best times to connect with another human being at a "cellular" level is when there's no cell reception.

In the Tao Te Ching we read, "It's the emptiness in the bowl that holds the thing we want." What author Lao-tzu is implying is quite outrageous. He is suggesting that the bowl itself is of less value than the emptiness it surrounds. In India, the great yogis tell us that "spaciousness" is the key to peace and joy. The great pianist Arthur Schnabel intoned, "The notes I handle no better than many pianists. But the pauses between the notes—that is where the art resides."

As counterintuitive as it may seem, when we listen to a beautiful song, what we mostly "hear" is the absence of sound. Emptiness. Think of it this way: What would it be like if we heard every single sound at once? Utter madness. So when we hear a beautiful song, what we are hearing is next to nothing. Almost zero. The composer very carefully picks the notes and places them in the vast eternity of silence or emptiness. So let us no longer be afraid of emptiness, stillness, or silence. It is from these things that everything has come into being. The universe included.

## Deep Thought

As I type these words, I am profoundly grateful for the technology that allows me to do this. I have taken time away to write. I have not checked my e-mail or used a phone of any kind for five days now. I feel alive, free, and at peace in a way I haven't known for many years.

## Chotchky Challenge

Pick one day, just one, in the next 30 days, to completely unplug from computers and phones and the like. I dare you. Send an e-mail telling everyone that it's part of this crazy Challenge you have accepted. They might just join you. Then, once you see that you can actually survive, and the fate of the world does not rely on you being plugged in like a machine, do it for a week!

Again, send out an e-mail and tell everyone. Challenge them to join you. Heck, meet up with them for lunch, face-to-face. I realize for your job you may have to use technology during work hours; however, with discipline, you can draw a line. Or just go on a vacation. A true vacation of the soul: maybe to Hawaii or maybe in your own house. It's amazing how far away you can go without going anywhere simply by unplugging. This will help restore your perspective, which many of us undoubtedly have lost. This will change your life and in no way is going . . . *overboard!*

## Truth or Fiction?

Since the year 1997 the time the average American spends in the bathroom has steadily increased by approximately 28 seconds per visit each year as a result of tinkering with their cell phone (yes, sometimes even conversing).

*Truth or Fiction?*

Just an observation.

With that in mind, let's now use the Internet to get closer to the soul. Click on the "@" sign on the secret site: **www.barryadennis .com/chotchkyvideos1**. As you will see, I'm up to "know" good.

Then continue to the next chapter and find out what happened when my youngest son and I went on an electronics fast for a week. (Spoiler alert: the world did not come to an end.)

# CHAPTER 10

# THE JOKE'S ON ME (ENTERTAINMENTOTCHKY)

*Entertainmentotchky: (a) movies, video games, television shows, and the like designed to take our time and money while our dreams become a fading memory; (b) that which even quality entertainment is when we watch it so long we become numb and desensitized couch potatoes, which eventually leads to osteoporosis of the body, mind, and spirit*

Entertainment is a wonderful part of life, especially when shared with loved ones. However, when it glorifies violence, degrades the sacredness of sexuality, and has little original creative thought, it simply becomes a bunch of Small Plastic Gophers running around naked on the screen with guns, bombs, and stilted dialogue that some part of the Hollywood machine decided to invest millions of dollars in.

The line here is gray; I understand that. We get to regularly accept the Challenge of self-inquiry.

I'll never forget taking my youngest son at age ten to see *The Dark Knight* with Heath Ledger as the Joker. CJ begged, I caved.

That night, after I tucked him in and turned to leave his room, he said, "Daddy, I'm scared. Every time I close my eyes, I see the Joker."

*Well, the joke's on me, and it's not funny.*

My son was traumatized because I joined the rest of the "sheople." Baaa! I got in a long line and paid good money to watch two hours of explosions, death, and psychotic madness. Basically, it was the Chotchky Mind at Mardi Gras on steroids captured on film.

Everything we pay money for, we are voting for. We are saying to the universe, "I want more of this, please," so the universe keeps making it. Entertainment is also a reflection of our consciousness. As we begin to shift our paradigm back to the soul, entertainment will reflect that shift. And I believe it is happening.

You can see the struggle for consciousness just by looking at what's playing in the theater. The next time you check out the movie listings, show the reviews to your soul and see which ones it chooses. You'll reap the benefits, and so will your children.

Television is another slippery slope. Once when my wife left town for a week, I simultaneously had a lull in my workload. The two things combined created a seldom seen window of time where I wasn't sure what to do with myself. I could go to the gym every day and really get in shape. I could work on my book. I certainly wanted to spend time with my youngest son, who was now kind of an "only child" as his older brother had recently gone off to college. I could even get caught up on all the TV I hadn't see over the last several extremely busy months, through the wonder of TiVo. *Yes, that's it,* I thought, *I will get caught up on all the TV. I deserve it. I've earned it.* I even went out and rented a few movies. (*The Dark Knight* was now on DVD. Just seeing it on the shelf gave me the heebie-jeebies.)

That Monday afternoon I watched several TV shows. Then when my son got home, after he did his homework, we watched several more TV shows and a movie. The next day I turned on the

TV again and channel surfed for a while, but nothing seemed to satisfy me. My tolerance level had risen. I needed "more" to get the same fix. More action, more violence, faster editing, a busier sound track, so I slipped in another DVD. After about 20 minutes, something truly frightening happened. More frightening than closing my eyes and seeing the Joker. I began to feel apathetic, numb, lethargic, complacent. It happened so slowly, I didn't really know I was feeling such things. It was a "subtle takedown" similar to the time our minivan caught on fire while I was driving down Highway 101 on the Fourth of July.

If I could take my brain out of my skull, put it on ice for half an hour, and then place it back in my head, I honestly believe it would be a comparable sensation to the numbness that had overcome me. I would not be surprised if drool had begun running out of the side of my mouth.

When I was a kid, I regularly saw myself from the third-person perspective, from up in the air. Sometimes I would see myself in the hallway opening my locker, sometimes at lunch with friends. It would just happen. I had no control over it. Some say this is a psychological phenomenon, others say it is spiritual. Either way, I can tell you that it is soulful. Now that I'm an adult, full of logic and reason, it doesn't happen much anymore. But that day . . .

*Suddenly, I saw myself sitting there on the couch from about ten feet up at an 80 degree angle. I watched me for quite some time. I was pathetic. I felt compassion for that stooge. He had dreams and great potential, but that was all shoved aside, forgotten. He wanted his life to have purpose, but he'd become so apathetic. "Get up, your life awaits. GET UP NOW . . . "*

And then, *boom!*

The "me" who was watching from up high was now in the me-on-the-couch, seeing through the eyes that were stuck, superglued to the boob tube. I popped up off the couch so fast you would have sworn it was an ejection seat.

"My book," I said to no one there, "my book."

I ejected the movie I had already invested 20 minutes of my time on, then grabbed the other two I had rented and returned them to the video store. Unwatched. You might be thinking, *What a waste of money.* If so, consider this. Wouldn't it have been a much bigger waste of resources had I sat there for the next eight hours, possibly days, while my soul was literally asking me to seize the day? Carpe diem!

I hurried back home and began to write. Hours passed like seconds . . . I felt invigorated, joyful, alive. Living from inside my passion, I got completely carried away.

Now that is a worthwhile goal for life: to get "carried away." To align ourselves so closely to our soul, with our passions, that it lifts us up, pulls us forward, and carries us away from our fears and excuses—away from our procrastinations and distractions into the pure joy and exhilaration of being alive.

In the blink of an eye, it was already 3:30 P.M. as my son came walking in the door. It felt as though I had just turned on my computer. What to do now? I wanted to keep writing, but I also wanted to spend quality time with my son. *I guess I'll have to stop for the night. Maybe we'll watch some TV together.*

*Noooo!*

And with that came one of the most radical, unconventional, rebellious, crazy, "backward" ideas I'd ever had. So backward in fact, it just might have been inspired by angels. I told CJ that for the next week, there would be no TV, no movies, no video games, and no YouTube. Every evening, when he got home from school, we would work together. The two of us, side by side, on the big bed in the master bedroom. He could help me with my book.

I expected mutiny. A riot, maybe. At least a household strike. However, what I got was, "Okay."

That night we laughed, talked, worked, and connected in a way and with a kind of depth we never had before. He fell asleep on my shoulder around 10:30. Sometime around 2 A.M. I finally let the glow of my laptop go dim as I picked up his ten-year-old, five-foot frame, carried him down the hall, and tucked him into bed. My heart was so full my eyes leaked.

We did this every night for a week. We both got carried away. Carried away to a place where time and space do not adhere to the rigid rules of Newtonian physics. A place where peace and joy are the only motivating factors. A place where dreams come true. This I know for sure, because, you see, you're reading the book.

## Tuning In

I know the amount of time we spend tuned in to TV, movies, YouTube, and such seems normal. And well, it is. But that's only because it's been culturally indoctrinated into us as part of the Chotchky Paradigm. Normal and soulful are often diametrically opposed. Sometimes I wonder if those like Mozart, Beethoven, Leonardo da Vinci, and Thomas Edison would have found their genius if those distractions had been around.

## Chotchky Challenge

Let's get carried away. I wish to create an opportunity for your life to be renewed. It's your life, the only one you have. Each second is golden. What would you do if all the Chotchky that takes your time and creates a false sense of purpose just disappeared? In other words, what "carries you away"? What lifts your spirit and bends time and space? What gives you energy just thinking about it? Miracles are in there. Write it down now:

_____

_____

_____

_____

_____

Now choose a week. Seven days—the number of Creation. During these most precious days, eliminate all distractions. This time, ditch the TV, video games, and movies. No distractions. Tell your friends and family that you are on a soul retreat. This, you can do anywhere. Transfer the time you would have spent on distractions and deposit that time into whatever carries you away. Use the computer for this soulful purpose. *Research it, scheme about it, get books on it, dream about it, feel it, practice it . . . do it.*

## Deep Thought

*You cannot use your time the same way you did in the past and expect different results.*

This week will change your life. Give your soul this gift. You deserve it. And so does the world.

Does what I'm suggesting stir something in you? If so, then make a go of it. This one week will likely hold in it more than any seminar, retreat, or therapy session you could pay thousands for, which, as you know, usually has no lasting effect whatsoever. With the completion of this one Challenge, there will be a shift in you. Remember, you have a great excuse not to feel weird about this. Tell everyone you are taking the Chotchky Challenge. Just the sound of those words awakens the soul; a part of them will understand. Ask them to join you. Look at your calendar now. Choose a week to get carried away.

### *Yogurt Sessions*

Heather and I have pretty much given up sitting down to watch TV. We don't flop on the couch; we do yoga in front of our favorite shows. The average person in America watches somewhere around five hours a day. If Heather and I watched five hours of TV per day, given the fact that we are often doing yoga and other exercises while doing so, we would be in the best shape of our lives. Now that's a Paradigm Shift.

In the classical sense of the word, however, I am not doing "yoga," per se. I actually make up my own moves; it's very freestyle.

Heather, who is a yoga instructor, calls what I do "yogurt." I think this is because it's so smooth. I've thought about even teaching this "yogurt" as a class. If it caught on, my yogurt would have a "culture" all its own.

I hope it does catch on, because by doing "yogurt" while the TV is on, we are moving counter-culture to the Chotchky Paradigm. TV is proven to affect the brain like a drug. Our natural filters fall away so the commercials and the "product placements" drop right in. Then we wonder why, while shopping, we suddenly "want."

However, by doing "yogurt" while enjoying your favorite TV show, you are not only improving your physical health, but as you allow yourself to look away from the screen from time to time, it keeps the Chotchky filters in place. This allows your higher consciousness to stay with you as enjoy some entertainment. Impulse buys are less likely to control your impulses.

Also, our yogurt sessions are actually quite intimate as we stretch together and give back rubs. We have also recently discovered that "commercials are for kissing." On several occasions we have actually said, "Why can't commercials be longer?" Now that's a Paradigm Shifting.

## Chotchky Challenge

Begin your own "yogurt" sessions the next time you turn on the TV. You will live longer. Create your own style. And if you're with that special one, remember what commercials are for!

For a supersized helping of inspiration, click on the balloon on the secret web page: **www.barryadennis.com/chotchkyvideos1**. I'm really getting carried away.

Then we're going to look at some "dirty" pictures of celebrities. Do I have your attention? I hope not.

✳ ✳ ✳

# CHAPTER 11

# INFORMOTCHKY

Are we in charge of the thoughts in our mind? Do we have free choice concerning the meditations of our heart? The answer is a very challenging *no*. We are bombarded with *informotchky: the never-ending stream of useless information designed to hijack our attention, causing our thoughts to dwell upon trivial, frivolous matters.*

What I'm describing is blatant Chotchky of the brain. Our mind may be the most precious storage space there is. What is placed within it creates our thoughts. Our thoughts create our reality. The logical conclusion is whoever controls our thoughts . . . controls us.

*"As a man thinketh in his heart, so is he."*

— THE NAZARENE

*"That which you dwell on, you fell on."*

— THE BARRY DENNIS

All five of our senses are a direct in-box to our mind. We do not have total control over what enters our senses, and the Chotchky Campaign has taken full advantage. Repeatedly cramming our in-boxes with information so that we begin to dwell upon what the campaign dictates. By raising our awareness of the information that is streamed into us, like a computer receiving random "cookies" from the Web, we can begin sorting through it and discarding whatever does not plant healthy thoughts in the fertile ground of our minds.

The "news" is a good example. So much is "sense-sationalized," which is to say, created to activate and enter our senses. Even the weather report plays this game.

I live in Oregon where the weather is quite mild. However, at least once every winter when there is a fraction of a chance that it might snow, it becomes "Winter Storm Watch." You would think it's Armageddon. Everyone begins to live in fear of a snowflake. People get in line to buy snow tires at Les Schwab like it's a soup kitchen during the Depression. And there are those hardcore winter tires with metal spikes that rototill the freeway. Come spring, you could plant corn on I-5. Then we spend countless millions of dollars having the grooves filled so we can do it all again next December. There's always some reporter at the highest point in the Portland metropolitan area with earmuffs, gloves, and a parka on, shaking in his boots, saying things like: "Moments ago, right here, I saw a *snowflake.* If you see this snowflake, call the number at the bottom of the screen. Do not, I repeat, do not let it hit the ground. Barricade your windows and doors. Tell the people you love good-bye. . . ."

The drama, fear, and sensationalism will continue until we stop supporting it. As we change, the news will change to reflect that shift in consciousness, which will in turn support and encourage the change in us, spiraling up and up. When you feel fear, anxiety, or a general malaise overcome you while watching the news or reading the paper, change the "channel" of your mind. Choose to allow something else to influence you. Do not let sensationalism overload your senses. Nine times out of ten, the story they're selling is not the whole truth. For example, snow rarely sticks in Portland.

## Miss Information

She runs amuck! Twisting facts, telling half-truths—only the parts that support her agenda. She's everywhere, including in you. Much of the time, we aren't aware of when she is speaking through us.

This is by virtue of the fact that we all have prejudices and agendas hidden even from ourselves. Regardless of how it happens, when we spread gossip, taking what we read on the Internet, or from a *friendotchky*, as gospel, she is us. And when gossip has become gospel, we all lose our way.

When we gossip we are: Gabbing Our Sacred Self Into Purgatory!

Gossip is a backward attempt at raising ourselves by lowering someone else. Our saving grace, however, lies in the peace of knowing that the key out of this purgatory is as close as our breath. As we watch what we say, our words become a feedback mechanism, letting us know when our thoughts are in error. Then we can change our words, which changes our thoughts, which sets our soul free. Any words that are not helpful, constructive, lovingly honest, or kind are *wordotchky*. They fill the space around us like broken toys clutter a playroom or pollution fills the air.

## Magazinotchky

Throwing myself with reckless abandon into researching informotchky, I bought, for the first and last time in my life, a *National Enquirer*. The incredible thing about magazinotchky is that it's a double assault on our senses. Not only is it a "thing" that takes up precious space in our homes causing clutter, but it is also direct Chotchky of the mind. *Talk about the Chotchky Effect!*

As I mentioned earlier, magazines and the like "airbrush" the lives of models and stars to reinforce and create a kind of idol worship that keeps us buying into a false idea of perfection. Incredibly, the opposite extreme is true as well. We love to tear them down. The front caption of the *Enquirer* read, "Cameron Diaz caught cheating!" And then there were photos of Cameron Diaz and other stars with a "stamp" over the pictures that said: "100% unapproved; the pictures the stars don't want you to see." *Then we shouldn't be seeing them!*

To help sift through the dirt, ask yourself these questions: *Is this information truly useful to my soul's journey? Or is it potentially hurtful or untrue?*

## Chotchky Challenge

Circle your answer after each of the following questions. (The correct answers are given at the end.)

1. Is the information in that gossip magazine potentially untrue? Yes or No

   (Hint: Is 1+1=3 untrue?)

2. Are most gossip magazines potentially designed to be hurtful? Yes or No

   (Hint: Is a hand grenade potentially hurtful?)

3. Is that magazine likely to support the evolution of all life? Yes or No

   (Hint: Would a giant meteorite headed for planet Earth?)

4. Is there any part of you, even a smidgen, that would like to see the unauthorized photos? Yes or No

   (Hint: You don't get a hint on this, or the next two, either.)

5.  Do you ever buy or read information potentially hurtful or untrue? Yes or No

6.  Do you ever feel an uncontrollable urge to read the seductive, hurtful, potentially untrue headlines of such magazines at the checkout stand? Yes or No

*Answers:* Numbers one and two are Yes; the rest are No.

If you got any wrong, don't fret; you are not alone. Approximately 7 billion others did as well. It just shows us where the work needs to be done. And for each one you knew what the "correct" answer was but were honest anyway, you get extra credit. In this way, you may have gotten 100 percent. (Go to the head of the class.)

I don't know Cameron Diaz, but I think she is a powerful woman who shares her talents with the world. So, why in the world do we want to hurt her? She is a part of our family. Why would we want to feed off of her pain and, more important, why would we want to create pain in her life?

Let's begin the shift now. Whenever you see sensationalized headlines designed to appeal to the lowest functioning part of your mind, say this little prayer for yourself, for all those tempted to read it, and for the person targeted by the gossip:

> *Bless you. I am so sorry we feel a need to pry into your private affairs. Please forgive me. I wish you peace. I release any part of me that may be jealous of you. I am ready to rise above the need for gossip. May all humanity join me. I no longer need to revel in others' misfortunes, real or sensationalized, to bring meaning to my life. I'm too busy making a Master Peace out of mine. And so it is. Amend.*

I know that may be a little much in the throes of magazinotchky. If so, just say, "I'm sorry. Bless you. Forgive me." It will change you at the core. Your soul will be freed from purgatory.

### True Confessions

I am not immune to such headlines. Sometimes I feel a strange and dark gravitational pull, a kind of Black Hole, around checkout stands. It's as if I lose all voluntary muscle function. My arms start lifting away from the body like creatures from *Night of the Living Dead,* reaching for the most sensationalized, most potentially hurtful headline. As Darth Vader said, that's the "power of the Dark Side."

During his training to become a Jedi master, Luke asked Yoda if the Dark Side was stronger. Yoda cleared his throat and replied, "No, more seductive it is." How true!

And today, the gossip has followed us into our kitchens, our living rooms, and right onto our laps. Wherever there is a computer, "Miss Information" has her say. Sometimes the power button of a computer virtually beams us to the grocery store checkout stand. But what if this is all part of our "Jedi" training? What does a master teacher do, whether it be an actual historical figure or a fictional one like Yoda or Grasshopper's master in the television show *Kung Fu*? They constantly challenge their students to choose between right and wrong, between the "world" and the soul. What if all the temptations the Chotchky Challenge has laid before us are the universe's way of training us? In this manner, we can see all the difficulties of a wayward world in a new way. We see them as our teacher. And just like Luke Skywalker or Grasshopper, when we choose right consistently, we become the master.

So now, when I feel the pull toward informotchky I see it as an opportunity to advance in my training. I ask myself, *What is it in me that is drawn toward something I know is designed to hurt others?* You see, this dark place inside of me would exist whether or not the temptation was there. In this way, the temptation is a gift that brings up my shadow, like a master teacher would do, so I can see it, acknowledge it, and heal it. I become acquainted with my own insecurities, shame, and fears. What if all the backwardness of the world is an opportunity for accelerated spiritual growth in disguise? I think maybe it's time for us all to slip on the robe and sandals, accept the Challenge, and become the Grasshopper.

### Let's Take a Moment . . . .

Since gossip is Gabbing Our Sacred Self Into Purgatory, it's only logical that our gossip affirmation is: God, Open Some Sense In People.

Read the following affirmation from your heart:

> *God, please, open some sense in people, especially me. Some sense of the sacred. I now choose to be a part of the evolving human consciousness. When I feel tempted by gossip in any form, I gracefully turn away. I bless those being attacked by it, for they are a part of my human family. This becomes easier and easier as I see every temptation as my teacher. I accept the Challenge.*

## Deep Thought

Food is a sacred thing, our energy source. To have this *source* surrounded by the low energy vibrations of gossip is challenging indeed. However, we can now bring sacredness back to our groceries and give thanks for the abundant supply.

Let that gratitude fill you, and the gossip itself will begin to fade away into purgatory where it belongs. Because . . . *the most powerful food is what you feed your mind.*

Let's check out some of these "checkout" stands and use them to check in to see if we can raise the bar (not a Snickers!). Click on the couple at the watercooler on the secret page: **www .barryadennis.com/chotchkyvideos1.**

Then carry on as you and I travel back to the 13th century for a lesson from an ancient master as we step into the fourth and final level: the Soul.

# LEVEL IV

# SOUL

You can see now how all four levels are connected. Physical Chotchkies affect our state of mind inducing the Chotchky Effect. Our state of mind impacts the health of our body, and the state of our body influences our mind. Everything then affects the "soul" of our being. It *includes and transcends* both body and mind.

Imagine a bubble inside a bubble, inside a third bubble. The outside bubble would be the soul—both a "part of" and "more than." Soul of course is a very ethereal concept. Just be aware, and feel it as you read. Notice how it's all connected.

# CHAPTER 12

# THE LOINCLOTH

### Truth or Fiction?

In the 13th century, a great master lived in a cave near a small village in Nepal at the base of the Himalayas. Today that village is known as Katmandu. At this time, however, there were fewer than 500 villagers. The master had renounced everything of the world. He had need of nothing other than his robe and sandals. He took only one new student every ten years. When the time came for a new student, several young men from the village made their cases but only one showed true promise. His name was Fu.

After a year of tutelage, it was time for the student to denounce all things of the world. He was to learn to trust the universe to provide, as did his master teacher, who proudly presented his student with his own humble, flowing garb. And so it began. The student found a cave nearby to be his home. He was to do nothing but meditate until the master returned from a spiritual trek for an undisclosed amount of time.

Fu was quite content. The universe did provide, and he was happy. He lived in harmony with nature and was greatly loved by the villagers. One day some friends came for a visit, and there was Fu, sitting blissfully on a rock in his cave.

"Fu, you would be much more comfortable with a loincloth," one of the villagers remarked.

Fu replied, "I have renounced all things of the world. I am content and happy with nothing but that which my master has given me to wear."

"As you wish," his friend said. After they left, however, Fu began to consider a loincloth. Maybe it *would* be more comfortable. But then he remembered his master teacher's words and was conflicted. It is said that he meditated on this idea for many months: to get a loincloth or not to get a loincloth.

Finally, one day he thought, *What could it hurt?* So he went to the village and, because he was so loved by the villagers, the cloth maker gave him a loincloth.

He used his loincloth religiously to sit upon as he meditated. He *did* have to go to the river every so often to wash it, which cut into his meditating time, but it seemed to be a fair exchange.

Then one day he came to get his loincloth off the branch of the tree where he hung it to dry, only to find several holes. It appeared as though rats had found the loincloth quite appetizing. He considered letting it go. However, he had gotten used to it. It was cushy. So, he went to the village to get a new loincloth, but this time the cloth maker wanted him to pay. He didn't have any money, so the cloth maker accepted an IOU.

Fu also got a cat, with a similar arrangement, to chase away the rats. This worked beautifully. The cat chased the rats so the monk could have his cloth. However, the cat became scrawny. He needed more nourishment than the occasional caught rat, so Fu got a cow for milk for the cat who protected the loincloth so Fu could sit on it and meditate. Soon, however, the cow became scrawny. There wasn't enough grass around the cave for the cow to graze upon. So Fu began to work the land to feed the cow that fed the cat that kept the loincloth from getting eaten by the rats so Fu could meditate.

Working the land, of course, cut greatly into his meditation time. He was making a little profit on the extra grass, so he hired his friends who had recommended the loincloth to work the land so he could get back to meditating. Soon there was so much grass he had to hire more people from the village. It became quite an enterprise. The villagers worked very hard and became strong. They made up songs and even danced as they worked the field. However, over time, they grew unhappy. They didn't like the working conditions and formed a village union. They made many demands. Fu spent most of his time now dealing with the unhappy villagers. He built a kind-of office and what today would be called a "break room" for the villagers. He also hired a manager.

Fu was stressed, but had very little time to meditate for release. At least when he did, he had a loincloth to sit on. The cave no longer seemed appropriate, so he built a home next to the office and the break room. He didn't sleep very well, though, because he was concerned about his loincloth. Each day he milked the cow that ate the grass that fed the cat that kept the rats from chewing on it.

The next season there was a great drought. They could not grow the grass that fed the cow that fed the cat that kept the rats from getting into his house and chewing up his loincloth. The business went under, and the villagers were very upset with Fu. Under so much stress he had forgotten to pay back the IOU for the cat and now he barely had enough to reimburse the cloth maker. When he tried to return the cat, it ran away while chasing the rats who had just absconded with his loincloth. He ended up paying the cat lady with his sandals and the robe off his back. He then became known as the naked beggar. Cold, dirty, and hungry all the time. A few years later, the master returned. He barely recognized his student, there in the street, nude.

He said to his apprentice, "My son, what happened?"

With great remorse, the student, unable to hold eye contact, finally confessed, "Master, I got a loincloth."

The master shook his head in grave disappointment and said, "You Fu!"

*Truth or Fiction?*

Let's just say "mythical."

What is the "loincloth" in your life? Everything we bring in comes with a whole enterprise. Choose your loincloths carefully, lest you end up "the naked beggar."

As Anonymous said,

*"At first it is something; after we possess it, it isn't."*

Truer words have never been spoken. To avoid playing the "Fu," let's say you're shopping or just walking down the street and all of a sudden you see that "something." It could be anything, really, whatever you desire at the time. Your "loincloth." Or maybe just the fact that it's there makes you yearn for it. That's how silly the Chotchky Paradigm can be. It could be a popular book, a fancy car, designer shoes, a new relationship, the latest gadget, whatever. There is a moment when you feel happy, whole, even joy: *Ah, there It is.* What is actually happening is quite profound; you haven't even bought the thing and yet you somehow feel happy and complete. How can that be? The thing isn't even yours. You don't even own it. "It" is not even set free from the packaging.

So how could this feeling be occurring? There's only one answer: it is not the thing itself we so desire. It is the feeling—of wholeness, completeness, happiness—that we all really want and, of course, we have.

The Challenge is not unlike a lab rat that receives a treat (cheese) for finishing a task (a maze). We have been taught that acquisition is the task and for each thing we acquire, we get a treat (a happy feeling). Like any treat, however, it is fleeting, so we must be about the business of constantly finishing the task again (like a good rat) through the maze of halls in malls and the like. The things we acquire as seen through the Chotchky Paradigm are triggers of worthiness. *I just finished the task (acquired something); therefore, I'm worthy, so I now get a treat (a cheesy feeling).*

Here's the thing. *You are not a rat.*

You are not only the receiver of the "treat," you are the giver of it, and you are worthy of receiving it right now, un-airbrushed, as you are. No Chotchky required. In this way, you begin to outsmart this troublesome strain of *projectionotchky: the act of projecting emotional well-being on to some "thing" out there.*

That's why the feeling dissipates so rapidly after you acquire something: the thing has no feelings to give us.

You are every outlet mall, every bazaar, garage sale, flea market, gift shop, car dealership, and yes, even every Nordstrom's. You carry the feeling, which is what you are actually shopping for, with you always. Deep inside of you that just-bought-it feeling is always available . . . in stock, in your size, in the latest style, in you!

## Chotchky Challenge

The next time you're shopping and that feeling of wholeness arises, catch yourself. Your True Self. Look at the "thing," hold it, sit in it, caress it, and let the spell fall over you. Then, like a wizard awakening to your power, say to yourself, *I already have this. It was mine before I got here because I brought it here with me.* In that moment, you are turning the tables, using the campaign that is designed to hide the soul, to find the soul. It's a big game of hide-and-seek and the ramifications are enormous.

### The Art of the Precycle

I don't expect any of us to make the complete shift to knowing our true nature in one fell swoop, instantaneously shattering the Chotchky Paradigm. For most of us, it will happen in increments. The simple awareness that you are not a rat and that the task is not to acquire but to live passionately, unafraid, is enough to lead us out of the maze and begin living from the inside out (and that's no piece of cheese!).

With this understanding, we can begin practicing the art of the *precycle,* which may be the most ecologically sound and psychologically transforming practice ever introduced to our slowly awakening world.

*Precycle: the act of returning a thing to the earth before it was even taken, saving our resources and creating a brighter future.*

Begin precycling today. You don't need special containers, and there's no hassle separating "this" from "that." Ah, the ease of it all! Everything stays right where it should be. Here's all you do: Before buying something, just consider all the resources it took to make it and all the work you put into earning your money. Money is your time and energy captured on a piece of paper. Time and energy is the essence of living. This means that for everything you buy, you are literally trading a piece of your life.

If it isn't truly a fair exchange, walk away. Feel Mother Earth breathe a sigh of relief as you put into motion a ripple effect that will help build a brighter tomorrow. The most perfect storage space for our resources is and always will be our planet. There they can be used in the future for something truly worthwhile.

It is helpful while learning the art of precycling to ask the following questions: *Will I "love" it or find it useful a month from now? A year from now? Or will it quickly join the ranks of the other Small Plastic Gophers ransacking my humble abode?* As important as it is to rid ourselves of Chotchky, *it's exponentially more important to stop bringing it in.*

Check it out, I'm precycling now. Go to the secret page, and choose the image of the earth: **www.barryadennis.com/ chotchkyvideos1**.

Next we'll take a trip to the drive-through for a "Happy Meal." Here, people are suing the fast-food chain for making them overweight, while I'm losing my mind because I can't find the "key" to my existence until I end up lost in Zimbabwe. It will all make sense soon enough. . . .

# CHAPTER 13

# "HAPPY MEAL"

There are people who have sued McDonald's because they got burned after spilling coffee on themselves. Recently, two teenage girls and their parents sued the company because, after relentlessly eating the fast food, the girls became obese. What's wrong with this picture? In both cases they are claiming "pain and suffering." And yes, I do feel great compassion for these consumers; however, what are your thoughts as you read the words of their attorney John Banzhaf?

> When we're suing on behalf of children, it's hard to argue that a 6- or 8- or 10-year-old child has to take full responsibility for their decisions when they're lured into McDonald's by the toys and the playground and happy meals. . . .

Hmm, if only we could sue the paradigm that made it acceptable for parents to continually feed their children happy meals. If only we could sue the paradigm that creates the tactics used by fast-food restaurants to "lure" in the children. If only we could sue the farmers who give the cows hormones and corn (not their natural food source), which make the cows grow faster and pass gas (more on this later), causing global warming just so they can keep up with . . . what? Our culture's demands for more cheeseburgers. *We're suing ourselves.*

Justice begins when we take full responsibility for our actions. Through the Chotchky Paradigm, however, everything appears to happen to us from "out there." We tend to live, then, as victims being continually harassed by circumstance. This creates a life chock-full of "pain and suffering."

That said, I have wondered if I might have a case against McDonald's for the pain and suffering my family has endured while pulling away from the drive-through with one of those "Happy Meals." I think it's safe to say there's no actual "happy" in there. And what about the pain and suffering inflicted upon my feet?

I have plans to walk on hot coals in an actual fire pit. There are seminars built around this practice. It sounds scary, but I assure you, it's relatively safe. Try walking through my kids' rooms barefoot in the dark after they have randomly discarded the broken, pointless bauble that came with lunch. This is a true test of one's pain threshold. At my workshops on the Chotchky Challenge, I'm seriously considering, as part of the mastery level training, having all participants walk over a pit of Happy Mealotchky. It would make this whole hot-coal thing seem like walking on marshmallows.

What "Happy Meals" fill our children with is the delusion that the emptiness they may feel on the inside, or will come to feel later on in life, can be filled somehow by a piece of plastic and a shake. There is no knickknack that can fill our children's yearning for love, purpose, and meaning. It does, however, give us something to put in our landfills. I guess that counts for something.

There came a point whenever my children wanted to order a box of this fodder, I would say, "Fine, but you can't get the toy." I tried to explain why. "You play with the thing for five minutes, then you fight over who got the best one, and then, no sooner than when you ripped it out of its bag, you discard it on the floor of my car. It sits there for weeks, during which time I will have to ask you at least on 12 separate occasions to pick it up.

"When you finally take it out of my car, you randomly scatter it about like big chunks of fertilizer that seem to grow more 'whatnot,' leading to physical harm as one of my heels, supporting my total weight of 187 pounds, comes down on top of a plastic pointy Smurf.

"I fall to the ground writhing in pain while other random doodads leave indentations on my skin. Eventually, it gets thrown out, which means it gets piled up in our landfills. You can't recycle these things—there are millions upon millions of Happy Meal toys strewn about in big gigantic holes that we dig for such hooey. All the while, more Happy Mealotchky is being manufactured across the oceans, shipped in fossil-fuel burning transporters, creating the greenhouse effect."

My kids looked at me with an expression that seemed to say, *What is this "landfill"? Can we go there? Is there an admission fee?*

Before the revelation that I did not have to accept the Chotchky that came with the "food," I had quite a Happy Meal runaround.

It began when I lost one of two of the most useful things I own: my car keys. There was only one other thing that I despised losing as much my keys: my wallet. (This was pre-whone.) I searched everywhere for my keys. Every nook and cranny. Every junk drawer. Then I thought that maybe my car keys were somewhere . . . in my car.

At the time, my car looked like a landfill. Happy Meal toys mixed and mingled with riffraff of every origin. The stress was creeping up on me as I waded through the wasteland. No luck. My keys were missing for over two months. I only had what is called a "valet key," which makes one wonder if valets are Munchkins. This key is really small! It actually hurt to open my door for lack of leverage.

*Keyotochky* comes with its own formidable grade of the Chotchky Effect. It fills our drawers and key hangers with jingly clutter while filling our mind with questions. We have no idea what they go to, yet we actually experience fear when we consider letting them go, "just in case." Just in case of what? Perhaps one of these keys is for some door we do not know exists within our own home, which leads to an alternate universe where the more you eat the less you weigh. Balderdash. Besides, I know that a universe where the more you eat the less you weigh sounds great, but with our current appetite, we may all vanish!

Recycle the keys and anything that gives you that "just in case" phobia. And if it's not recyclable, throw it all away. Your house and car are not a landfill. Then say the "Throw Away Prayer," which is a key to higher consciousness:

*As I discard this, I am committed to becoming a more con-scious being. As a result, I throw away less and less trash be-cause I buy less junk. And so it is.*

After two months of using that tiny valet key, I dreaded the thought of unlocking the door or trunk or starting my car. Then one day the unthinkable happened. I couldn't find my wallet!

Gone. No keys (except the valet toothpick) or wallet. Every time I needed a credit card or my driver's license, I felt a sense of panic.

Now, not only was it extremely difficult to start my car, but when I did, I was driving without a license. I was "on the lam."

I spent countless minutes, precious time, looking for my wallet. Stressed. Going around town "on the lam." What happens for me in these situations—and maybe you can relate—is that when I am searching for something that is important, I acquire very powerful Chotchky Vision. Once I have searched everywhere and then begin again where I started, Chotchkies start flying. In the throes of such lunacy we may think or even say things out loud like, "What in the hell is all this junk?" Correct! In that moment we're in hell. Inferno is not a place somewhere in the center of the earth where Happy Mealotchky melts into a giant plastic ball; it is a state of consciousness experienced when living through the Chotchky Paradigm from all of the fruitless searching.

There is a sense to which the Chotchky Paradigm turns our mind into a plastic ball. And since like attracts like, we begin seeking out other things of its kind. We attract "plastic" relation-ships, "plastic" experiences, and we feel "plastic" emotions in self-imposed dramas captured brilliantly in Shakespeare's *Much Ado About Nothing*.

In fact, there is a giant plastic "island" in the middle of the Atlantic Ocean. It's approximately the size of the continental United States, and it's made up of countless tons of synthetic trash we have thrown into the ocean as a result of our plastic relationship to life. Mother Earth has gathered all this refuse into one giant clump so we can see it, face it. Like any good mother, she is giving us some tough love, saying, "I love you so much, I'm saying no. This is not okay. Please wake up."

As we accept the Chotchky Challenge, we begin to reclaim the miracle that is our mind—an indescribably creative, free-thinking expression of life. In turn, the Plastic Island will slowly disappear as we no longer add to its bulk through shallow living.

So there I was, in hell. It was my fifth time rummaging through my house and office, reaching greater and greater levels of despair, when I determined to ransack my car once again in hopes that I had somehow overlooked my wallet the first few go-arounds. This time, I would tear it apart if I had to. The anxiety of being on the lam was growing exponentially.

With Chotchky flying out of the doors, I emptied the entire contents of my glove box, cup holders, side-door compartments, and trunk. Then I simply removed everything that was not bolted down, which consisted of floor mats, the trunk mat, and a spare tire. I moved both seats as far back as possible, then climbed in upside down so my head was under the steering column in the space designed for feet. My feet now fumbling around the head rest, I reached in underneath the seat, desperately grasping, only to feel several small plastic toys from Happy Meals gone by, mixed with other miscellaneous itemotchky. I threw them out the door in disgust. At my wit's end, I said to the space under the car seat while blood slowly filled the space in my head, "Please, God, where is my wallet?"

That's when I realized, as the small plastic toys hit the cement garage floor, that there was a "cling" sound. Happy Mealotchky is made exclusively of plastic, and "clacks" rather than "clings." I looked at the pile on the floor, and smack dab in the middle of it, there lay my *keys!*

It took another few days to find my wallet, which ended up being in a drawer in my office. The drawer, of course, was at least 50 percent full of *office supplyotchky*—an excess of pens and pencils, many of which were broken and did not work, several big erasers, and three staplers. Three staplers, all of which worked flawlessly. I actually tested them. Shot staples up into the air like fireworks.

What am I doing with three staplers? I had looked in that drawer several times, looked straight at my wallet, but was rendered blind by the chaos, the landfill that had become my drawer. The day that I found my keys while looking for my wallet was the moment I stopped letting my children get the "free toys" with their Happy Meals. I finally took full responsibility for my circumstances. The time, pain, and suffering the "free" toys cost me, my family, and the planet cannot be quantified in dollars.

We all want to make the most of our time. It is the essence of life and we know there is a limit. Yet we go about our days as if they will last forever, allowing Chotchky to creep in, stealing this most precious of things. Inherently, time is never Chotchky, but sometimes, by unconscious living, we create *timeotchky: the ticking away of the clock while we search for things that really do matter but have become lost in a wasteland of the irrelevant.*

## Deep Thought

Approximately 98 percent of us, myself included, have not fully outgrown the Happy Meal deception. We still buy into it. As adults, it just gets more costly. The Chotchky Campaign is relentless: "Act now and get six more for free!" "We're giving it away!" "Everything must go!" I once saw a watch for sale in a magazine that came with a "free" car. I'm tempted to explain all the ways that a car is so far from "free" it makes Russia, pre-1989, look like a democracy. Instead, I'll ask you. How many different ways could this car end up costing more than the watch and the car are worth combined?

## Chotchky Challenge

Consider having a real discussion with your children the next time they want a "happy meal." First, make it clear to them that "free with purchase" makes no sense at all. Then describe the troubled journey of the "happy" toy from the pillaging of the land for the materials to the pollution from the production of it and the transport. Eplain how, because your kid will not find any genuine happiness in it, it will end up in a landfill, causing a kind of constipation for Mother Earth. Mostly let them know that happiness is an inside job that comes from living a life of purpose and self-love.

### *A Real Happy Meal*

We heard there was a stream maybe five miles down the red gravel/dirt road from our bungalow in the bush of Zimbabwe. We were there for a couple of weeks doing volunteer work. It was nearly 100 degrees out. You wouldn't think of taking this journey without water and at least rugged hiking shoes.

So with a combined 64 ounces of $H_2O$ and our designer, high-tech, scientifically tested footwear, Heather and I were on our way. After about a mile, we were greeted by an ostrich that seemed to be attempting to interrogate us: "What are you doing in my bush? From whence did you come? Do you have a passport? I want your shoes!" Once we finally got past "ostrich immigration," it was a long and desolate path. Nothing and no one for miles. Heat rose from the ground, bending light in that mirage-inducing way. That's why I wasn't sure whether or not to believe my eyes when I thought I saw movement ahead. Slowly, as we came closer, six children materialized.

I need not elaborate much. We have all seen it on TV. The children were barefoot and scrawny by our standards, and wearing what we would consider "filthy" clothes. We, as Westerners, naturally feel sorry for these people. And I am not saying we shouldn't have compassion. However, we often fail in such situations to look at ourselves, at our own hidden "poverty."

As we drew near, we noticed they were eating something from their hands. While they nibbled, they laughed with great joy, grinning from ear to ear. I later learned it is called *sudza,* a staple food similar to rice. It does not come with a toy and yet, those kids were so happy! We greeted them with "Hello," which exhausted their knowledge of English.

In my travels I have found two things that break all language barriers: music and juggling. I often bring my guitar when I travel. I didn't, however, take it on this walk. So instead, I picked up some rocks and began to do a juggling/clown act. The kids erupted with laughter. Joy is not something they hide away in the storage closets of their mind. In no time we were deeply enamored, all eight of us. They took us by the hands and when our hands were full, the others took our arms and began leading us. Where, we didn't know. To paraphrase a very famous carpenter: "Let the children lead you to the Kingdom of Heaven." Well, this has never been more literal.

After about three or four miles of walking, we saw a village on a hill. We asked if this was where they were taking us. *They laughed.* It occurred to me that if we hadn't been wearing our high-tech, air-sole, computer-chipped sneakers, our feet would have been raw and bloody. *They wore no shoes.* Their feet were so callused, they most assuredly could even walk on Happy Mealotchky without consequence.

Soon we were in the heart of their village. I don't know its name—I simply refer to it as the Village of Nothing! It's fitting. They had no electricity, which translates to no heat or air conditioning, no running water, and no refrigerators. No TV, toasters, microwaves, hair dryers, and Xbox 3 millions. Each family lived in grass huts no more than ten feet around. Dirt floors. In this village, however, there was a true abundance of a very rare commodity in the Western world. It overflowed from every nook and cranny. A bounty of *nothing.* Nothing to deceive them. Nothing to cloud their minds and snuff out the soul. This nothingness seemed to be the container of their joy.

There, at the center of the village, I began to juggle rocks. The laughter of the six children was like a bell that rang through the heart of the Village of Nothing. Soon all the children of the village surrounded me. This became one of the wackiest, most inspired, joy-filled times of my life. I dropped the rocks, lifted my arms in the air, and began singing and dancing with a combination of moves that can only be described as a cross between something Jim Carrey, Steve Martin, and Pee Wee Herman might choreograph on the fly. The joy of Nothing is contagious.

The kids' laughter only egged me on as they mimicked my moves to near perfection. Then I began clapping and stomping in rhythms so complicated one should not be able to replicate them without many years of disciplined musical study. And yet they copied me without missing a beat. And then they would laugh. Oh, that laugh!

I danced around the grass huts kind of like a slightly crazed Gene Kelly in *Singin' in the Rain,* except this was *Singin' in the Heat of the African Sun in the Village of Nothing.* In some ways this village made our slums appear more like five-star hotels and yet, in its own way, it was meticulous. The villagers took great pride as they swept the dirt floors of their huts. Really!

Suddenly I stopped, went to my knees, putting one finger to my lips. "Shhh."

All 50 mimicked. It sounded like pouring rain. Then I drew a circle in the dirt. I hadn't the slightest clue of where this was going.

I sang out, "This is the circle!"

They all echoed what they heard, to the best of their ability, with a delightful mix of sounds at the top of their lungs, which, phonetically, might look something like this: "Dis ees dah surckoo!"

"The circle is love."

"Dah surckoo ees luv."

"In the circle we are one."

"Een dah surckoo we ahh wooon."

Then we did the Chicken Dance! This is universal.

A teenage girl was observing this spectacle of spontaneous celebration, smiling, laughing in the background. Somehow she had quite a command of the English language. While I did the Chicken Dance with the kids, Heather introduced herself to the girl.

Before we'd left on our walk that morning, Heather grabbed a long-sleeved white shirt to protect herself from the sun. I don't know how it came up, since at this point the kids were playing "pile up on the funny white man," but she offered it to the girl. As Heather held out the gift, the girl stood motionless.

"For me?" she said, unbelieving. "Thank you, but no, I can't."

Heather insisted, "Please, I really want you to have it. It would be a gift to me, to give it to you."

The girl reached out, accepting it, and then held it to her chest as slowly, eyes closed, tears came. Tears of Nothing. "Thank you, thank you. This will be my favorite shirt. I will cherish it forever."

The irony, of course, is that back at home we probably had enough shirts for every person in the Village of Nothing. And maybe even the neighboring one, the Village Next to Nothing.

When it came time to leave, the children stuck to us like Velcro. Holding on to our hands, arms, elbows, and pant legs, we moved like one big blob back toward our bungalow as the sun began its slow descent over the African plains.

On our journey home, I pulled a fairly new container of sunscreen out of my pocket. This was something completely foreign to them. I used it like face paint, applying it with one finger to my lips, cheeks, and nose, making me a clown. Only now do I realize before that moment these kids had never seen nor heard of a "clown." With no context, there's really no way for us to imagine what a striking image this must have been. Then I did my best Charlie Chaplin routine. I must have appeared quite mad. They gathered around, holding out their palms. I quickly emptied the entire squeeze bottle as they, laughing hysterically, began rubbing it all over each other's faces. The look of the bright white sunscreen against their dark-as-night skin was art in motion.

Saying good-bye to their now-painted faces was oh so bittersweet. We had to pry their hands from our arms.

"Byee-Byee. Weee luv eeyooo," they sang over and over as we made our way back to our hut down the long red-dirt road.

That day, Heather and I went looking for a stream. What we found was a river of joy with no beginning and no end. It miraculously sprang up from Nothing. What those children have is the Holy Grail. What many people have in our Westernized world, with all of our riches, is a backward kind of poverty. A poverty of happiness, a poverty of the soul.

*The Chotchky Challenge is to live in the heart of the Village of Nothing, while residing here in our Village of Way Too Much.* That is true enlightenment and will transform the world; that is Heaven on Earth.

## Chotchky Challenge

Circle the degree to which you believe you are taking full responsibility for your experience regardless of circumstances:

10%  20%  30%  40%  50%  60%  70%  80%  90%  100%

## Let's Take a Moment . . .

Let's take a moment for some SPF 100. Take a deep, cleansing breath. Allow your mind to empty into Nothingness:

*I know that the Village of Nothing is a state of mind. I, too, can live there. I choose to let go while living in the Village of Way Too Much. And so I see myself putting bright white sunscreen on my face. As I do so, I realize that this is no ordinary lotion. It offers 100 percent of Soul Protection and Freedom, or SPF 100. It blocks 100 percent of the harmful rays of excess. I see my face covered in it, and I smile as the rays of false information from my well-meaning culture bounce off my skin. I know that I am perfect and whole. There is nothing more I need to be in joy.*

Click on the image of the grass hut on the secret page now:
**www.barryadennis.com/chotchkyvideos1**. The Village of Nothing is near. As we continue, you will meet some friends who were
haunted by a throw pillow followed by an encounter with a wise
master in Japan who is rebelling against the norm of his entire
culture (as all great masters before him).

* * *

# CHAPTER 14

# GIFTOTCHKY

*Giftotchky: the prevalence of gifts given that are not wanted and, in fact, become a burden on the receivers as they are riddled with guilt, unsure of what to do with the thing given out of a sense of obligation*

Once a year, a ritualistic gathering takes place around many parts of the world that forms a hybrid of such stuff. It sneaks up on us, wrapped in good intentions. The players generally mean well: grandmas, in-laws, mothers, brothers, second cousins, neighbors, friends, and even strangers who seem to appear out of the woodwork. Everyone contributing to the glorious pile of gifts that will, not long after its unwrapping, create varying degrees of confusion. What I speak of is none other than . . . *Christmasotchky.*

In the name of *Jesus.* A man who came to free us from the *shackles of Chotchky.* Children around the globe regularly experience complete meltdowns from the jolting amount of gifts. After opening several boxes, they begin to get overwhelmed and anxious. Their behavior resembles that of a manic-depressive. Hyper, bouncing off the walls one minute; possessive, fearful, angry, sad, and teary the next. And if brother or sister gets something they did not get, then that is what they really wanted, and it is "unfair."

So we buy more Chotchky to make sure they both get even piles. Both pieces of battery-operated plastic, of course, are completely forgotten the next week if not the next day, taking up more space in our homes, our minds, and our souls!

On Christmas and any other gift-giving occasion, in an effort to be polite, rooted in a sense of obligation, there are inevitable moments of uncomfortable posturing as we, well, fib; "Oh, um, cool. I . . . I love it."

*Obligotchky: The feeling that if you don't give a gift, you are a bad person, even if it means burdening others with something they don't want and now must put in storage because, out of a deep-seated guilt, they cannot bring themselves to get rid of it. In turn, they feel obligated to return the burden by buying something out of obligation for you, perpetuating the cycle of guilt as we all wonder which gift was given and by whom because they're on their way over, so we better get something out of storage, quick.*

To add insult to injury, now we must write a thank-you card for that which we did not actually want. The guilt builds the longer we put off the writing. I once sent a thank-you note for something I had already regifted. Oh, the hoodwinks.

### "The Case of the Throw Pillow"

A friend who leads spiritual retreats once told me that after each of her weeklong retreats, everyone is gathered together for a group photo. (You know the one.) On one occasion, a participant of the retreat took said photo and somehow infused it on a number of throw pillows. I don't know if the outer layer of a throw pillow is called a "case," but if it is, these throw pillows were now covered in *cases with faces*.

She hand-delivered one of these faced cases as a gift to my friend. Allow me to compress a long conversation with her and her

husband into three words: they hate it. From it, they actually receive "the creeps." However, they are guilt-ridden for not liking it.

There are indigenous peoples on the planet who believe that
when you take their picture, you take their soul. I used to think
this was silly superstition until I saw one of the "cases with faces."
It seemed almost plausible that these people's souls really were
compressed onto the pillow.

Out of guilt, they used the thing for a while. They "threw"
it on the couch for padding. However, somehow, they never felt
comfortable, sitting on the faces. Desperately, they asked what
I thought they should do. I explained that it was obvious, right
there in the name of the article: throw it away. They felt so much
guilt around it, though, that they were powerless in its presence.
Immobilized. It's their kryptonite! I told them they have two
choices: they can keep it for *life* or get rid of it.

This, of course, is clear, but in the throes of giftotchky, someone has to be the voice of reason. It's a great opportunity for us all
to face the facts. If someone really loves you, is a real friend, there
is no way they would want you to feel such turmoil because of
something they gave you. If they would, how could they be your
friend?

Get rid of any and all giftotchky and the guilt that goes along
with it. You may even consider having a heart-to-heart conversation and being honest (there's a concept), especially if it's a friend
or relative who regularly arrives bearing Small Plastic Gophers.

You might lovingly and gratefully say something like: "I really
appreciate the love with which you give. That love (or sincerity or
. . . ) is the real gift to me. Thank you. And I'm at a place in my life
where I'm letting things go and creating more space in our home.
I'd feel *so* loved if, from now on, you'd give me the gift of your
presence, rather than presents. If you really want to wrap something up, how about a gift that doesn't take up long-term storage
space—a basket of fruit, tea, movie passes, flowers, a meal out, a
pass for a yoga class, three hours of babysitting, and so on."

Honest communication may be uncomfortable at first; however, you will deepen your relationships as you become more and more authentic.

## Chotchky Challenge

Is there anything in your life that is or has become giftotchky? If so, let go of it and the guilt associated with it. Heck, even regift it, but only if you are sure the intended second receiver will actually like it. Do not spread STGs (Socially Transmitted Guilt).

At this point, you may be wondering if the Chotchky Challenge requires a "gift-free" world. This, of course, is not the case. *The Challenge is to give authentic expressions of the heart by bringing consciousness to everything you purchase.* In this way you will be giving something soulful.

### *Presents with Presence*

In Japan, there is a tradition of gift giving called *omiyage,* pronounced "oh-me-yah-gay." If this tradition keeps going at its current rate, the Japanese islands could surpass Venice as the fastest sinking land mass on the planet. It just can't support the extra weight.

The tradition dictates that whenever a visitor comes from a different region or a different country altogether, they must bring gifts. They actually have banks created for the sole purpose of storing the excess omiyage. People pay monthly to store gifts they do not want in what is one of the highest priced real-estate markets on planet Earth.

My oldest son, Xander, recently returned from Japan as part of a Lewis & Clark College study abroad program. While there, he discovered that even the Japanese are becoming disturbed by omiyage. They are beginning to refer to it instead as *gomiyage.* This is quite significant because the word *gomi* means trash. By adding a letter, they are in essence saying that the practice has become the tradition of giving each other trash. They know this and yet they keep on "gomiyage-ing."

While there, my son met an old man who is a major player in a kind of revolution. He refuses to partake in gomiyage. Some are offended by this. Changing paradigms is never easy. Instead, after getting to know someone, he then returns home and finds something that is relevant, meaningful, and actually useful to his new friend. This is beautiful. This is giving presents with presence.

However, the more we understand the Chotchky Challenge, the more we begin to realize that the greatest gift we can often give is nothingness. Consider, for a moment, the exchange that occurs in conversation. We believe we are the ones giving the gift when we are doing the blabbing. And sometimes this is true. Often however, talking is *taking*. Listening, which is the act of *adding nothing,* can be a much more meaningful gift. A gift with *presence*. Besides, we can learn things by listening. Things that the universe may be trying to give us as a gift.

I suggest, as we shift our paradigms, that we give more of the most precious thing we have: our time. Give the gift of being together—slices of your very life. Take someone for a ride in a hot-air balloon or a horse-drawn carriage. Go row a boat on a lake. Bring someone to your favorite secret place. Buy someone a massage or give someone a massage. *Get creative.*

Such gifts do not pile up in our closets or attics, or bring guilt. They create happy memories that nourish and heal the soul. In my family, we have also given charitable gifts in the name of our children to those who go without.

Let's join the old Japanese man on a mission of soul: just say "nomiyage" and you will begin to feel the holy presents . . . in your presence.

## Chotchky Challenge

Think of someone you love who is having a birthday soon. Or maybe Christmas is near? Or maybe just because.

What could you give this person that would truly have presence? What experience could you share? The gift of time? Think outside cultural norms. What stirs your soul and brings joy to your heart? These are the gifts the soul wishes to give and receive. Why would you give anything else? Now take the steps needed to prepare this gift of the heart.

I have prepared such a gift for you, and it's not Chotchky. Go to the secret page and click on the gift: **www.barryadennis.com/ chotchkyvideos1.**

Next we're going to discover why the aliens have not shown themselves yet and what it's going to take for them to make an appearance, a *close encounter of the third kind.*

# CHAPTER 15

# FLIMSY EARLOBES ABANDONING ROCKS

So why do we gather, corral, herd, hoard, collect, keep, hide, and store? The reasons for these phenomena are sprinkled throughout this book. However, I have gathered, hoarded, corralled, and collected them all into one four-letter word. I couldn't help myself. It's what we do. *FEAR.*

It's been said that fear is False Evidence Appearing Real, or Forget Everything And Run. I personally like to think of it as Flimsy Earlobes Abandoning Rocks. My reasoning for this should be quite clear. It makes no sense whatsoever.

Something like 98 percent of all fear makes no sense. It is excess emotion. It's been passed down to us by our long-lost distant relatives who actually had a good reason to be fearful. They were being chased by woolly mammoths with large flimsy earlobes. They were forced into abandoning all hope and throwing rocks. It just doesn't make any sense now. There are no more giant flimsy earlobes. We had them all for lunch.

At the time, fear was useful, but now it has turned on us and become our own worst enemy because, psychologically and physiologically, we still think "they" are coming to get us. We're stuck in the past. That's why we resemble squirrels in the fall collecting nuts. Our ancestors were hunters and gatherers.

When we feel fear, we are actually afraid for our life. We may be receiving some constructive feedback from a co-worker. Suddenly it feels as if they have large flimsy earlobes, accompanied by the urge to abandon all hope and start throwing rocks. Or maybe we have a presentation to give. We look out and it feels like a packed house of saber-tooth tigers.

Just before I called my wife to ask her on our first date, I was petrified. I stared at the phone for so long it felt like I was out on the plains, stalking Wally the Woolly. Now, 14 years later, and very happily married, as soon as she says "Honey, we need to talk," the clock turns back 50,000 years. Wally is near as I nervously begin reaching for loose rocks to assist me in doing battle.

Our life is not in mortal danger, but the ancient part of our brain is convinced we are.

Almost all fear is Chotchky! When you are afraid, call it for what it is. Call it on the carpet. And then roll it up, tie it tightly with some twine, take it out into a field, and abandon it.

I was once co-facilitating a retreat on Maui at a place called Shangri-la. Down a very steep hill, there is a lush tropical trail that culminates in a 15-foot cliff, down which one must belay using an old rope tied to a scrawny little tree. At the bottom, there is a 12-foot waterfall that pours over lava rock frozen thousands of years ago. The crystal-clear water pours into a pristine pool overlooking the ocean. Every day I would hike this trail, belay down the rope, and, with total abandonment, run and jump into the air, splashing down into this nature-made water park.

One day a 60-ish-year-old woman from New York City heard the splash from above. She was maybe 5'3" inches tall and fairly, well, "plenitudinous." Very gingerly grabbing hold of whatever branch would accommodate her bounty, she made her way down the trail to the top of the cliff where the rope dangled precariously.

I did not want to show it, but I was astounded to see her there. She wanted to come down. She wanted to jump in.

I am never one to stand in the way of a fellow human being facing their fears. These are glorious moments. However, this was not ancient-brain, unfounded fear; it was real. She could seriously be hurt and she wanted me to help her down. Did I want to be held responsible for what could happen?

I asked her several times, "Are you sure you want to do this?"

"Yes" she said, fighting back the tears. "I'm so afraid, but I really want to jump in."

I climbed up the rope to meet her and explained that she would need to turn around, putting her back to the drop-off below, and face the cliff. She apprehensively turned and, getting down on her tummy, began to shimmy over the top. Her feet were approaching my face as my toes wiggled into the cracks in the ancient lava wall. As she continued to "scootch" over the edge, I realized I was in way over my head. How does one prepare for such a thing?

And then . . . she slipped.

There's no gentle way to put this: Her butt slammed into my face. I managed to grab her thigh with one hand while continuing to hold the rope with the other and hoisted her over my head, placing her squarely on my shoulders. If you could somehow recreate this feat, it would make for a great moment in a Cirque du Soleil show.

With a lot of trembling on her part and bravado on mine, somehow we made it to the floor below.

Finally standing on horizontal ground we slowly approached the precipice that revealed the pool below. She began shaking, tears welling. Her soul wanted to jump, but the fear, oh the fear. When staring down at the water, you generally cannot see the bottom; instead, what you see is your reflection looking back. It's a giant mirror, an illusion, like most fear.

We project our fret into the unknown. This tendency was helpful when woolly mammoths were real. As a result, the evolution of our mind occurred steeped in fear. But beasts no longer roam the neighborhood looking for a meal, we don't live in caves nearly freezing to death, and hunting is a sport in which we now have quite the unfair advantage. The very things we feared are no longer lurking. Our projections, however, are.

The woman was terrified that the water wasn't deep enough or that some "thing" was in there even though I submerged myself repeatedly, proving beyond a shadow of a doubt that there was nothing to fear. The logic was sound; the evidence indisputable. She knew this. And yet still, the worry overwhelmed her. She feared for her life. If we are not vigilant, the beasts of our projections will rule us and, ironically, bring about our untimely demise. Worry and fret, the offspring of fear, create poor mental and physical health, illness, and disease. It's fear that kills us, not that which we are afraid of.

She finally took my hand and allowed me to walk her to the edge. While she was visibly shaking, I told her to "watch with your heart, not your eyes" as I released her tight grip on my hand and lunged forward into the air and down again. Now, when she looked down, no longer was there the illusion of herself looking up from the water in fear, but me, encouraging and smiling.

"You can do this! There is nothing to fear."

Her body suddenly became still. The sweet release of surrender seemed to fill her every cell. She took a deep breath and then, one step forward, letting out a screech that ricocheted off the cliff walls, she jumped.

Awkwardly, at an angle, she plummeted, followed by the kind of "kasplash" that occurs only from a sideways entry. I'm sure all of her worries concerning the depth of the water disappeared as quickly as she did. Down, down she went. Gone, akin to a stone. And just as I began to wonder how long she could hold her breath, she emerged. Screeching with joy! Alive. Beautiful. Glorious. Baptized.

Before we ascended that 15-foot cliff back up the trail that day, she transcended her fear, repeatedly jumping off that ledge like a little girl without a worry in the world. That pool, that jump, is not unlike almost every fear we face today: False Evidence Appearing Real. On the other side awaits new life. A new beginning. What is your fear?

Let's jump in . . .

What is it that you are afraid of right now? Making a difficult phone call? Going on a job interview or quitting a job? Con-
fronting a loved one? Change? Whatever it is, there is virtually no
difference between it and what my friend faced before she went
kasplash. You are projecting ancient history into the present. It's
time to jump in. Your life awaits.

*Now imagine doing the thing that needs to be done. If you will just
see it, feel it, this can transform the fear into excitement. As you move
through the fear, you will be like my friend emerging from the water.
Reborn. One of the most dangerous things you can do is live in fear. It
can destroy us. So jump now, knowing that fear literally is a thing of
the past.*

I have come to believe wholeheartedly that FDR was on to
something when he said, "There is nothing to fear but fear itself."
Well, that and "someday."

When we live for "someday," we're kind of like "the jerk" in
the classic Steve Martin movie of the same name. He breaks up
with his girlfriend and, wallowing in self-pity, as he leaves her
behind he proclaims that he does not need her or her stuff. But as
he begins to walk away, he can't help but grab an ashtray. Then a
paddle. Then the remote. In the end, we see him walking down
the street dragging every appliance he ever owned behind him.
It's pathetic. But it's us.

No, we generally don't have our Chotchkies in tow, but they
occupy a place in our psyche. Imagine what it would look like if
we could suddenly see what every person is dragging around. We
would all look like walking garage sales. Pulling behind us everything from the people we're holding grudges against, to pieces of
art that we never hang, to high-school trophies from track and
field. *Oh, the good old days.* Let's not be "the jerk." It's "poverty consciousness," the state of living, thinking, and feeling that there is
never enough. In poverty consciousness, no matter how abundant
we may be, we can never let go of the anxiety of "not enough." If

we live in a castle and continually live in fear of losing that castle, then we are the Kings of Fear.

## Chotchky Challenge

What is your "someday"? What if the someday you have been waiting for is today, and the one thing your soul has been waiting for all this time is for you to let go of the past? Can you feel the freedom? It's time to begin trusting in the Youniverse. It's a game changer. Let's say today is your "someday." What are you going to do now that it has arrived?

Pick one thing you will now let go of from your past or something you are ready to begin, and write it down here:

_____

_____

_____

_____

Oh, how good it would feel to actually do it.

## *Choose a Major*

Fear also rears its illusionary head when we begin to feel this most blessed nudging called "divine discontent." These are times when our soul is pushing through the Chotchky Paradigm, trying to get our attention, tapping us on the shoulder with a feather and a whisper. Much too often, when we feel this nudging, we ignore it, often leaving the soul no other option but the proverbial two-by-four to the head, a tragedy that forces us to change. We don't want to listen because we're afraid to face the fact that we have been wasting our life away and so, instead, we continue . . . wasting our life away.

There is this thing we do in college called "choose a major." Sometimes, by our final year, we realize we want to change to a different major, but we've already invested so much time and money toward this one, we can't bring ourselves to change. Every day, people become lawyers, doctors, or accountants, knowing in their hearts they will be miserable.

We get married, have children, and then feel completely trapped. Then, on our deathbed, we think, *If only I had changed majors!*

Whether it's our stuff, a relationship, or a career, if the only reason we won't get rid of it or stop doing it is because we've invested so much in it, then it's now costing us more than all the tuitions in every Ivy League school combined. Besides, there's only one major: Life.

And the most direct route to getting your master's degree is to stop doing things out of fear and start living.

## Chotchky Challenge

If you're not happy, change your "major"! Otherwise, what you're doing "for a living," day in and day out, is Chotchky.

Come now, let's change majors together. Choose the graduation cap on the secret page: **www.barryadennis.com/chotchky videos1**. Then in the next chapter, we're going to get a sunburn and a hot dog in Palm Springs. There are monkeys, meditation masters, Michael J. Fox . . . you've got to read it to believe it!

# CHAPTER 16

# GNP

Thank heavens for financial crises, for they are not what they seem. The truth is that they are crises of consciousness reflected in our relationship to money.

Once while visiting the sleepy town of Lincoln City, Oregon, I noticed a little shop called the Cyber Café and Bookstore. Lincoln City is a regular getaway for my family, but I'd never seen this place before. It was as if it had just appeared, and it was "groovy." The server was the most genuine and sincere I had ever experienced. It was an honor to be seated in her section, and I really wanted to tell her that. We often have such urges to speak from the heart, but we become conflicted, afraid of looking silly, being vulnerable, or playing the fool.

I try to listen to those whispers because I believe that only good can come of it. I finally said to her, "I would like you to know that you are the most genuine, present person I've ever had the pleasure of being served by. You're just so sweet. Do you own the restaurant?"

She smiled. "Thank you so much. I'm actually part of a meditation community that owns the café together."

Then I asked the first question that comes when living through the Chotchky Paradigm: "How's business?"

She knew what I meant. A very patient, compassionate expression shone through her eyes, like one might convey while teaching a small child. "Business is good, but we didn't buy the store to make money. We bought it simply to be in service. It's part of our practice."

Her name is Jyoti. We became fast friends and the café became my favorite haunt on the Oregon coast. Every time I was in town, I couldn't wait to see her and just experience the "vibe." One day years later, much to my dismay, there was a "for sale" sign hanging on the front door. Jyoti told me they were getting so many requests to teach meditation that they no longer had the time to run the restaurant. About six months later it sold. Who wouldn't want to buy it? It had become a very successful business.

That was over six years ago and the restaurant has changed hands more times than I can count. No one else has been able to run the cyber café successfully. This should not come as a surprise. You see, we have it backward. Jyoti and her friends were not running the café to make money; they were running the café to be of service to humanity. And from that soulful place came, not only the joy of being a little light in everyone's day but also as a "side effect," more success than they needed. We've all heard the old cliché, "Don't put the cart before the horse." You might say Jyoti was living from a "don't put the cash before the soul" philosophy. A young carpenter who later became known as Christ (which means *light*) put it this way: "Seek ye first the kingdom . . . and all these things shall be added unto you."

This confuses the Chotchky Mind like a monkey with its hand caught in a jar, trying to get a nut. This is how some monkeys are captured. A jar of nuts is affixed to the ground. The monkey then reaches in and grabs them, but once its fist is closed, it's too big to pull out of the jar. "Oh no, here come the people. I must let go, but I want those nuts. If I don't let go, I will spend the rest of my days in a zoo where people eat entire bags of nuts while looking at me behind bars. *Ahh!*"

The monkey is then captured, and guess what? He never gets his nuts.

This is how economies crash. We can't let go. We try to leverage ourselves like a monkey trying to get its hand out of a jar. It's not going to work. If we can't afford the nuts, we can't have them. We have to let them go. Our nuts, of course, are our homes, cars, clothes, plasma screens, "fourth meals" . . . things that the Chotchky Campaign, in all of its monkey business, has convinced us we must have.

Darwin's theory is that we evolved out of monkeys. If it is so, the next stage in our evolution might just be to let go of our nuts. Or given the national debt, this could become . . . *the planet of the apes.*

### GNP or GNH?

"How much money is enough money?" a reporter once asked John D. Rockefeller, the richest man who ever lived. He supposedly replied, "Just a little bit more."

In the country of Bhutan, they measure their success by what they call GNH, or Gross National Happiness. That has soul! The Declaration of Independence speaks of the pursuit of happiness. The Founding Fathers understood GNH. However, somewhere along the way, the pursuit of happiness got mixed up with the pursuit of Chotchky. We call it GNP. Remember the advice Victor Lebow gave President's Eisenhower's Council of Economic Advisors: "Our enormously productive economy . . . demands that we make consumption our way of life, that we convert the buying and use of goods into rituals, that we seek our spiritual satisfaction, our ego satisfaction, in consumption . . . we need things consumed, burned up, replaced and discarded at an ever-accelerating rate." And we took his advice.

My wife and I recently watched a television special called *Adventures of an Incurable Optimist* with Michael J. Fox. It documents his journey with Parkinson's, a disease that slowly erodes one's motor functions to the point of uncontrollable shaking. On this show, we witnessed what I would consider the miraculous. While he was visiting Bhutan, his symptoms actually disappeared. He went off his medication. He climbed a mountain and even sat motionless during a tea ceremony. There is no logical explanation for this. Just seeing Michael, still, on a mountaintop, sipping tea in silence was deeply moving. As he became immersed in a culture solely committed to happiness, he was able to find stillness.

### Cause and Effect

Everything, including the economy, is always an effect of a prior cause. The cause of financial crises is most often due to a bankruptcy of spirit. When we are out of touch with the inside, the outside falls apart.

Therefore, I do not see "crises," I see opportunity. This is beautifully captured in the Chinese symbol for the word *crisis:*

Credit: Alecmcconroy at en.wikipedia.

The first character means "danger," the second represents "opportunity." Through the Chotchky Paradigm, we see only danger in the crisis. However, as we begin to live from the soul, we are able to recognize the opportunity.

Thus, I see financial crises as an opportunity to shift our focus onto what really matters. We begin to see that how we have measured our success is, in some ways, a measure of our failure. If we measure the health and growth of our society by how much we consume, then the opposite is true as well: we could just as easily measure the health of our economy by how much we throw away!

Your trash collector can tell you how "healthy" our economy is with the same accuracy as the government and its expensive accounting systems that track our spending. In this way, our trash collectors are economic experts. We think guys with expensive degrees, whom we pay millions of dollars of tax money, should sit around in plush rooms wearing Armani suits theorizing about our economy. Backward. They should all be in coveralls picking up our trash.

So through the Chotchky Paradigm, we are experiencing a financial crisis whenever the trash bags weigh a little less. But from the perspective of the soul, what is it that we are experiencing? Economic growth!

*True economic growth: a deep understanding that the economy is a delayed reflection of human consciousness.*

Like everything else, as we shift toward the soul on the inside, we slowly see a more soulful, balanced world around us. Everything we do today has ripple effects reaching into tomorrow. Understanding this is key. Otherwise, as things improve we take it for granted and begin to slip back into old habits, which create the cycle of "crises" all over again.

After 9/11, there was this sentiment to return to "normal." Even in the President's address, we were told to go back to normal. Please, God, *deliver us from normal.*

Normal has never been the genesis of greatness, brilliance, excellence, or any sort of transformation. Try telling a butterfly to go back to normal.

The same thing seems to happen every time the economy tries to create a cocoon from which we are to emerge. Instead of allowing for the proper gestation period so we can fly, the cry is for everyone to go back to being a caterpillar—to spend more, to buy things we don't need, and to create another false economy like before. Every day, we have an incredible opportunity to create a new normal! The soul is crying out for it. In 2009, the government dumped approximately $800 billion into the system to "stimulate" the economy. This kind of lunacy will work . . . only if the lesson within has been learned. The government could dump all the money in the world into our economy and it would only, ultimately, do more harm if we simply go back to normal.

## Let's Take a Moment . . .

Let's take a moment to give ourselves a raise. Breathe deep, and allow peace to well up from within. Pause, and then reflect on this:

> *I know there is only one economy, the economy within. This is the only truly free enterprise. I choose to give myself a raise today. I'm going to write a check that can't bounce: a reality check. The happier I am with what I have, the richer I become. This is a raise in consciousness to the top floor, corner office of my mind. A raise no one can take away.*

## Chotchky Challenge

When a kid tells another kid what to do, the response often is "You're not the boss of me!" It's a weighty proposition. No one is the boss of you but you. In fact, *you are the boss of your own mind, the manager of your money, the owner of the business of your soul!*

Here's a fun way to invest in your soul. Get a small notepad or create a place in your smartphone called "Chotchky Cash Converted to Soul." Every time you are tempted to part with your time and energy (money) for Chotchky, stop. Write down the amount and walk away. Then at the end of the month, tally your savings. Put that money toward a dream, your favorite charity, or anything else that lifts your spirit. You might even consider opening a separate bank account called a "soul account" and watch the shift that's occurring inside of you as the balance grows.

### Water Wedgie

One rainy winter day, CJ and I hopped on a plane to sunny Palm Springs. He was nine, an age when just being together is enough. We had no plans. What more could we want? Father and son . . . good times.

Everything changed, however, as we entered Palm Desert air space and spotted something that appeared to be an enormous water park. We couldn't be sure, as we were still 1,000 feet up and peeking through one of those little egg-shaped, warped windows. It sure looked like a bunch of tubes twisting and descending. It could, however, be some kind of factory, or worse, a giant bowl of spaghetti. But soon as the "buckle your seatbelt" sign lit up and our ears began to pop, it became clear. This was no factory or bowl of spaghetti, it was a full-blown, water-wedgie-giving, sunburn-makin', hot-dog-sellin' water park!

There was a time, just moments earlier, when the success of our trip relied on nothing. We were truly happy just to be together, come what may. But now, a deep wanting had arisen in us. We *wanted* the waterslides, cotton candy, and leftover pig parts compressed together into the shape of a torpedo.

Now the success of the entire trip rested on one thing: *a water wedgie*. We decided to go there on day three. The only glitch in our plan was that we were no longer present, always daydreaming of cannonballs and bloodshot eyes. To this day, I cannot recall anything that happened leading up to day three; however, day three itself is forever etched in my memory. Our wanting had reached a kind of delirium. At 10 A.M., we threw on our bathing suits, grabbed the sunscreen, hopped in the rental car, and followed the sight of zigzagging tubes suspended in air.

The parking lot felt like a scene from one of those apocalyptic Hollywood productions. I expected a tumbleweed to enter, stage left, at any moment. *We must be early,* I thought. *Probably opens at 11.* We parked and then ambled toward the gate. I knew we were close; the undeniable tangent odor of chlorine filled the air. It seems these "water" parks are actually 50 percent water, 50 percent chlorine. Swimming in them is akin to undergoing radiation treatment with the whole neighborhood.

Upon reaching the gate, CJ grabbed hold and pulled his face right up to the metal wiring, mouth gaping as he gazed upon the paradise sprawled out before him. I looked for some kind of sign, any information that might put to rest the now creeping feeling that things were about to go terribly wrong. I found my sign soon enough. There it was in black-and-white: "Opens March 7th." It was March 3rd and we were booked to fly out of this vacation get-away/retirement commune on the 5th.

*Nooooo!*

I didn't know how to break it to CJ. In his mind, he already had a water wedgie. It was one of those moments you dread as a parent, kind of like the "sex talk."

I took him by the shoulders, looked him in the eyes, and said, "I'm sorry, son. It's closed."

The contorted expression that slowly morphed onto his face reflected his internal anguish. A kind of "water wedgie" of the mind. *It wasn't pretty.* Then without a word, he got back in the car, and we drove to the hotel in silence. I thought maybe he had reached some level of acceptance. At least he wasn't whining. I, myself, was still having a hard time fully acknowledging reality. I wished with all my heart that the water park had been open. *I wanted a hot dog and a sunburn, darn it.* This, of course, only brought suffering. Fighting against reality always does. Through the trial and error of living, I have reached a profound conclusion:

*Wishing for what isn't, is never going to get us what we wish for.*

This is true because, ultimately, underneath all the Chotchky, the only thing we really want is to be at peace, truly happy. Wishing for what isn't and can't be only creates suffering. The Chotchky Mind is constantly wishing for what isn't, arguing with what is, wanting something different, more, bigger, now.

By the time we got to our hotel room, CJ was still silent. He just started packing his bags, which made no sense. Then he rolled them past me and went out the front door while muttering the first words I'd heard out of this nine-year-old kid's mouth in about an hour: "Good-bye. I'm going to the airport. There's no point in being here now." He left. Shut the door behind him. As if he could drive! Or maybe he planned on rolling his bags all the way to the gate.

He actually did say, "There is no point in being here now." Being here now could possibly be the *whole* point. Somehow, we had allowed the "creation of wanting" to completely take us out of the moment, out of Palm Springs, out of our vacation and out of our minds.

The Chotchky Campaign exposes the average North American to 3,000 images per day, each one designed to create within us the same feeling that CJ and I were burdened with the moment we saw the twisting tubes from on high. It's a feeling of discontent with whatever we already have, even if it's each other. Make no mistake about it; there is a battle for our attention, and once our attention is gotten, the *creation of wanting* is the goal. We won't be happy until we get "it." Then, after we get it, it's not all it was cracked up to be. We are suddenly saddled with the same desperate feeling CJ and I felt staring into the park through the gate next to the "closed" sign.

The Chotchky Campaign is designed to create more wanting. Getting the thing only brings fleeting satisfaction; stringing you along like an addict who needs a fix, so you long for the next "improved" or "updated" version. Manufacturers have learned to design things to break or quickly become obsolete, so we need more, more, more.

My first iPhone did not have moviemaking capabilities or a real GPS. This astounded me because before that, I had an "unsmart" phone. With it, I could video my kids one minute and the next be led down the road by a smooth-talking British female voice, turn by turn. Soon a new version of the iPhone was to be released, which promised video and GPS capability. I said to a Mac "genius" at the store, "I can't believe they couldn't have included all of this in the first version."

For the flash of an instant, he gave me a look that had all the informative power of a Shakespearean soliloquy.

*Oh, you poor, sniveling, naïve little man. Don't you know? They could have. They have "updates" chronologically scheduled and psychologically tested for the next several years to keep the Chotchky cycle spinning. With each new release, you will feel discontented, unhappy with what you have. And this is the best part: As others get the newer version before you, you will feel "less than," all of your insecurities validated.*

What I'm saying is that we never get into the "water park"! The creation of wanting keeps us in a state of thinking that "happiness is in something I don't have." From that thinking, how can we ever have happiness?

What CJ and I forgot when we were mesmerized by the sight of giant slides from up yonder was the true location of the only "water park" that matters. The joy, the peace, the fun, and even the "water wedgie" are all an inside job.

## Chotchky Challenge

Put this simple truth into action. It's like magic. Memorize it and cast it like a spell at any situation you have no control over—traffic jams, closed water parks, wiped hard drives, and so on: *Wishing for what isn't is never going to get me what I wish for.*

Why? Because the only thing you ever really want is to be truly happy, at peace.

Click on the Chinese symbol for *crisis* at my secret site and see the opportunity, right there: **www.barryadennis.com/chotchky videos1**. Next, we'll travel back to the beginning of time. To our very origins where we learn from a cheetah whether or not humanity has a chance, and we will discover that it was never the Communists but the cows who may be our greatest enemy.

# CHAPTER 17

# GLOBAL "WARNING"

Some say climate change is nothing to fear; that we are simply experiencing a regularly occurring cycle and that all will change back in good time. Others say that climate change is primarily caused by humans. Contrary to popular concerns, however, if climate change is real, it is still not the number one issue of our time. That would be facing, addressing, and changing the aspect of humanity that would allow such a thing to occur: the Chotchky Paradigm! Regardless of what is happening around us, what is truly needed is a "climate change" on the inside.

Everything that happens on Earth, like the economy, holds within it a message for humanity. It's a *global warning*. Abraham Lincoln said, "America will never be destroyed from the outside. If we falter and lose our freedoms, it will be because we destroyed ourselves."

This is not only true for the United States, but it is also true for the human race. Climate change or not, we are consuming at a clip the planet is not designed to sustain. There is no need for debate on this. All you need to do is ask, for example, the West African black rhino. Oops, you can't—it's extinct. Through poaching, the Chotchky Paradigm has snuffed them out. The earth simply could not keep up with the human demand for black rhino horn. Taking all forms of life on the planet into account, it is estimated that between 50 and 200 species go extinct per day, in great part, because of our ravenous appetite.

Here's the Challenge. "Hunting and gathering" is embedded in our DNA as a survival instinct carried forward from millions of years of barely surviving. Because of this, over the last 100 years we have used our advanced technology to alter our surroundings. We've refined "hunting and gathering" to a science. Everything now comes to us—in stores, on display, in boxes, and sometimes frozen and packaged with preservatives. Canned, with a shelf life that seems, well, impossible. We are that powerful. The deep-seated problem is . . . we haven't altered our behavior to match our new surroundings.

Psychologically, in many ways, we are still Zug dwelling in a cave, wondering how we will make it through another day. And then we wander into the supermarket or the mall and, I'll be darned, everything is right there. How on Earth did this happen? Our instinct says, "Get everything now while it's still here, quick." The irony is this instinct for survival has become our demise. The time to evolve is now.

And, I think it has begun.

When I was a kid, I was quite enamored with cheetahs, the fastest land animal on the planet. In the seventh grade, I wrote a paper on them. I will never forget the day my father told me that he had business in South Africa and that the family was going along for a vacation. There was a lot on our itinerary; however, the only thing I could think about was the two days we would go on safari. With all my heart, I wanted to see a cheetah.

We flew out of Johannesburg in a small twin-engine airplane. A couple of hours later, we landed in the African bush on a gravel landing strip in a place called Londolozi. For a 12-year-old kid, it was almost too much. Like a dream. We gathered our luggage, threw it in the back of a Land Rover, and were off.

On the way to our hut, we came upon a giant pile of elephant dung in the middle of the road. The tracker, a native from one of the local tribes, hopped off the front of the Land Rover and began walking in front of us, pointing the way. After traversing a river and covering many miles of bush, there it was: a huge elephant eating the branches of a tree. We watched him for a while and then he took off running. The chase was on. It didn't take long for the elephant to shake us, but it was an unforgettable encounter. To me, it felt as though I had just seen a velociraptor or a Tyrannosaurus rex.

When we finally made it to our huts, we received an orientation and then were headed on our first official safari.

At one point our guide asked, "What would you like to see?"

Without hesitation, I threw my arms up and shouted, "A cheetah! A cheetah!"

"That's very unlikely," he answered. "There are just a few left, but we'll keep our eyes open."

Being an incurably optimistic kid, I still believed I would see one. Over the next few days, I kept one eye scanning the horizon. We saw a couple more elephants and were told they were a few of the only surviving ones left in the world. We saw one white rhino, and our guide made it clear to us that this was a great honor. The white rhino was predicted to be extinct within a few years. We saw a few giraffes, a pride of lions, a couple of buffalo, and one hippopotamus. Each sighting was a thrill for me. However, I was always hoping for that rare cheetah encounter. Or at least a leopard. That would be a close second.

The days flew by and soon our time on safari was over. As we loaded onto the little plane, my heart was broken. I sat by the small round window, peering out—yes, still hoping to see a cheetah or maybe a leopard. When we took off, I hid my face from my brothers because I didn't want them to see the tears streaming down. It made no sense to me that we would destroy all those animals, many already gone, the rest on the brink. Right there, a few hundred feet off the ground, I promised that if the cheetah somehow survived, I'd be back.

Thirty-one years later, when my youngest son was 12, we boarded a small twin-engine plane in Johannesburg, South Africa, landed on a tiny airstrip in a place called Londolozi, and hopped in a Land Rover.

On the drive to our accommodations, our guide asked us, "What would you like to see?"

Without missing a beat, I of course said, "Cheetah!" I was not much different than I was all those years ago.

The guide replied, "That's a tough one, but we'll keep our eyes open."

During our safari, we saw hundreds of elephants, a thousand buffalo, several prides of lions, about 20 giraffes, and rhino around every bin. One night, we parked next to a tree with a leopard dangling from a branch while her two cubs wrestled just feet away. There is only one reason all of this was possible. Between 1980, the first time I was there, and the fall of 2010, an "internal climate change" occurred in the heart of humanity. A shift. Something happened that is, to me, miraculous. I got to share with my family something that, at one time, I thought would never be. We can change! We have. We are moving closer to the soul. And yet there is still a long way to go.

The cheetah is still extremely endangered, as there are only about 1,000 left in all of South Africa. As we made our way back to our hut to get packed for our flight home, a familiar tear began to fill my eyes. No cheetah sightings, and this might have been my last chance.

Then it happened: an hour before our plane was to take off, our guide received a call from another group: "We've spotted a cheetah." My heart rate tripled. Our guide said it was about 20 minutes away and that if we hurried, we might be able to make it in time to catch our flight.

"Should we go?" he inquired.

"Are you kidding? *Go!*"

We flew! Fifteen minutes later, there I was with my son, the same age as I was when I dreamed of seeing this very sight. Thirty feet away, the fastest land animal in the world sat gazing across the plains. You could feel his speed even in the stillness. The shape of his head. The power of his legs. The color and design of his coat. Did you know, as part of a cheetah's coat, there is a black "tear" dropping out of each eye? It's quite something. For me, now, the cheetah's tear is both a tear of sadness and of joy. A tear of sadness for what has been; a tear of joy and hope for the changes that have come and can be. An internal climate change is happening. It's a return to a truth we all knew at one time. Everything is connected. Knowing this may be our salvation.

When we hear "we are one," it is generally said as a spiritual concept. And yet, there is a sense in which it is true even in our physicality. Let's go back to our origins. Billions of years ago a star exploded in space. The dust created from the explosion began dancing together in a most extraordinary way, heating up to form a ball of magma. Eventually, the outer crust cooled into rock. That's us. And the cheetah. And everything else! We are those rocks come to living, breathing consciousness. Through and as Mother Earth, we are one.

Many indigenous cultures knew this truth without the aid of modern science and technology. With great humility, they walked upon the Earth knowing the footprints they left upon her were footprints on themselves.

But then we created a complex infrastructure. A shortcut between us and Mother Earth. You see, hunting and the actual need for gathering played a spiritual role in our existence. It kept us humble and connected to the delicate and most perfect balance that moves through our planet. From this connection came a kind of wisdom that is just now reawakening.

Before making any important decisions various indigenous cultures would consider how their choices today would affect seven generations in the future: "How will what I am doing now affect my children's children's children's children's children's children's children?" In other words, if I kill this cheetah for his coat today, I will actually be reaching into the future and taking this magnificent breed away from my children.

Reincarnation is an intriguing spiritual philosophy. In fact, many people on the planet believe in it or something similar. Consider this: If reincarnation or something like it is real, then you will be the seventh generation your actions today are affecting in the future.

## Let's Take a Moment . . .

Take a moment to open your hands and heart to the earth:

*Take a deep breath, knowing every inhale and exhale is Holy Communion. As you breathe out carbon dioxide, Mother Earth takes it in and breathes out oxygen for you. Thank you, Mother.*

*Imagine now that you are looking down upon the earth from space. You can feel the abundance of life on each continent and in the oceans as she spins. How beautiful. Can you see what a gift to the universe she is? This tiny blue marble suspended in the vastness of it all. You are so blessed. Bring a greater awareness to every decision you make, consciously, gently, and masterfully creating your collective Master Peace with all of humanity.*

## Chotchky Challenge

On a scale from 1 to 10, rate your ecological awareness level, with 10 being the highest:

- I turn off lights that are not in use. ___

- I recycle everything I can. ___

- When I brush my teeth, I turn off the water. ___

- When I purchase things, I make sure they are healthy for the environment. ___

- I consider how my actions could affect generations in the future. ___

- I know that everything I do has repercussions, either creating peace or confusion. ___

If you scored less than 60, as I did, there is improvement to be made. Realize that these things we do are not an inconvenience; they are part of the curriculum of the soul here at the "University of Earth." Everything is connected. The six practices in this Challenge, done consistently, will help save the cheetah—and all life on Earth.

### But What about the Cows?

Cows play a big role. In fact, this is one aspect of Al Gore's film *An Inconvenient Truth* that leaves me suspicious. Why didn't he mention the impact of cattle on the atmosphere? How can you not? Irrefutable scientific studies have shown that cow flatulence has a huge impact! And one thing is clear: cow emissions are produced by Chotchky demands.

To make bovines grow faster and plumper, in an effort to keep up with our hankerings, we've introduced to the world "corn-fed cows." Corn is not a cow's natural food source. Corn gives the cows gas. Not that they aren't prone to breaking wind on occasion—it just adds a lot more volume. But when you consider that it is estimated the average cow emits between 50 and 132 gallons of methane per day, and that methane is 23 times more damaging to the environment than carbon-dioxide emissions, it seems worthy of our attention. A friend of mine said it is because of our appetite for red meat that people aren't ready to hear the truth. Just go for a walk in a pasture. Trust me, you will hear it. In fact, I think Al Gore should consider a whole new slide presentation: "An Inconvenient Toot."

I'd like to introduce you to Mother Earth now. Join me on this safari by clicking on the elephant at the secret page: **www .barryadennis.com/chotchkyvideos1**. As we continue, you're about to learn a powerful lesson from a guy who, scientifically speaking, is the happiest human alive.

# CHAPTER 18

# BE IN THE WORLD OF CHOTCHKY, NOT OF THE WORLD OF CHOTCHKY

Two thousand years ago, a very wise prophet hung out a lot with 12 others, all of course, in robes. These 12 were quite inquisitive. One evening, to answer their questions in one sweeping motion, the wise prophet said to them and anyone else who would listen: "Be in the world, not of the world."

This sums up the Chotchky Challenge quite nicely. I believe it's more than fair to say that this great teacher was deeply aware of the Chotchky Challenge. In fact, his mission was to help humanity overcome it. Further, his way of teaching, using parables, included "Challenges" designed to inspire in the listener the awareness needed to transcend the "world." And so let's take this Challenge, which was given 2,000 years ago, and has become more relevant today than ever.

What do you think the deeper meaning is, hidden in this little gem of wisdom? If we are not to be "of the world," then what are we to be of? Jot down your answer here: _____

_____

_____.

The wise prophet is saying that despite the influence of the world, we are to be of our true essence, our spirit or soul; to live from the heart. The "world" refers to the consciousness that pervades the masses: Chotchky. As we shift to the soul, we will see that there is a reality where the suffering and dramas of the world are transcended. All the great teachers who ever lived embodied this simple philosophy. They rose above the accepted paradigm or "common sense" of their place and time, and instead lived from the uncommon sense of the spirit.

When being "of the world" and being "of the spirit" are the same, when "spiritual sense" becomes common, the shift will be complete, and I have an idea to help bring about the change. Have you ever seen the bumper sticker that says something to the effect of: "He who dies with the most toys wins"? It is an eloquently condensed reflection of the Chotchky Mind. I'm thinking of creating one that reads: "He who dies with the most *joys* wins."

## Deep Thought

It is more than likely that you, like me, have way more than the most affluent people had not long ago. What do you think the great wisdom teachers of old would think of the world today? Once, in deep meditation, the following came to me as if from the voices of the ones in robes:

*If the accumulation of worldly goods has become unconscious, habitual, ritual, or a pacification, you have forgotten who and what you really are.*

## *What's Wrong with Having Toys?*

Nothing, necessarily. The problem occurs when our toys begin to play with our priorities.

Once, a very wealthy man came to the aforementioned prophet and said, "Master, I will do anything you ask of me so that I might enter the Kingdom of Heaven."

The master replied, "Get rid of all your Chotchky and follow me."

Okay, so the original translation did not actually use the word *Chotchky*. (Although, since he was Jewish, it is possible.) Translating the passage thusly, however, captures the intent.

What's interesting is that the world's prophetic masters all taught that this kingdom the rich man is seeking is close at hand; in fact, it couldn't be any closer. In the ancient Judeo/Christian Gnostic books of the monks of Nag Hammadi, it was written: "The kingdom of the Father is spread out upon the earth and the people don't see it."

Why? Because the Chotchky in our closet and mind is clouding our vision. We have even begun to look for the kingdom of heaven in the piles. Does this mean we should all become monks and relinquish our worldly possessions? Feel free, but that's not my plan. There are many wealthy people who use their influence for good in the world and actually spread the Kingdom of Heaven with it. But for the wealthy guy seeking guidance in our story, he had become so attached to his possessions that they were a distraction keeping him from experiencing heaven.


## Truth or Fiction?

During the economic shift of 2009, a German billionaire lost approximately 500 million euro, which made him "just" a millionaire. Despondent, he then committed suicide.

*Truth or Fiction?*

Truth!

It sounds crazy, I know. And yet, imagine if you had millions of dollars and overnight—poof—say 95 percent of it was gone. Now you're just an average millionaire. If we are honest with ourselves, I think we will find that we would be extremely distraught. I know I would. I also believe it's crazy.

During a talk I gave to a room of over 200 people, I told the true story about a group of Buddhist monks who gave Western scientists permission to study their minds. The scientists ran a battery of tests, including brain scans that can actually measure the level of peace and happiness in the brain. Cool!

They had been studying the minds of people from many different backgrounds for years. This, however, was like nothing they had ever seen. Soon, the scientists began realizing they were in the presence of some of the happiest human beings on the planet. Not only could they feel it in their company, but the science proved it. The parts of the monks' brains that create tranquility, peace, and happiness were constantly lit up.

While measuring the monks' heart rates and brain waves during meditation, the scientists even stood directly behind their subjects and shot a pistol to try to rattle them. The monks did not flinch. There was nothing the scientists could do to take away their happiness. One monk's mind showed so much peaceful activity they finally came to the conclusion that they may very well be in the presence of the happiest human being alive. The monks, of course, had almost nothing but the robes on their backs.

When I finished telling the story, I then asked the audience the following question: If I had $50 million in my right hand and the essence of the monks' consciousness in my left, and you could have either one right now, which one would you pick? Recognize as well, if you choose the monk, most of your worldly possessions would probably disappear.

## Chotchky Challenge

Which one would you choose? Check one below:

$50 million ___ or the consciousness of the monks ___

After I asked the audience the question, the place got uncomfortably quiet. I stood there waiting. You could feel the struggle between the Soul Paradigm and the Chotchky Paradigm. Confusion!

Then one honest man yelled out into the silence, "I'd take the money!"

Everyone burst into laughter. We all knew the correct answer was to accept the enlightened consciousness. Logically, we understand that everything we would do with the money would be an effort to capture the peace, joy, contentment, and happiness that the monks had already found. And yet, the seduction of the world, the clutches of the Chotchky Paradigm, is so strong that we struggle with what we know to be true.

Also, why do you think, along with choosing the monk's consciousness, most of your worldly possessions would likely disappear? Logically, if you have the consciousness of the happiest person in the world, you would no longer have a desire for most of your possessions. You would know your wholeness so you would, by your own volition, let go of your stuff. It would make no sense in such joy and happiness to spend so much time on the care and feeding of your stuff.

It has been said that "money is the root of all evil." This, however, is a grave misquote. The actual statement of truth is, "The love of money is the root of all evil." Adding those few words makes all the difference in the world. When we think we actually love money, we then neglect everything else that really matters, such as our health, our significant others, and the good we could be doing in the world with it. The love of money creates greed, scarcity, and fear, masterfully captured in Charles Dickens's most famous character, Ebenezer Scrooge.

There is a reason that *A Christmas Carol* is one of the most beloved stories in television/movie history. Scrooge embodies the spiritual struggle going on in the world. We are all Scrooge, to some degree or another, hoarding, guarding, counting, collecting, and living in fear. After he is visited by three spirits, he experiences the paradigm shift to the soul in one night. If only we could all be visited by such ghosts. They scared the living Chotchky right out of him!

How would you fare if the ghosts of Christmas past, present, and future visited you tonight? I'm willing to bet each of us would change our ways. Uh oh, here they come . . . *boo!*

Name one thing you would do differently if you really were just visited by the ghosts of your own past, present, and future.

_____

_____

_____

_____

_____

Maybe such a visit would be enough to rid us of one of humanity's most prevalent and disabling mental conditions: *procrastinationotchky.*

We've all had the feeling, not that it's ever really acknowledged. Often, because it's become so habitual, we don't even know we're doing it. Actually glad to see more e-mails to deal with, laundry to be laundered, dishes to be unloaded. Comforted by clutter, disarray, or lack of organization. We get to play the victim/hero: "Look at me. I'm so busy with all the busywork. There is no end to it. I am so unappreciated—you have no idea. Woe is me." This is textbook *procrastinationotchky: a self-destructive behavior rooted in the fear of our own potential that uses busyness as an excuse to keep putting off what really matters.*

It's a detrimental strain of avoidance, as it's the avoidance of life itself. Heck, we not only welcome these distractions, at times we manufacture them. They give us a false sense of purpose as we brush our souls to the side. As C.S. Lewis said, "You can't get second things by putting them first; you can get second things only by putting first things first." The truth is that most of us live our lives doing second things expecting great returns. When I think I might be doing this, I ask myself, *Is this really important? What am I avoiding? What am I afraid of?* For example, when I'm inspired to write a song, if I see it as something that is important, I must allow myself to stay connected to the inspiration. If I don't stay connected, the inspiration will disappear as I worry about trivial things like the placement of pens on my desk. So, *when I'm in the flow, I let the outer go.*

People who know me well may step into my studio and, upon seeing things in disarray, say, "Ah, you have been very productive lately." Staying physically organized at times becomes an excuse to avoid soulful organization. When I'm writing a song, scraps of paper fly everywhere, cups of tea stack up on my piano, e-mails pile up in my computer. Things can become quite a mess, and yet a well-written song is one of the most profoundly organized things in the universe. Every note in its place, every word with its rhyme, every beat just in time. Finishing the song has helped keep my insides in order. Only once it's done do I take the time to get the office back in place.

*Note:* During these times of passionate work, make sure to schedule in enough breathing room to address your family-related responsibilities. There have been times when I have gotten so involved in my projects I lost track of time and neglected family commitments. For this I am greatly sorry. It is a balancing act, and over the years I have gotten better and better at walking that fine line. My greatest "project" is my family, my wife and children. I love you all very much.

I recently had, however, a funny observation:

*Being "anal" can keep us stuck on our "buts."*

*But I don't have enough time or money to follow my dreams.* Really? Somehow there seems to be enough time and money for cable, countless movies, expensive dinners out, racks of clothes, junk food, Snuggies, giant plasma TV screens, surfing the Net, gossiping, texting, lattes, drugs, alcohol, cigarettes, and Red Bull!

We usually have enough time and money, or at least *some* time and money. We just don't have enough commitment. Through the Chotchky Paradigm we actually learn to think that these distractions are necessities. For example, many of us believe we can't function without a latte to start our day. It makes one wonder how Leonardo da Vinci was able to get up in the morning, paint the *Last Supper* and the *Mona Lisa,* design entire cities, compose music, create designs for flying machines, and consult world leaders— without a latte?

I find this hard to believe. Among all those inventions, he must have first concocted some rudimentary espresso machine. Then he finished the *Mona Lisa.* (Either that or he had a Starbucks card.)

If you buy one latte a day for a year, you just drank roughly $1,368.75. That's just one latte without a pumpkin scone (my favorite addiction). Then things really add up. We have enough time and money; we just need to get off our Chotchky **Buts.** Through many years of leading workshops and giving counseling to people who are ready to make their dreams come true, I have found that most of us are living an exhausting and shame-inducing dichotomy. At the core of our beings, our priorities are all much the same, beautiful and soulful. Sincerely ask anyone what their true priorities are and before your very eyes you will actually witness a being switch, for a moment, to the Soul's Paradigm. Priorities are eternal and universal. They are embedded in us as a kind of "true north." We speak of such things as truth, love, peace, our "work" in the world, that which gives purpose to our life and joy to our heart, family, friends, health, passions, integrity, giving, and much more.

But when we analyze how we spend our time, money, and energy in general, there is often a vast discrepancy. Our actions simply do not always line up with our own professed values. We become confused as to why our life isn't working better. There is a level of shame attached to this confusion. The work we are doing here in the Chotchky Challenge is realigning the two by bringing together this holy union between that which we know matters and how we use our lives. I have asked literally hundreds of people what their true priorities are, their deeply held values, and to this day no one has ever said money, TV, shopping, gossip, or junk food.

Let's take a page from the life of the master Leonardo da Vinci. I believe he died with a lot of joys. I, for one, thank God for his presence on Earth. He wrote, "As a day well spent brings blessed sleep, so a life well lived brings blessed death." May we each live in such a way that we one day know this truth, no **buts** about it.

## Chotchky Challenge

How much do you think you're stuck on your Chotchky "but"? Circle the percentage:

10%  20%  30%  40%  50%  60%  70%  80%  90%  100%

Whatever amount you choose represents the percentage of your life for which you are making excuses. Excuses lead to a life of regrets. The Challenge? Become aware of when you make excuses and remember, *this is your life.* Your miracle. Don't let it slip away!

## Deep Thought

You could spend your entire life organizing things that might not be Chotchky, but the time you wasted obsessed with organizing it all could be.

✳

We're about to be visited by the spirit where excuses are a thing of the past. Find the "Scrooge" at the secret page: **www .barryadennis.com/chotchkyvideos1**. As we continue, you're going to discover, once and for all, what your true purpose in life really is.

# CHAPTER 19

# PURPOSE IS AS PURPOSE DOES

### Truth or Fiction?

Medical science has recently proven that having a sense of purpose is the most powerful "medical" prevention for Alzheimer's, heart attacks, and strokes.

*Truth or Fiction?*

Truth!

In an ongoing study of healthy aging by Rush University Medical Center in Chicago, researchers asked thousands of retirement-age men and women to complete a questionnaire in order to rate their "sense of purpose" in life. Those with the highest sense of purpose were half as likely to develop Alzheimer's.

Here is a condensed version of the questionnaire, which can help you ascertain your level of purpose. On a scale from zero to ten, how true are the following statements for you?

- ___ I don't give my future any consideration.

- ___ I try not to think about the future because it almost always brings new problems.

- ___ My daily activities often seem trivial and unimportant to me.

- ___ I used to set goals for myself, but now it seems like a waste of time.

- ___ Sometimes I feel as if I've done all there is to do in life.

Add up your total when you're finished. If you scored 35 or more, since this condensed test is similar to the Rush study, you may run a high risk of dementia and early death. If you scored 10 or less, you are likely among those predicted to live a long, healthy life. No matter what your score is, know that you can improve your outlook.

I hope it has become clear how Chotchky, in all its forms, distracts us from living a deeply purposeful life. This is scientific proof that it can even cause Alzheimer's, not to mention a general shortening between the time of birth and the time of our inevitable date with the Grim Reaper.

I must say that I don't agree with this gloomy association with the one who comes to take us at our time of death. The many documented near-death experiences give us a vastly different picture. Those who have stepped on the other side will most assuredly tell you that it is only "grim" if you have not lived a purpose-filled life. The grim comes in when you have allowed your attention to be overtaken by the meaningless.

I recently read an article interviewing the oldest man in the world. At 114, he stated that the most important factor in living a long and happy life is to live a life of purpose. Reflecting on his 114th Christmas, he said that people's preoccupation with things doesn't make sense to him. This man intuitively knows about the Chotchky Challenge. His time of passing may very well be coming soon, and when it does, I'm thinking there will be no "grim" for him.

"Purpose" is like the pair of glasses we can't find when they are sitting on top of our head. It's similar to this crazy notion of "the one." The idea that there is just one human being for us "out there" and that we must find that one is crazy-making. On a planet of over six billion people, the chances of finding that one individual is inconceivable. It would mean that, in the search for love, 5,999,999,999 people are Chotchky. In reality, there are countless thousands of people who would make wonderful partners for life, for each of us. My wife and I feel very lucky we found each other. However, we don't pretend there isn't anyone else in the world we could and would love. Why? Because like a pair of glasses we can't find on our head, "the one" is with us all the time. This notion has more to do with being happy with ourselves than it does with being happy with someone else. This makes you "the one."

It is the same with this elusive "purpose." For each of us, given our unique combination of gifts, there are many things we could do with great purpose. Having a purpose gives life meaning, yet it doesn't necessarily need to be something massive in scope.

For some, our "purpose" may lead us to become something as clearly outstanding as the first African-American President of the United States. For others, our "purpose" may lead us to serving food in a restaurant. Remember my friend Jyoti? Whatever the case, the critical "peace" is to give your whole self to it because . . .

*Purpose is as purpose does.*

As we live with purpose, whatever we are doing inherently becomes purposeful.

Since my father was a child, he has given purpose to everything he has done, whether it was delivering the paper on his Schwinn or selling Crescent wrenches door to door. In fact, he was so good at selling those wrenches, at the age of 16 he thought it would be his life's work. Dad was devastated when his supervisor told him he wasn't going to get promoted. His supervisor's reasoning was that he believed my father to be "destined for something much greater than selling Crescent tools."

What did his supervisor see in my father that he didn't recognize in himself? Was he more talented than he realized? More intelligent? More capable than the ones who did receive a promotion? Not necessarily. I believe simply giving purpose to whatever we're doing leads us to become more capable. It's the chicken or the egg scenario . . . which comes first, the ability or the willingness to become able?

It was a sense of purpose the supervisor saw that led my father to eventually become one of the most successful franchisees of the Dale Carnegie courses in the history of the company. He later started his own leadership-training company and has since written 15 books on the subject. What is the thread that led my father from the age of 16, as a Crescent wrench salesman, to a bigger life than he could have ever imagined? One thing: He gave purpose to whatever he did and the universe responded in kind. This is a pure example of what many refer to as the Law of Attraction. When we give our heart and soul to whatever it is we're doing, make it purposeful, the universe will lead us to a more meaningful life than we could have ever conceived.

Our first step is simple and yet so feared. We must commit. Through the Chotchky Paradigm, we become paralyzed, afraid of commitment because we think whatever we are doing can't be it. Therefore, committing is always seen as a waste of time. It's got to be something else, somewhere else. This leads nowhere.

## Deep Thought

Ultimately, every human being on the planet has the exact same purpose. It is the purpose of this book: *to live from the soul in our own unique way.* How we express this one purpose can be as varied as the number of people on the planet.

What do you think your individual expression of the one purpose is at this time in your life? Write it in the space below:

---

---

_____

_____

_____

Now, move your feet.

An added bonus to living life on purpose is that the greatest diet there happens to be is purpose itself! To be excited about something that has meaning takes empty cravings away. We no longer look for meaning in food, dysfunctional relationships, drugs, or junk.

I've got a palm full of purpose waiting for you now. Go to the secret web page and click on the hands: **www.barryadennis.com/chotchkyvideos1**. Next we take a trip to Ireland, where my wife accidentally annihilates the entire trip. You'll see.

# CHAPTER 20

# MOMENTS, NOT MEMENTOS

To stay connected, inspired, in the flow of a life lived with purpose, it helps to build in a pause and regularly reflect. It keeps us in tune with our soul. Incredibly enough though, one of the most stressful things we often do is go on vacation. That stress is sometimes created by the Chotchky Mind's desire to capture, collect, and hold on to every moment through mementos and photos. When we spend too much time trying to make mementos out of moments, we lose momentum. Life is moving in a pure, sweet, glorious pace like a river moving through a valley on a spring day. Our preoccupations can dam that river.

As the Chotchky Mind tries to grab every moment, the moments actually begin to slip right through our fingers, like trying to grab the water in the river. We simply aren't present. What is right before us is better than any gift-shop Chotchkies. The true vacation is in the Now—and that doesn't cost anything nor does it take precious suitcase space, only to be put in storage if it doesn't break before we get home.

I'm not saying we shouldn't ever buy a keepsake. I am saying it helps to bring some Chotchky Awareness to the gift shops with you. Almost everything you will see while walking through any tourist section of any city is designed to trigger the Chotchky Trance, rendering us unconscious to the point where we are actually pulling out our credit cards, cash, and even traveler's checks to buy trinkets when, at home, we actually think about the price of groceries.

On the other hand, it can be quite a cultural experience to wander around the local markets. I bought some juggling bags at a medieval festival on an island in Sweden during a family vacation. The experience itself was priceless, and I love those juggling bags. I'm a juggler. It's something I do. This makes sense. However, some stuff I bought at the medieval festival was just, well, evil. Stuff that we lugged around the world, only to wonder why we bought it when we got home. Like this "flint" we purchased. I think that's what it's called. It makes sparks. The Chotchky Mind sees something that makes sparks and thinks, *I can't live without it.* You actually think you will take it home and use it to light a fire. But why? Nostalgia? Do we miss the old days, before lighters and matches? This is how the Chotchky Mind works, especially on vacation. That flint is still floating around our house somewhere.

"Moments, not mementos" also means bringing awareness to the amount of time you spend putting an image-capturing device between yourself and the actual experience you are trying to capture. There is a fine line. I know that taking pictures can add greatly to an experience. Sometimes stopping to take a picture helps us to be present to the moment. Other times it becomes a preoccupation.

When I was 21 years old I went to Russia as part of a group of around 500 people working for peace. At the time I was a member of the *paparotchky*. I took so many pictures and videos that when I think back on the experience, I actually see images in my mind of a blinking red light telling me the video camera was in record mode. I feel the underlying stress I felt trying to "capture" everything. I truly missed half of the experience.

Today, I allow myself to experience a whale breaching before I try to take a picture. I want to really see it. To feel it. This has helped reduce the overwhelming piles of pictures and terabytes of memory cluttering my drawers and hard drives. I try not to let a "Kodak moment" become more about the Kodak than the moment.

Once in the middle of a tour of Ireland, over dinner, we began viewing all of the pictures we had taken with our new digital camera. My wife accidentally pushed the "reformat" button, not knowing it was another word for "delete all." For a moment, we actually felt like we lost our past—as if all the joy we had experienced didn't count.

I finally said to Heather, "There's nothing you can do about it. Let it go. *Let it go!*"

And the truth is, *phototchky* can keep us stuck in the past, reminiscing about "the good-old days," when the best day, the only day, is today.

My advice: Take no pictures on the way up the mountain. Everything you see on the way up will be there on the way down. This goes for any experience. On the way back, you will know what really matters because you will have experienced the moments. You will have clear memories and feelings of the "mountain." That's living. Then on the way down, you will be much more conscious and aware of what really matters. You can spare yourself all the phototchky to wade through later, but most important, you will have experienced life from the first-person perspective.

Moments are not Chotchky. Moments are life. But we sometimes create *momentotchky* by mindlessly spending money on souvenirs and constantly putting a wall between us and reality in an attempt to capture it when the greatest image-capturing device in the universe is between our two ears. Use it, and you won't need a flint to make a spark, for your life will be a flame.

## Deep Thought

The ability to long for the past is uniquely a human trait. If lower life forms had this ability, we would never have evolved from the primordial goop we may have once been, *for fear of moving on.*

Realize that every moment is a miracle. Time and space are an illusion. This is not conjecture—it is tested, proven science. Therefore, within each moment is magic; God's sleight of hand whipping up a miracle before our eyes for the enjoyment and enrichment of the soul. Each moment is to be fully lived in. Reflecting on the past, learning from the past, appreciating rich memories is beautiful. Dwelling there, however, in the past or the future, we skip right over the splendor of now. One is gone and can never be had again. The other will be, but will be missed if we are not present.

*Every moment is the memento, every year the souvenir.*

I've got quite a moment for you. Click on the beach chairs at the secret site: **www.barryadennis.com/chotchkyvideos1**. Then we're going to begin performing miracles!

# CHAPTER 21

# PEOPLOTCHKY

As I mentioned at the beginning of this book, if you do a search on the word *Chotchky*, you will find many spellings and definitions. One of the actual definitions is "a dolled-up woman who looks good on a man's arm." She is Chotchky—literally. What is being described is a "trophy wife" or "rent-a-date"—a person whose purpose is to keep up appearances.

*Peoplotchky: anyone who encourages and
enables behaviors that do not support your soul*

As we go through life, our self-defeating habitual behaviors must be addressed to give the final paint strokes to our Master Peace. When a self-sabotaging behavior has been acknowledged, and you are ready to change, it is vital to surround yourself with people who encourage you. This is probably the most powerful aspect of Alcoholics Anonymous. First, ask the people in your life to support the change. If they are unable or unwilling, then those individuals have become peoplotchky. It is written that the Nazarene who walked on water could not perform miracles in his own town, *in Nazareth*. There was too much *friendotchky* around. He had to make new friends—those who would support his desire to transcend the Chotchky Paradigm—and surrounded himself with the men would become known as the 12 disciples.

He could not perform any miracles until he left town and made new friends.

If you don't believe in the miracle stories, then maybe this example does little to inspire. If you feel, for example, that no one could walk on water and that it's all "just" a myth, it is important to understand that myths arose from our collective consciousness in an attempt to explain spiritual truths. And, by the way, miracles do exist. Like for example, your life.

The question is: Are we allowing this miracle to reach its grandest expression? The truth *within* the story or "myth" that he could not perform miracles in his own town, historical or not, is undeniable. In order for the miracle within our lives to come to full fruition, we must surround ourselves with "soul mates": friends at a soul level. There is an opportunity here for all of us to rise together. What a gift it would be to ask our friends and loved ones to support us: "I am letting go of [insert Chotchky behavior] and focusing on my soul's purpose. Will you support me in this?"

There is nothing more loving than asking friends to support the change moving through you now. If they are unable to reciprocate, then the most loving thing you can do might just be to let them go. A friend of mine used to meet regularly for lunch with a specific group of gals. She began noticing that whoever happened to be missing from the group became the subject of the conversation, and it was not flattering! My friend began to feel out of integrity just by showing up for lunch. She also began to wonder what they said about her when she wasn't there. She finally told them she could no longer be a part of the group. She "unfriended" these individuals.

It wasn't easy. However, looking back, she can clearly see it was the most loving thing to do for everyone.

## Chotchky Challenge

Let go of any "friends" who do not support the very best in you. Then reach out to friends or loved ones and give them the gift of asking for their support in your transformation. Can you identify any habitual behaviors that are creating a wall between you and your best self? Think of one. Impatience, anger, defensiveness, gossipy tendencies, tardiness, procrastination, judging? Or overindulgence in alcohol, food, and the like? Think about it, and then jot it down in the space below.

*The behavior I am letting go of is:*

_____

_____

_____

What a gift it would be for your loved ones to have another human being say, "Can you help me be a better me?" Pick up the phone or write an e-mail stating your intention, asking for their loving support. Most likely, this invitation will not only transform your life and theirs, but your relationship might also take the glorious leap to "soul mates."

### *DNA—the Chotchky Inside of Us*

We can't really blame those who are walking, breathing, talking Chotchkies in our life. We all have a friendotchky list. The sobering question is: Whose list are you on? Yes, you and I are someone's peoplotchky! We can't help it. It's in our DNA. Which is why facing our Chotchky may be the next step in evolution. This is illustrated by the avatars of the ages who teach that our internal reality becomes our external experience: "As within, so without."

One day while tossing rocks off the bank of a river, I began telling a friend about the Chotchky Challenge. She became visibly intrigued as one of my rocks skipped right across the top of the water in a way that, to me, seems quite miraculous. She is currently a premed student and began to see a connection between our DNA and Chotchky.

Her eyes lit up as another rock bounced across the water. "It's so true. You won't believe this. Over 90 percent of our DNA is Chotchky. It's useless; it serves no purpose. Only a small amount is actually needed by our bodies to form and maintain the human organism. No wonder we make so much Chotchky. It's in our DNA. Maybe facing the Chotchky outside of us is the next step in evolution."

She then tossed a rock that seemed to bound across the river and, at the halfway point, as if by magic, it made a left turn. *Like it changed its mind.*

As we face the Chotchky outside, it represents and is a reflection of the Chotchky inside. Evidence of this is the number of random, inconsequential, flighty, distracting thoughts that incessantly barrage our mind. That's *DNAotchky* floating around like sediment in a river. Many of these "floaters" are our worries.

*"I am an old man and have known a great many troubles,
but most of them never happened."*

— ATTRIBUTED TO MARK TWAIN

I would venture to say that something in the neighborhood of 90 percent of the things that trouble us never happen. Those worries are Chotchky controlling our life. And arguing with these thoughts just adds more sediment. The trick is to let them settle to the bottom of the river of our mind so that clarity can come to us. From there, we too can change direction like a rock on a magical skip.

### Let's Take a Moment . . .

Let's take a moment for clarity itself. This is an exercise you can do whenever the Chotchky-based world that feeds it creates tension and stress.

This is our DNA meditation: Our Dog's Natural Awareness or Divine Natural Awareness; it's just that most dogs seem to stay connected to this divine state. We all know that, generally speaking, a dog's natural awareness is that of love and acceptance. And since we are created in the "image and likeness" of these godly attributes, it is our natural state as well. With all the sediment floating around in our Chotchky-filled lives, however, we forget. At times we become angry, resentful, and grumpy. We complain about the weather as if complaining could change it. We worry as if worrying had magical powers. I've never seen a dog fall into such madness.

Let's remember our divine natural awareness right now:

*Simply breathe in right now, in this moment. Then hold it . . . and release.*

*Breathe in through the nose and out through the mouth, and continue to focus on your breathing.*

*If thoughts arrive, let them be a rock skipping across a river. Gone. The sediment of the mind now becomes still and drops to the bottom.*

*Now take a deeper breath, allowing your diaphragm to expand. Hold it and release. Close your eyes and do this three times. No thoughts, just breath.*

*Relax and allow your breathing to settle into a natural flow, the ebb and flow of your body, much like the tides of the ocean. Let a gentle, soft, barely noticeable smile come to your face. A genuine smile of being, like you may have seen on a dog at times.*

*Allow peace, happiness, and joy to simply be in the "cup" that is your being. This is natural, an awareness you were born with.*

*You may wish to simply contemplate for a moment what you are grateful for. Grateful for the food that you eat, grateful for your livelihood, your loved ones, this body for your soul. Grateful for your Dog. Grateful to the Divine Natural Awareness rising in you now. This is your true DNA.*

## Chotchky Challenge

Do this or a similar simple breathing meditation once a day. When done with consistency and discipline, peace and happiness become your default mode. It is so very easy and yet in the Chotchky-based world, we get so busy that we often don't take the time to become centered and listen to our soul.

If you do this meditation just once a day, it may change the tenor of your very life.

Okay, my friend, I have a peaceful moment for you. Choose the dog at the secret site now: **www.barryadennis.com/chotchky videos1**. Coming up, we go for a ride in a minivan through a very exclusive neighborhood. Embarrassed?

※　※　※

# CHAPTER 22

# SILLY UTILITY VEHICLES

You may remember my friend who asked me to perform her own funeral. The ceremony was beautiful. As I watched the horse-drawn carriage trot toward the funeral home, the sound of the hooves clopping rhythmically against the ground transported me back to a simpler, more peaceful time.

*Then a Hummer drove past with music blasting through its tinted windows.*

I wondered what my friend would have been thinking as she looked down upon the scene from heaven. I'm thinkin' she was thinkin' . . . *Chotchky!*

Is an SUV inherently Chotchky? Of course not. If you use it to carry utilities and go off-road on a regular basis, your money has been well spent. I know people who regularly go to the mountains for winter play. SUVs are perfect for such activity, but many are never taken out to play. Those two extra wheels of power and that extra suspension for going over big rocks and crossing rivers is sadly left unused.

> *SUVotchky: the prevalence of "utility vehicles" that will never carry "utilities" or go "off-road" as they are designed to*

*do, which is the reason they cost so much—bought and paid for through the Chotchky Paradigm!*

Some SUVs are a physical manifestation of the Chotchky Mind's insensibilities around money and its constant stance in fear, provoking the "just in case" response: *I need one of these just in case a meteor lands in my front yard. With this, I should be able to scale it and still get to the mall.*

The Chotchky Mind also, of course, must have the latest thing, keep up with the Joneses, and associate its worth with the cost of its possessions.

Even if an SUV was used a few times to go off-roading or drive in snowy conditions, I hope those few experiences came with caviar, champagne, and a butler in the fold-out seat, because if you amortize out the extra approximately $4,000 you spent, that would come to something like $1,000 per off-road excursion. (Not to mention the fact that the trip may not have been enjoyed from worry that the off-road vehicle might get dirty.)

Many people who drive SUVs might actually be more comfortable and find more use in a minivan. However, the Chotchky Paradigm wouldn't allow it. Through this flawed vision, cars have become a status symbol. *We often buy cars that we can't afford in an attempt to fit in or put on appearances while we hold our soul in the trunk for ransom.*

I recently met one of the richest men in Oregon, and he happens to drive a VW Bug. He gets it.

My wife and I both used to think we would never be caught dead in a minivan. So far, luckily, we're correct, although we have been caught alive and well driving one right in front of our neighbors. I was only a little embarrassed, which faded as my paradigm shifted, moving closer to the soul.

Interestingly, we fell so in love with our minivan, we bought another one. The second minivan turned out to be one big giant chunk of Chotchky. It was almost never used. Just took up tons of space and filled us with guilt for not driving it. We're back to one van that we actually share with other people when needed. Cool.

I have a friend who bought a very expensive SUV. He had never, not once, used it for anything SUV-ish. He could have been driving a 1967 VW Bus or even a Bug, a Mini Cooper, or even, possibly, a mini-scooter. (Now that I would like to see.)

Then one day it snowed out. As I've mentioned, when it snows in Portland, it's like the Day the Earth Stood Still, especially in the Willamette Valley where I live. ("Willamette" is Native American. Native Americans could have actually used an SUV. There were no roads!)

So it almost never snows in this region, and when it does, it melts. Well, one day about an eighth of an inch actually accumulated. My friend, who spent several thousand dollars extra for four-wheel drive and truck suspension for just such an occasion, wouldn't leave the house. Thousands of dollars wasting away in the garage. Not that you need a four-wheel-drive vehicle to drive in an eighth inch of snow, but I suppose it wouldn't hurt. Other people drove to his house and picked him up—people who, by the way, were driving regular old two-wheel-drive vehicles.

My wife and I used to drive an SUV, but never really did any SUV stuff in it, except occasionally hop curbs. (That was fun. It was worth it.)

It was hard for us to let go of it. I enjoyed driving it around, knowing at any moment I could slog through two feet of mud, climb a rock wall, or get air off a sand dune. Too bad none of these occasions ever presented themselves in the city. Letting it go truly was a paradigm shift. One clear day, we just sold it and bought a Prius. It is now my wife's favorite car ever. She's a very successful business owner and truly could drive any car she wished. One of the reasons we love it so much is because it takes up less space. Imagine that. Liking something because it's smaller. The only bummer is that it gets around 50 miles per gallon. We're not sure what to do with the money we save.

## Deep Thought

We all share an SUV, it's our Soul Universal Vision. Our actions, however, do not always line up with that vision. It is a vision in which all are treated equally. Cars and homes and other things add no value to a human being, for a human is already priceless. Judging others based on what they own does not support this vision, nor does being driven by status symbols. When we do this, our possessions possess us.

## Truth or Fiction?

• The executive VP of North American auto operations at Honda said, "People who buy SUVs are in many cases buying the outside first; they are buying the image of an SUV."

*Truth or Fiction?*

Truth!

This statement was based on studies by the car industry itself.

• SUVs kill 3.4 times as many pedestrians per year as do regular cars.

*Truth or Fiction?*

Truth!

This is from a study published by the journal *Injury Prevention.*

## Chotchky Challenge

Take a moment for true self-refection. What percentage of you is driven to drive, or would like to drive, a certain kind of car for the status it has come to represent? Motivation is everything. The "why you do" is more important than the "what you do."

0% 10% 20% 30% 40% 50% 60% 70% 80% 90% 100%

If you drive an SUV but never really use it for true SUV stuff, consider selling it! Get a vehicle that actually fits your lifestyle—maybe a minivan—and then as you transcend "status symbolism," use the money you saved to fuel a dream. Make sure that "what" you do is motivated by a pure and true "why."

I have to check in with myself on this regularly. I truly have no issue driving our old family minivan though any neighborhood regardless of its socioeconomic status. But, when I'm in my BMW, do I want to be seen? Ah, there is the soul check.

### *Where Is the "Soul"?*

The Tao Te Ching is widely considered among the greatest dissertations on wisdom ever written. Roughly translated, it means "the book of the path to enlightenment." It contains an elaborate and complex passage that shows that even thousands of years ago Chotchky was challenging.

I have reproduced it here in its entirety, as it is worthy of your consideration. Please take the time to study the following and then thoughtfully consider the subtle nuances and innuendo:

> *"Have stuff . . . be confused."*
>
> — TAO TE CHING

Let's go for a ride now through a neighborhood that transcends status! Choose the "neighborhood" at the secret site: **www .barryadennis.com/chotchkyvideos1**. And for the grand finale, we're going to paradise.

# FORWARD

---

Truly one of the most powerful and challenging songs ever written is "Imagine" by John Lennon. Among many other soulful images, he asks us to imagine having no possessions. And that, if somehow we could really understand what he is saying, there would no longer be a need for greed or hunger. It is true, is it not? He is suggesting a complete paradigm shift. A move to the soul.

I'd like you to meet a friend of mine who I think can help. His name is Jay. This is not his actual name; it's his English nickname. He was born, raised, and has never left the island of Bora-Bora. If there is a physical spot on Earth that could actually have been the Garden of Eden, it is Bora-Bora. When you approach it, it's dreamlike, as the crater of a volcano slowly appears to rise up from the depths of the ocean. This crater is the island. The water is a color so blue-green that it gives the impression of thickness, as if it were a gigantic bowl of lime Jello. Jay and his native "family" of friends fish with homemade spears and still travel the ocean in catamarans as did his ancestors thousands of years ago. It's a place so cut off from the rest of the world that they live, in comparison to us, backward.

When I first met Jay, he said with exuberance, "I'm Jay, and this is my island!" He took my family and me to the top of the volcano where you can see the curve of the earth, and when the sun went down, I felt as though the heart of Gaia was there beneath my feet. As we gazed out, transported to another time, Jay spoke: "Here, we are all family. We know that what we do to one person, we do to the other; we do to ourselves. We know that here on this island." Then he paused, swallowed, and squinted his eyes a bit. "But I think the rest of the world has forgotten."

Jay has very little in the ways of worldly possessions. He lives in a small hut and has nothing but the bare necessities. And yet, he is a millionaire. Quite literally. He explained to me that he owns 50 acres on Bora-Bora and that he could sell those acres to developers for several millions of dollars. Yes, he could buy a yacht, drive a Hummer, have a woman on each arm, and eat caviar by the spoonful. The Western mind reels. *What on Earth is he doing living in a hut on an island where there's nothing to have and nothing to do? He must be out of his mind.* Maybe. Or, just maybe, he never lost it. There's no Chotchky to confuse him, to take his heart and turn it against his soul.

Without reservation he explained, "Living off the land and sharing it with my family means much more to me than any amount of money."

Bora-Bora is a part of what is known as French Polynesia, under what is called the "French protectorate." Jay laughed. "I don't know what they are trying to protect us from," he said.

The natives don't need protection from anything. Except perhaps the Chotchky Paradigm the French are introducing.

The word *protectorate* is propaganda. In fact, in Bora-Bora, where people have lived in relative harmony with the land and each other for thousands of years, one might even say the French are Chotchky. They are taking up precious space on this island, causing tension and confusion, taking the natives' minds off of what is truly important. They are attempting to force the islanders to live by their laws and accept their morals. There is even a silly little jail as a constant reminder.

On Bora-Bora the "unconditional love" many of us strive for is commonplace. Bonds between mothers and children are exceptionally strong, rooted into the culture and passed from one generation to the next. Loving bonds in the community extend beyond what we normally see in "developed" countries, even between the best of neighbors.

Jay told me this story of one local mother. On a beautiful, warm afternoon her 18-year-old son, Mick (not his actual name) was playfully wrestling in the sand by the shore with one of his friends. They often got in quite a tussle. This day more so than most. Mick jumped on the back of his friend, who then flipped him over his shoulder. Upon landing, Mick's head hit a rock. He died instantly.

Under French law, Mick's friend had to be arrested for "aggravated assault." For murder. This concept is foreign to the natives. Even so, the boy was sent to the silly French jail. Before the "French protectorate" arrived, the natives had never heard of such a thing. When the police came to take him away, Mick's mother, who had just lost her son by the hands of this boy, got on her hands and knees and begged the police not to take the boy away. She tried to explain that "This boy, too, is my son. All the children are my children." This made about as much sense to the French police as "jail" made to the natives. She followed on foot to the steps of the jail cell. She wept as she pleaded with the police to let the boy go. She told them that he was in great pain, and he needed to know that she loved him, as she did the one he killed.

This woman came with the boy's biological mother for months, every day, asking for his release. She never needed to say "I forgive you" because to say such a thing would mean that at one time, she was angry, felt victimized, or held a grudge. In the old ways, these are foreign ideas. The concept of forgiveness, as we know it, is not needed. It is transcended by acceptance and love. From the paradigm of the soul, there is nothing to forgive because the soul does not hold grudges or feel victimized, ever.

This woman, pleading at the steps of the jail, kneeling at the feet of these foreigners who have infiltrated her world, is, for me, the very image of our soul, pleading at a jail around our minds and hearts, petitioning us to remember a truth far above that which we have accepted and allowed to become normal.

Through her steadfast and unwavering devotion to the ways of her ancestors, to the ways of her soul, she refused to give up trying to free the one who killed her son. I know, it seems backward, but I assure you it is not. The "native" or original mind knows we are one. Therefore she knows he is, in spirit, her son, too. And on the island, they intuitively know there is no freedom in hatred, anger, grudges, and spite.

Intuitively, we all know this. We once locked that truth behind prison bars of Chotchky, shackled by attachments to "things," to being "right," or our addiction to drama, excuses, worry, and fear. We have been slowly clearing this emotional clutter from the first page of this book. With every Challenge we have taken, underneath, behind, and through each clearing of excess, there has been a deeper work going on. Directly and indirectly, we have been chipping away at the most detrimental form of Chotchky, which is directly connected to the soul: emotionalotchky. Let's go there now.

## Let's Take a Moment . . .

Take a deep breath, and allow your body and mind to be still.

*I ask you now, who do you need to forgive today? Recognize that any anger you feel has no effect on the person. It is hurting you. You know this intuitively, and its logic is sound. Allow this wisdom to soak in every cell of your mind, clearing out any ill will toward another human being. Ill will is ill-logical, for it only creates illness in you. It is like drinking poison and expecting the other person to die. So, begin the heavenly work of forgiving.*

*Can you understand that those you need to forgive have a past just as you do and that there was hurt in their past? Can you see that underneath all of the dysfunctional behavior, they are crying out for love? What if you allow these truths to bring compassion to your heart? As you do, you are being set free from your own bondage.*

*Think of the ones you need to forgive now. Hold them in your heart, knowing their pain. And now, with all your heart, to set your mind free, say to them, "I understand you want to be loved as much as I do. I forgive you." As you do this work, you forgive yourself. Therefore, the most "selfish" thing you can do is to forgive.*

## Deep Thought

We all are natives on an island. Blue-green, round, and magical, the earth floats in the sea of empty space. We have all gathered here to learn the lessons of the soul.

### *And So It Begins . . .*

Mick's mother did not give up. Eventually, the boy was released and welcomed into her family as one of her own. With the same steadfast devotion, we too can free our "innocence" from the foreign influence that is Chotchky.

This is oh-so-clear since you have just victoriously taken the Chotchky Challenge. This is, of course, only the beginning. The Challenge is laid out before you each and every day. It is everywhere. It is the Challenge we face as one human family. What you have now are the tools to create your true Master Peace. Therein lies . . .

*Liberotchky: the complete and total freedom from all things Chotchky.*

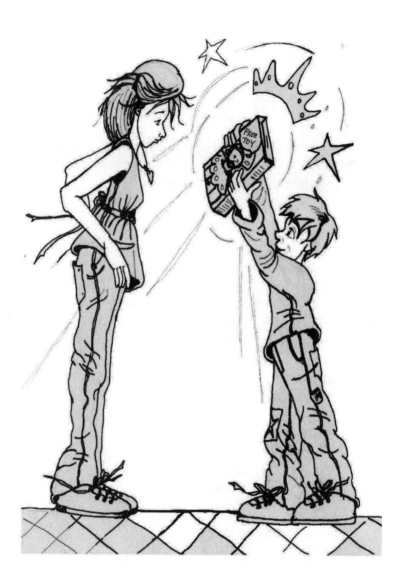

# HOW IT ALL STARTED

It all started with a box of fortified kid's cereal,

The words "free with purchase" on the outside;
    what a deal!


There was a prize! A free prize inside.

So I begged my mom "please," I begged till
    I cried.


"I'll do my chores as soon as we get home" . . .
    but I lied.

I'd do anything for the toy in that box
    of cereal, fortified.

It looked like it was alive from the picture on
   the box,

 It looked like it could talk, and bounce on its
   shocks.


When I got home, why, I didn't care.

That sugar coated cereal flew everywhere.

Clearly the toy was all that really mattered.

Not the cereal that now crunched under foot . . .
scattered.


As I reached into that box and felt
the magical prize,

I ripped it out with all my might, gazed with
longing eyes.

But it didn't look at all like the picture on the box.

"What a rip off," I yelled. "It's tiny, and doesn't even have shocks."

My mom looked at the thing and nodded
  with disgust

As she got out the broom to clean up the spots
  of dust

Maybe that toy would never be what it seemed.

Could it ever live up to what a little boy dreamed?

So, I put it on my shelf with all the other odds
and ends.

Things that I thought would somehow be my best
friends,

Things that I thought would fill an emptiness in me.

That box started a cycle; I'd take anything
for "free."

And every trinket for a deal on the QVC,

Maybe this thing or that is what's missing . . .
could be!

Always so excited for that box to arrive.

Always so disappointed when I looked inside.

There came a point when I knew I was fooling myself:

I would buy stuff and then just put it on the shelf.

But the day that changed everything, the day
    I'll never forget

Was the day I tripped on a Chia Pet growing
    on the 12th step.


I fell down those stairs through piles of
    collectible junk.

Broke several bones at the bottom, on a
    storage trunk.

And while the days passed in that well-made
hospital bed,

Things began to clear up, at least inside of
my head.

When I finally got home, on crutches, and in
    stitches,

I organized all my junk, from bad art to gift
    store dishes.


Then I had the biggest yard sale ever held on
    planet earth.

I got pennies on the dollar, still, much more than
    it was worth.

I gave toys to children in need, and to gangsters, I gave my "bling."

I had truckloads and truckloads of recycling.

Then in a huge bonfire, I let the last of it go.

I even roasted marshmallows in the fire embers' glow.

The only thing I kept was that prize from the
cereal box.

That "free" toy from my childhood that didn't
have any shocks,

That piece of plastic made in China is how the
    cycle got started,

How me and my soul were so duly departed.


It holds a prominent place on the kitchen window sill

Though it was thirty years ago now, somehow, still

It reminds me when I'm tempted, of the lessons
    I've learned,

Of all the misplaced clutching for that which
    I yearned.


The insight I gained truly set my soul free.

You see the prize was inside,

But the box . . .


Was me!

---

I would like to say good-bye, so go to the final link on the
secret site and choose the key: **www.barryadennis.com/
chotchkyvideos1**.

# ACKNOWLEDGMENTS

I'd like to begin by thanking my wife, Heather, for not making me sleep on the couch after I let the van catch on fire. I suppose that episode encapsulates one whole dynamic of our relationship. Thanks for loving and putting up with the little kid in me. You're one in a billion. I'm so blessed to have all your support. I love you.

Harold Bloomfield—it was you, your Birkenstocks, and your Moses bloodline that unleashed the Chotchky! Thanks, brother.

Betsy, thank you for helping me with my book proposal, which eventually got me the book contract. Jenna Glatzer, my editor, thank you for your sense of humor and gentle guidance. Thank you to Reid Tracy and Cheryl Richardson for selecting me, and for all the support at Hay House.

Kirk and Page, thanks for letting me shack up at your place and cogitate upon the philosophical ramifications of the subject herein. Your enthusiastic support is always felt.

CJ, our shenanigans have become many of my most cherished memories. Being your dad is my greatest honor. You are my teacher, my buddy, and my cohort. Thanks for giving the shirt off your back to the boys of Lovemore. I *love* you *more* than you may ever know. And Xander, you too are my teacher, and being your stepdad is a blessing beyond anything I could have ever imagined. I really think that you, maybe more than anyone, get me and the ideas in this crazy bit of work. Thanks for teaching me how to fix anything (technotchky).

And finally, to my parents, for always being such an incredible support system. Mom, I'm so glad you were able to forgive Dad the day he threw away your Chotchky. And Dad, I'm so glad you threw Mom's Chotchky away! Love you both so much.

# ABOUT THE AUTHOR

**Barry Dennis** is a world-renowned singer-songwriter, inspirational speaker, and cutting-edge spiritual teacher. He is the founder of Celebration Church in Portland, Oregon; as well as the groundbreaking "Coexist Celebration," a movement without walls whose mission is to create peace of mind, heart, and planet through understanding and joy. The Coexist movement includes leaders from all the world's spiritual traditions and is held in different locations around the globe.

Barry has performed his music around the world and has recorded three CDs, *One Among the Many, Make Me an Instrument,* and *Livin' in This Love.* He has written several hundred short stories and poems and has created over 50 life-enrichment programs, which are available in CD form and downloads. All of this can be found on Barry's website, including the innovative "Exceptional Life" online course.

Website: **www.barryadennis.com**

✳  ✳  ✳

We hope you enjoyed this Hay House Insights book.
If you'd like to receive our online catalog featuring additional
information on Hay House books and products, or if you'd like
to find out more about the Hay Foundation, please contact:

**INSIGHTS**

Hay House, Inc., P.O. Box 5100, Carlsbad, CA 92018-5100
(760) 431-7695 or (800) 654-5126
(760) 431-6948 (fax) or (800) 650-5115 (fax)
**www.hayhouse.com®** • **www.hayfoundation.org**

***Published and distributed in Australia by:*** Hay House
Australia Pty. Ltd., 18/36 Ralph St., Alexandria NSW 2015 • *Phone:*
612-9669-4299 • *Fax:* 612-9669-4144 • www.hayhouse.com.au

***Published and distributed in the United Kingdom by:*** Hay House UK, Ltd.,
292B Kensal Rd., London W10 5BE • *Phone:* 44-20-8962-1230
*Fax:* 44-20-8962-1239 • www.hayhouse.co.uk

***Published and distributed in the Republic of South Africa by:***
Hay House SA (Pty), Ltd., P.O. Box 990, Witkoppen 2068
*Phone/Fax:* 27-11-467-8904 • www.hayhouse.co.za

***Published in India by:*** Hay House Publishers India,
Muskaan Complex, Plot No. 3, B-2, Vasant Kunj, New Delhi 110 070
*Phone:* 91-11-4176-1620 • *Fax:* 91-11-4176-1630 • www.hayhouse.co.in

***Distributed in Canada by:*** Raincoast, 9050 Shaughnessy St.,
Vancouver, B.C. V6P 6E5 • *Phone:* (604) 323-7100
*Fax:* (604) 323-2600 • www.raincoast.com

**Take Your Soul on a Vacation**

Visit **www.HealYourLife.com®** to regroup, recharge, and
reconnect with your own magnificence. Featuring blogs,
mind-body-spirit news, and life-changing
wisdom from Louise Hay and friends.

Visit **www.HealYourLife.com** today!